LATIN CHURCH MUSIC
IN
ENGLAND
c. 1460–1575

Da Capo Press Music Reprint Series

MUSIC EDITOR
BEA FRIEDLAND
Ph.D., City University of New York

LATIN CHURCH MUSIC
IN
ENGLAND
c. 1460–1575

by
HUGH BENHAM

DA CAPO PRESS · NEW YORK · 1980

Library of Congress Cataloging in Publication Data

Benham, Hugh, 1943-
  Latin church music in England, c. 1460-1575.

  (Da Capo Press music reprint series)
  Reprint of the 1977 ed. published by Barrie & Jenkins,
London.
  Bibliography: p.
  Includes indexes.
  1. Church music—England. 2. Church music—
Catholic Church. I. Title.
ML3031.B46 1980 783'.026'242   79-25063
ISBN 0-306-76025-8

This Da Capo Press edition of *Latin Church Music
in England* is an unabridged republication of the
first edition published in London in 1977. It is
reprinted by arrangement with Barrie and Jenkins Ltd.

Published by Da Capo Press, Inc.
A Subsidiary of Plenum Publishing Corporation
227 West 17th Street, New York, N.Y. 10011

Manufactured in the United States of America

LATIN CHURCH MUSIC IN ENGLAND

c. 1460–1575

LATIN CHURCH MUSIC
IN
ENGLAND
c. 1460–1575

by

HUGH BENHAM

BARRIE & JENKINS
COMMUNICA · EUROPA

First published in 1977 by
Barrie and Jenkins Ltd
24 Highbury Cresent London N5 IRX

ISBN 0 214 20059 0

TO R.M.B.

Contents

List of illustrations

Preface

The church music discussed in this book ranges from the contents of the Pepys manuscript of *c.* 1460 to the *Cantiones* which Tallis and Byrd published in 1575. The principal aim is to study in greater detail than has yet been done a body of elaborate large-scale music for the Latin rite of Sarum written between about 1475 and the Reformation which is one of the finest flowerings of English music in any age. The earliest of this music is in the Eton choirbook, its leading composers John Browne, Walter Lambe, Richard Davy, William Cornysh and Robert Wylkynson. The tradition is continued by Robert Fayrfax, Nicholas Ludford and John Taverner, and in some pieces by Thomas Tallis, John Sheppard and Christopher Tye. Study of early Elizabethan music enables us to record the last traces of the tradition, and to see the first maturity of the new imitative style which had begun developing in the second quarter of the sixteenth century. We can also follow through to their ends the careers of composers of Latin music active under Mary Tudor, when the Latin services, banned under Edward VI, were briefly restored: Tallis is of course chief among these composers, but other considerable figures are Robert Whyte, William Mundy and Robert Parsons. The 1575 *Cantiones* form a fitting conclusion to our study because they represent the climax of Tallis's career and the first powerful emergence of William Byrd, whose work in full would be a study in itself. The music we are to deal with is not very widely known: it has not enjoyed the more or less continuous tradition of performance of music for the Anglican church. Much of it is not 'familiar' in sound or immediately accessible, but it has a strong appeal once appreciated.

As our title indicates, we are not concerned here with the music written for the English liturgy under Edward VI and Elizabeth: this has been admirably treated in another volume in the present *Studies in Church Music* series, Peter le Huray's *Music and the Reformation in England 1549–1660*. We shall do no more than mention the liturgical pieces for organ by such men as John Redford and Thomas Preston, for these are discussed, again in the present series, in Francis Routh's *Early English Organ Music from the Middle Ages to 1837*. The archival material of the pre-Reformation period appears to have been so fully covered by Frank Ll. Harrison in his masterly study *Music in Medieval Britain* (especially in Chapters 1 and 4 'The Institutions and their Choirs' and 'The Institutions and the Cultivation of Polyphony from 1400 to the Reformation'), that I have felt it necessary to devote very little space to this subject.

All musical examples are given at the original pitch and with note-values quartered. Editorial accidentals and reconstructions of missing parts are given in small print. Quartering of note-values is now more or less standard for editions of late fifteenth- and early sixteenth-century music, but I have adopted it even in those later works where halving is customary (and often more suitable) for the sake of uniformity, and to show as clearly as possible changes in the choice of note-values towards the end of our period. I ask the indulgence of those for whom 'quartering' of say late Tallis will inevitably seem awkward or annoying.

In the text names of notes in italics refer to pitches in specific octaves, and follow Helmholtz's system (i.e. from the C below the bass stave to B a seventh above, capital letters are used: *C–B*; for the three octaves above, the notation is *c–b*, *c′–b′*, *c″–b″*; the octave below employs the symbols *C,–B,*).

A Table of Works is provided for each composer to whom a section is devoted. The manuscript sources for these works, if not mentioned in the text, will be found listed in the printed edition indicated at the end of the Table and/or in *Die Musik in Geschichte und Gegenwart* and other works cited in the Bibliography. Only collected editions are listed in Tables and in the Bibliography; many editions of individual works have a short life before being out of print, so that publishers' catalogues (especially those of Chester, Novello, Oxford and Stainer and Bell) are the best place to find out what is currently available.

Notes for all Chapters appear after the final Chapter. Full titles of publications referred to in footnotes are given in the Bibliography.

I should like to acknowledge the great kindness shown to me at the Libraries I have visited, and in particular to Mrs E. Prior of the Thorold and Lyttleton Library, Winchester, Canon F. Bussby of Winchester Cathedral Library, the Staff of Southampton University Library, Dr

M. A. Baird of the University of London Library, Mr Patrick Strong of Eton College, Miss Miriam Miller of the BBC Music Library, the Staff of the Bodleian, Christ Church and Cambridge University Libraries, and of the British Museum. I am extremely grateful to Mr Alan Thurlow for lending me transcriptions of Sheppard's responds, hymns, psalm-motets, and antiphons, and to Mr Bruno Turner for supplying copies of Sheppard's Masses; to Dr John Bergsagel for making available copies of Ludford's Masses *Benedicta* and *Christi virgo*; and to Dr Margaret E. Lyon for permission to have her thesis and transcriptions of the Lambeth and Caius choirbooks reproduced. I wish also to record my thanks to the Carnegie United Kingdom Trust for permission to quote passages from *Tudor Church Music* as musical examples; to Messrs Stainer and Bell for similar permission regarding *Musica Britannica* and *Early English Church Music*; and to the American Institute of Musicology, publishers of *Corpus Mensurabilis Musicae*. Finally my thanks go to Mr Paul Courtenay for drawing the musical examples so beautifully, and to Mr J. G. Pattisson and Mr James Moore of Barrie and Jenkins for their kind help and advice.

Chandler's Ford, Hampshire,
September 1974.

I

Introduction

'In College or monastery it is still the same: music, nothing but music'. Thus Erasmus wrote, early in Henry VIII's reign, after complaining about the inaudibility of the words in the church music of England at that time, and the singers' inability to understand the Latin they were singing.[1] In 1521 the Scottish historian John Major also mentions the great vigour of English musical life in the early Tudor period; *he* is full of admiration (and remarkably free of national prejudice): 'Though in France or in Scotland you may meet with some musicians of such absolute accomplishment as in England, yet 'tis not in such numbers'.[2]

When we today look at the surviving early sixteenth-century repertory we may find it difficult to understand such remarks about the extent of musical activity in England: for example, our list of Fayrfax's works (Table 6, Chapter 8) contains only twenty-three titles (while the French composer Josquin des Prez, who died in 1521, the same year as Fayrfax, has roughly this number of Masses alone to his credit). Several English works that have been lost are mentioned in Tables 6, 7 (Chapter 8) and 8 (Chapter 9); in fact many entire manuscripts have fallen prey to the natural ravages of time or to mid sixteenth-century iconoclasm.[3] But the comments of Erasmus and Major about the extent of English musical activity do of course cover other types of music as well as such great Masses, votive antiphons and Magnificats as make up Fayrfax's surviving corpus. Such large-scale pieces were special items for important occasions, and were, there is no doubt, beyond the capability of many smaller choirs—so a great number of smaller-scale works of the same nature as Ludford's Lady Masses and the pieces discussed in Chapter 7 have presumably perished. Various kinds of improvised polyphony (notably descant and faburden) were part of every musician's training;[4] but naturally, *because* they were forms of improvisation, we have few written examples of them. But it is essential to remember that plainsong formed the bulk of pre-Reformation church music, even simple polyphony being only an occasional alternative to it or embellishment of it.[5]

The foundations with the most generously endowed choirs, in which the more elaborate polyphony was naturally most extensively cultivated, were colleges (including Eton, Magdalen, Oxford and King's, Cambridge), collegiate churches (including St Stephen's, Westminster and St George's, Windsor) and household chapels (among which the sovereign's Chapel Royal was pre-eminent). In secular cathedrals musical provisions were rather less generous, with only the more expert men and boys tackling polyphonic music. The larger monasteries sometimes employed lay choirmasters and lay singers outside their own services in devotions which the laity could attend. Some larger parish churches hired singers for periods or specific occasions, but did not support them all the time.[6]

Such early sixteenth-century works as Taverner's *Gloria tibi Trinitas* and *Western Wynde* Masses and Fayrfax's *Aeterne laudis lilium* antiphon were possible only because of that remarkable musical rebirth of the late fifteenth century which is known to us today from the contents of the Eton choirbook. We have to speak of 'rebirth' because while English musicians in the early 1400s had been at the forefront of European musical development—for the one and only time—there was afterwards something of a barren period. English music, hitherto most generously represented in Continental manuscripts, now appears scarcely at all. The loss of influence and international standing came about because there were no new English composers of the class of John Dunstable (d. 1453) and Leonel Power (d. 1445); but undoubtedly the fall of the French dominions was also important, in that fewer composers can have had the opportunity of working and travelling abroad.

Not only did the English cease to influence foreign composers, they also appear to have had only very limited knowledge of developments on the Continent in the second half of the fifteenth century. Although the Wars of the Roses, most acute in the 1450s and 60s, would probably not have borne directly on musical life to any great extent, they do mark a 'turning inwards' to which the new musical insularity seems subtly related. The Pepys manuscript of *c.* 1460 is the only large collection of music now surviving that was copied during the worst years of civil strife. It contains mostly small-scale pieces for two and three voices, which are not of outstanding merit.

In about 1476 Johannes Tinctoris, the Flemish theorist and composer, contrasted the key role of earlier English composers, notably Dunstable, with the current position: 'While the French contrive music in the newest manner for the new times . . . the English continue to use one and the same style of composition, which shows a wretched poverty of invention'.[7] We do not know what recent English music Tinctoris had heard, but it is clear that by the time he made his rather acid observations the ascent from the nadir of English musical fortunes had begun. For it is highly probable that the earliest music in the Eton choirbook belongs to this period—it may even be a few years older—since William Horwood and Gilbert Banester both died in the 1480s. For Eton College itself the 1470s were a time of rebirth. In 1476 the ornaments and books of the chapel were restored, having been made over to neighbouring St George's, Windsor in 1465, four years after the founder of Eton, Henry VI, had been deposed by the patron of St George's, Edward IV.[8] Nationally there was greater peace and new prosperity, for Edward IV had re-established himself firmly as a very efficient ruler after his deposition and restoration in 1470-1. While it is natural to think of the Eton music as 'early Tudor', because most of the work on the choirbook seems to have taken place in the 1490s, it is right to remember that its earliest development is Yorkist.

The Eton choirbook is the most important single source from our period; its most widely represented composer, John Browne, must occupy one of the highest places among English musicians of any age, while the sizeable contributions of Walter Lambe and Richard Davy are very impressive. The scale of musical thinking is much broader than in earlier English work: the length of pieces is generally greater; and writing for five voices instead of three has become the 'norm', while six-part pieces are quite plentiful, and a few very successful ventures are made into seven-, eight- or nine-part writing. The growth in the number of voices is accompanied by an extension in the total compass of choirs, both upwards and downwards. The highest boys' parts, reaching a'' flat or b'' flat in terms of modern pitch (see Chapter 3, section on Vocal scoring, pitch and transposition) give a brilliance not shared by contemporary Continental music. Rhythmic and melodic differentiation of the various voice-parts is very important; the words that best describe the style are complex, elaborate and florid.

The Eton composer's attitude to the text is often very casual. Long phrases on single syllables are common, and the rhythmic complexity is such that, in the words of Erasmus, 'the congregation cannot hear one distinct word.'[9] There is scarcely any evidence of deliberate expressiveness: music for the Eton composer was God-centred, a vehicle for devotion, an aid to it, part of the church's ceremonial, and a reflection of divine order, not a form of entertainment or a means of depicting human emotion. The Eton composer would have fully understood what John Wheathamstead, Abbot of St Alban's, had said about half a century earlier when he made provision for polyphony at the Lady Mass: 'wherever the Divine Service is more honourably celebrated the glory of the church is increased and the people are aroused to much greater devotion.'[10] John Stevens puts it very neatly when he says that 'up to the sixteenth century good moral results and devotional stirrings were regarded as the natural by-product of good music.'[11] The connections between music and mathematics, arising from the Boethian beliefs that music was 'number made audible' and that 'all things that are beautiful are subject to the power of number and can be explained by it'[12] are investigated in Chapter 4 (section on Length relationships) chiefly in terms of formal planning.

The preceding remarks will help to answer a question which use earlier of the word 'rebirth' may have raised: what connection is there between the Eton music and that wider rebirth, the Renaissance? Music so clearly God-centred, in which the listener's role is very passive, is obviously not yet influenced by the humanistic spirit of the Renaissance, but is still firmly part of the medieval tradition (which in Northern Europe was very slow to surrender to Renaissance attitudes and ideas).

In music the term 'Renaissance' is an awkward one to define.[13] But by any reckoning the concept of musical unity is of fundamental importance: that is to say, the various voices of a composition tend to be broadly similar in pace and general rhythmic character and to share melodic material instead of being differentiated in content and manner. Unity is most powerfully expressed through imitation—indeed this must be considered the key Renaissance technique. Imitation was adopted in a large way in about 1500 on the Continent, Josquin playing the crucial role in its development. Earlier movements towards musical unity, which had involved a reduction in the functional distinctions between parts rather than a sharing of material, may well be regarded as signs of transition from 'Gothic' to Renaissance, rather than as in themselves producing a Renaissance style.

Imitation still occupies a very limited place in the Eton music, as we saw earlier. In early sixteenth-century English music, particularly when we come to Taverner, it is more frequently used, but it generally retains an incidental character. We may see it almost as decoration of a basically differentiated structure, something 'grafted on' rather than something which actually pervades or generates the music. There are interesting parallels here with some early Tudor architecture, where

we find Renaissance ornament on Gothic structures. At Hampton
Court for instance (begun 1514) 'the plan and construction . . . were
entirely in the medieval tradition, and the general style of the fabric
was not far removed'[14] from that of Henry VII's reign, yet we find
such embellishments as the terracotta plaques of Roman emperors.
In Winchester Cathedral Bishop Fox's choir-screens of 1525 are
decorated with *all'antico* motifs.

Neither these *all'antico* motifs nor the Roman emperors at Hampton
Court are English in inspiration; both show the influence of the Italian
re-discovery of classical architecture—the Roman emperors are actually
by an Italian, Giovanni da Maiano. So to what extent was the adoption
of the Renaissance device of imitation in English music the result of
external influences? In the case of Taverner's *Meane Mass* (in which
imitation is much more important than usual in his work) its handling
is very obviously indebted to Josquin's practice, and later composers
would never have written all that they did without knowledge of
Continental models—Byrd's 1575 *Cantiones* pieces are a particularly
important case; but in general contacts between English and foreign
musicians in the early years of the sixteenth century are limited and
unclear.

English craftsmen could see the Italianate masterpieces of Henry
VII's tomb by Torrigiani in Westminster Abbey and the screen of
King's College Chapel, but were slow to adopt the Renaissance style
whole-heartedly. English composers were similarly conservative; as
already said, Fayrfax, whose music is in most important ways similar
to that of the Eton composers, died in the same year as Josquin. It is not
until the mid sixteenth century, in Elizabeth's reign particularly, that
English music began in earnest to 'catch up' with that being written
in France and the Netherlands. By this time we find imitation dominant; rhythms (already somewhat simplified by Taverner) very much
less complex, with simple chordal textures enjoying some use; harmony
more 'tonal' in feeling; dissonance used purposefully for the harmonic
tension it can give, not merely as decoration; very often a more unified
formal structure, without the block contrasts of full textures and
reduced groupings employed by the Eton composers and Taverner;
and much greater respect for words, with lengthy melisma usually
eliminated, verbal rhythms matched more carefully in the rhythms of
the music, and some occasional expressive response to a text.

There was an obsession with words and their clear interpretation
in early Tudor England. The humanists were rediscovering the classical
literatures of Greece and Rome. From the mid 1490s when John Colet

lectured at Oxford on the Epistles of St Paul, new methods of biblical scholarship were being developed which paid attention to the 'natural' meaning of the words instead of to the allegorical, moral and ana-gogical ones preferred by the schoolmen.[15] In 1516 Erasmus (whose pre-occupation with words is already obvious) published an edition of the Greek New Testament, together with a newly-made Latin transla-tion. Although the translation was not much better than that of the Vulgate, the Greek manuscripts being poor ones of no great antiquity, 'it was much to have begun the use of Greek manuscripts' at all.[16] Erasmus not only advanced Biblical scholarship, he also directed bitter satire against the wholesale corruption he saw in the Church; according to an old saying, which is at least partly true, he laid the egg which Luther hatched.[17] By the early 1520s Luther's ideas based on personal faith and responsibility and on Scripture (which should be available to everyone in his own language) rather than on papal authority and ecclesiastical tradition had gained very considerable ground in England, particularly at Cambridge where Erasmus had been.

The rapid changes in belief and in liturgy which followed the rise of Lutheranism—limited reform under Henry VIII, the further pro-gress of Protestantism (including the introduction of English services) under Edward VI, the return to papal allegiance and Latin liturgy in Mary Tudor's reign, and the Elizabethan Settlement of 1559 which restored the English Prayer Book—all had profound effects on the extent and character of church music. If Erasmus had been alive to visit England in Edward VI's reign or in Elizabeth's he would have been delighted to find a major reduction in musical activity, for like him many Reformers considered that far too much time, talent and money had formerly been spent on church music. As a result of the Chantries Act of 1547 many choral foundations were dissolved; after this 'fully choral services were to be heard . . . only in some forty or so cathedrals, churches and chapels . . .'.[18] An Act of 1550 sanctioned the surrender and destruction of all old service-books, to ensure universal adherence to the new English Prayer Book;[19] but fortunately a sizeable number of service-books and even a few musical manuscripts survived this particularly nasty piece of legislation. Of course there were always plenty of people who valued music in their worship—including Queen Elizabeth herself—and a quite considerable amount of church music *was* written under Edward and Elizabeth. There were simple functional settings of English texts which show a new concern with projecting the message of the words clearly for the edification of the people. But works with Latin texts continued to be composed. Some of these may well have been performed in connection with a Latin translation of the Prayer Book which appeared in 1560, and some may have been used by Papists for devotional or recreational use; but the perpetuation of the old tradition under Elizabeth may be attributed in large measure to purely musical and antiquarian motives (see Chapter 10, section on Latin church music and the Reformation).

2

Polyphony and the Pre-Reformation Services

Most of the music to be discussed in this book was composed before the introduction of the first English Prayer Book in 1549 or during the restoration of Roman Catholicism between 1553 and 1559. We can begin to understand it only if we know something of its place in the Latin worship of the unreformed church; for its composers were not individualistic artists, but servants of that church and its liturgy, and always members of some community, chapel, church, college or monastery, which existed 'for a wider purpose than a purely musical one.'[1]

In pre-Reformation England, where most music sung in church was plainchant, polyphony was generally reserved for important services and feasts, for liturgical texts of particular interest, and for important devotions. It was a mark of ceremonial distinction which, like any other, was valued for its special ability to honour God and the Saints, to increase the glory of the Church and to foster the devotion of the faithful. Its essentially decorative function is obvious where it is made to alternate with unaccompanied plainsong (as in most music for the Proper of the Mass and for the Office) and particularly so where it incorporates as cantus firmus the plainsong it 'replaces'. Works with plainsong–polyphony alternation, which sometimes involved the two sides of the choir, sometimes a solo–chorus contrast, are usually described as *alternatim*.

Before the Reformation there was not the complete liturgical uniformity which Edwardine and Elizabethan Acts imposed, but the use of Salisbury (or the Sarum Use as it is commonly called) was followed by the great majority of churches, apart from monastic ones, and we do not need to consider any of the other independent (but in most important respects very similar) uses. The 1549 Prayer Book Preface, in commending the new uniformity, not unnaturally somewhat exaggerates the former position: 'heretofore there hath been great diversity in saying and singing in churches within this realm:

8

some following Salisbury use, some Hereford use, some the use of Bangor, some of York, and some of Lincoln'.[2]

The worship of the pre-Reformation church may be divided into three main parts: the Mass, the Office, and extra-liturgical devotions.

THE MASS

The Mass was celebrated daily. In addition to the principal 'Mass of the day' one or more votive Masses might be offered. The Mass of the Blessed Virgin Mary (the 'Lady Mass'), originally prescribed for Saturdays, was celebrated daily in many places from the thirteenth century onwards, and became a focus of popular devotion (as to a lesser extent did the Jesus Mass).[3]

The order of Mass consisted of the Ordinary, parts which did not change according to the season or feast (although some might be omitted on occasions) and the Proper, parts which did change. The Ordinary, in addition to numerous prayers, included the Gloria in excelsis, Credo in unum Deum, Sanctus and Benedictus, and Agnus Dei. (Since in the Sarum rite the Kyrie eleison often had a seasonal or festival trope, it was almost part of the Proper.) The Proper itself included chants (Introit—or 'Officium' as Sarum called it, Gradual, Alleluia and Sequence—sometimes omitted, Offertory and Communion); prayers (Collect, Secret and Post-communion); and readings (Epistle and Gospel). The choir's chants for the Mass were recorded in a book called the Gradual[4] (except that sequences were sometimes found in a separate volume). The Missal,[5] which was designed for the celebrant to use at the altar, contained the words of the Mass and the music of the few passages he had to sing, such as the Preface.

On Sundays and festivals the Mass of the day was celebrated with great splendour. Polyphony might replace plainsong in the musically most important items of the Ordinary, namely the Gloria, Credo, Sanctus and Benedictus, Agnus, and (sometimes) the Kyrie eleison. The Lady Mass attracted not only settings of the Ordinary but also of some texts from the Proper.

From the early years of the fifteenth century the old practice of writing isolated movements or pairs of movements for the Ordinary was largely abandoned in favour of the composition of complete four- and five-movement Masses unified by a common cantus firmus and/or a recurring opening passage. (Of course all the movements of a Mass were not sung in immediate succession as in most modern performances, for various prayers, readings and proper chants separated one item from the next.) Mass cantus firmi were normally taken from the chant of the Office, although non-liturgical tunes appear in a few works. Melodies from the Proper were avoided. So were chants belonging to any of the Mass movements themselves—presumably because composers were unwilling to let plainsong proper to one text invade other movements.

It seems likely that each Mass was written in the first place for the festival from whose Office its cantus firmus came: Robert Fayrfax's *Tecum principium*, for example, uses the Christmas antiphon of this name, and so was probably first performed at Christmas. But it seems unlikely that the work was sung no more than once a year in view of the labour involved in composing and rehearsing it. On the other hand the great length (from about 600 to 800 bars) and elaborate character of many Masses would surely have limited them to very important occasions, the highest achievements of the polyphonic art thus accompanying the ultimate in religious ceremonial. Shorter less ornate settings, usually without cantus firmus, obviously found a place on less important occasions.

The Kyrie eleison (although always present in Continental settings) was much more often than not omitted from English Masses in our period. As already pointed out, its text was often troped in the Sarum rite; this inevitably meant, despite some freedom in the choice of trope, that the inclusion of a Kyrie limited a Mass's usefulness. The earliest English composers of Masses were content with such limitation: for example, all three Masses attributed to Dunstable had troped Kyries.[6] But five-movement Masses written after about 1450 always have the untroped Kyrie required for lesser festivals and for the Lady Mass. Thomas Packe's *Gaudete in Domino* and *Rex summe* were probably for lesser festivals. Ludford's seven three-part settings were certainly for the Lady Mass, because items from the Proper are included; so one assumes were the Masses by William Mundy and William Whytbrook, for their Kyries use the same cantus firmi as some of Ludford's. These cantus firmi seem to have been known as 'squares', because Mundy and Whytbrook entitle their Masses 'Apon the square'. The history of squares is very uncertain,[7] but we do know that they were not plainsong melodies. Several of the squares which appear on the fly-leaves of British Museum MS. Lansdowne 462, a fifteenth-century Sarum Gradual, have the names of early fifteenth-century composers—Dunstable, Leonel (Power), and Leroy (Henry IV or V)—attached to them. They may well have been extracted from polyphonic works by these composers, perhaps in the first place as bases for improvised polyphony; the tune which Ludford used in his Wednesday Mass has in fact already been traced back to the tenor of Thomas Damett's Credo in the early fifteenth-century Old Hall manuscript.

There are some isolated Kyrie settings. One, from the Pepys manuscript of *c.* 1460, has the trope 'Deus creator omnium', and possibly was used in conjunction with four-movement Masses on those principal feasts for which 'Deus creator' was prescribed. A group of Kyries appears in the mid sixteenth-century Gyffard partbooks, interspersed with Alleluias. All this music was clearly intended for the Lady Mass, because some of the Alleluias incorporate proper Marian plainsongs, and two Kyries (Taverner's and Hyett's) have squares as cantus firmi. Kyrie-Alleluia pairs may well have been linked with four-movement Masses independently composed: this would explain the Gyffard scribe's placing seven such Masses immediately after the Kyries and Alleluias, and might be deduced from his then presenting a Mass *with* Kyrie (Sheppard's *Playnsong*) and another with Kyrie and Alleluia (Appleby's). It is possible, however, that Kyrie-Alleluia pairs provided all the polyphony used at some celebrations of the Lady Mass, especially since the Gloria was omitted in Advent and Lent, the Credo on ferias and lesser festivals, while a Kyrie and Alleluia were always sung. A sequence was also always sung at the Lady Mass, and a setting of this could apparently be used as well as the polyphonic Alleluia or just with the Kyrie, since the accounts for 1521-2 of St Mary-at-Hill, London mention a 'pryksonge boke of Kyryes Allelyas and Sequences',[8] and a 1529 Inventory of polyphonic music at King's College, Cambridge refers to 'iiij bokys of paper havynge Sequenses and Taverners Kyries' and 'Taverners Kyries with the Sequensis.'[9]

Although the Kyrie had nine invocations, it is usual for only three to be set in polyphony, in the order Kyrie, Christe, Kyrie. Ludford's seven Kyries used squares from a special fourth book to supplement these sections—the same squares which appeared as cantus firmi in the polyphony. A Kyrie not based on a square, such as Okeland's from the Gyffard group, presumably used plainsong for the non-polyphonic parts. But as normal with *alternatim* works, the copyist did not provide the chant, for this (like a square in Ludford's case) was obviously performed by someone not using the polyphonic partbooks. An organist may have played the chant or even improvised upon it, because the organ is known to have been widely used at the Lady Mass.[10] Or it may have been sung—in which case solo performance could be suggested by analogy with the solo–chorus relationship involved if an organ were used with vocal polyphony.

The normal pattern for a Kyrie must have been plainsong or square for the odd-numbered invocations, polyphony for Kyrie II, Christes I and III (the same music for each) and Kyrie V. A few settings, including Tye's, provide different music for Christes I and III. Mundy's Masses *Apon the square* both set six invocations, leaving (presumably) Kyries II and V and Christe II to be sung to the square. Exceptionally, Whytbrook's Mass treats the Kyrie complete.

The reason for having *alternating* Kyries is not altogether clear; just possibly it arose by analogy with the Alleluia and sequence, only parts of which were polyphonic. Alternation is occasionally extended to the Gloria and Credo of small-scale Masses, notably in five of Ludford's Lady Masses. Such treatment of these long texts would considerably ease the burden of singing a Mass upon a small group of singers—more obviously so than in the Kyrie.

In Ludford's five *alternatim* Glorias and Credos the squares employed in the Kyries re-appear both as cantus firmi and as the music for the non-polyphonic sentences. The phrases provided for the non-polyphonic sentences probably received (solo) *vocal* performance. The argument that instrumental performance was intended because their text is often incomplete may be dismissed; the words given are usually too generous for mere instrumental cues, and examples of somewhat similar incomplete underlay do occur in a number of passages from the Eton and Forrest-Heyther manuscripts which are unquestionably vocal (see Chapter 4, section on Cantus firmus treatment).

An *alternatim* work of special interest is the Organ Mass by Philip ap Rhys.[11] Here the organist is 'upgraded' to the primary role of supplying the polyphonic sections. The alternation scheme now involves polyphony for a soloist and (presumably) *choral* plainchant, instead of solo chant or square (organ or voice) and polyphony for the choir. Since the organist is of course still the 'solo half' of the solo–choir contrast (despite his upgrading) he still plays at the same points in the text as he would in a piece where he alternated with vocal polyphony; or, to put it another way, the sentences Rhys sets for organ are those which do *not* receive polyphonic treatment in *alternatim* works with vocal polyphony. This reversal is paralleled in other liturgical forms for which both organ and vocal settings survive: thus organ settings of hymns, Te Deum and Magnificat treat the odd-numbered verses, while it is the even-numbered ones that are the subject of vocal polyphony.

A characteristic of otherwise fully polyphonic English Masses in our period is the customary omission of part of the Credo (normally several consecutive sentences from near the end).[12] Sections from the

plainsong Credo (or any other material) were clearly not inserted in such cases, not least because there is sometimes no break in the music where the omission begins. The resulting disruption of the liturgical text by the musicians was presumably tolerated because the celebrant would recite the text in its complete form at the altar. Credo omissions cannot have been made simply to curtail the length of the service or the length of the musical setting needed, because only a few sentences were affected and because the remaining text was often treated quite expansively.

Incomplete setting of the Credo almost certainly developed from the practice, found particularly in English settings before 1450, of 'telescoping' the text—that is, of having two sets of words from it sung simultaneously. The history of this development is obscure, but there is a kind of intermediate stage where a scribe curtails or suppresses text in one voice of a telescoped setting, so that (on paper at least) some text is not provided for; this happens for example to one of Dunstable's Credos—in the Trent Codices 90 and 93, but *not* in the work's English source.[13]

The earliest surviving Masses which have 'true' omissions are probably those in the late fifteenth-century Ritson manuscript and Fayrfax's settings. Although deletions generally concern the second half of the Credo, occasionally a section nearer the beginning is left out as well (normally 'Deum de Deo . . . Deo vero'). Omissions vary considerably, but there are several 'standard' patterns. Three of these make a cut before 'Et in Spiritum Sanctum', resuming in turn at 'Et exspecto', 'Et vitam venturi' and 'Amen'; a fourth, resuming at 'Et exspecto', has a longer omission starting after 'sedet ad dexteram Patris'. The pattern a composer adopted may well have reflected current fashion or local preference. Indeed, the fourth pattern seems to have been used almost exclusively after *c.* 1525: it occurs in Tye's Masses, Tallis's *Salve intemerata* and unnamed four-part setting, Alwood's *Praise Him Praiseworthy*, and the most 'modern' of Taverner's settings, the *Meane Mass*.

A few Masses do have a complete Credo—or, in the case of *alternatim* settings, one in which only a single sentence has ever to be supplied between one polyphonic section and the next. Such Masses are chiefly by Ludford, who makes deletions only in *Benedicta* and *Lapidaverunt Stephanum*. The Gyffard settings *Apon the square* are also of this type. Counting Ludford's seven Lady Masses, most 'complete' settings are for the Lady Mass; however, there are no cuts in Ludford's *Regnum mundi* (named after a respond for the Common of a Virgin and Martyr) or *Inclina* (named after a respond of the Epiphany 'Inclina cor meum Deus').[14]

Most polyphonic settings of the Proper were for votive Masses, obviously because these could enjoy regular and frequent use, instead of being restricted to a handful of performances each year as Propers for other Masses would be. The Lady Mass Alleluias and sequences were the favourite texts: this was no doubt partly because they in particular gave the Lady Mass its special character, for an Alleluia and sequence were always available there, even when excluded from the Mass of the day.

A plainsong sequence was performed in simple alternation between the two sides of the choir, one side taking the odd-numbered verses, the other the even-numbered. In Ludford's settings polyphony is provided for the latter, the plainsong for the former being given in the soloist's book.

A plainsong Alleluia began with a short solo phrase on the word 'Alleluia'; this was repeated by the choir, who then added a new, longer phrase, the *jubilus*, on the final syllable. The verse was then sung by the soloists, until the last couple of words or so, which were sung by the choir (the melody of the 'Alleluia', with *jubilus*, being re-introduced). There followed a repeat of the 'Alleluia', solo part only if a sequence was to follow, but with the *jubilus* as well (sung by the choir) if there was to be no sequence. In very early settings the solo sections (including the first part of the verse) were given polyphonic treatment, the choral parts retaining their plainsong. This arrangement, applied also to other responsorial chants (Graduals and Office responds), was adopted because polyphony was originally always the preserve of soloists (i.e. there was one singer to each part), as it was considered beyond the capability of the main body of singers. But settings in the Pepys manuscript are of all or some of the choral sections.[15] In some cases the music of the Alleluia with *jubilus* is re-used to set the last words of the verse and its *jubilus*. This arrangement, which recognises the fact that polyphony was by this time frequently sung by choirs (with several singers to each part) instead of by soloists, subsequently became the common procedure (for example, see Ludford's and Taverner's settings).

THE OFFICE

The services constituting the Office were Matins and Lauds, often sung at night or very early in the morning, the 'little Hours' of Prime,

Terce, Sext and None, and the evening services of Vespers and Compline. (Elements from Matins, Lauds and Prime were incorporated into the Anglican Mattins or Morning Prayer; Vespers and Compline were antecedents of Evensong.) The main constituents of (Sarum) Matins were Venite with Invitatory, Hymn with versicle, and then, depending on the importance of the day, one or three Nocturns. A nocturn had three psalms, each preceded by an antiphon, and three lessons, the first preceded by a versicle and each followed by a Respond. Te Deum concluded Matins on most Sundays and festivals. Lauds, Vespers and Compline had Psalms with antiphons, a *Capitulum* or very short reading, a Respond, Hymn with versicle, Gospel canticle with antiphon (Benedictus at Lauds, Magnificat at Vespers, Nunc Dimittis at Compline) and prayers. Much of the plainsong of the Office was contained in the Antiphonal,[16] but for the hymns one must go to the Hymnal,[17] for psalm-tones to the *Tonale*.[18] The Breviary,[19] commonly without any music, contained the Lessons as well as antiphons, responds and some other items, but was an 'abbreviation' in the sense that it did not have the Psalms with their ferial antiphons (these are in the Psalter) or hymns.[20]

Polyphonic music for the Office consists mainly of settings of Magnificat, responds and hymns. It was Vespers which attracted most of this music, but the awkwardly-timed Matins and Lauds had some, and Compline a little.

All works for the Office involve a plainsong–polyphony alternation. Except in most settings of Magnificat, the polyphonic sections do not normally replace the proper plainsongs altogether, but incorporate them as cantus firmi, usually in equal notes. The continuous presence of a plainsong helps to give overall unity to a piece, and emphasises the essentially decorative nature of the polyphony.

Magnificat, the canticle of the Blessed Virgin Mary from Vespers, was a favourite text, as was natural in an age which laid so much stress on Marian devotion. The service-books refer to it as a psalm, appropriately in view of its manner of performance: a psalm-tone was used, the two sides of the choir alternated, and Gloria Patri followed the scriptural words. Like individual psalms or groups of psalms, Magnificat was always 'framed' by an antiphon, which varied according to the season or feast. On some major festivals the antiphon was sung complete both before and after the canticle, the first few notes in each case being sung by a soloist, the remainder by the choir on the soloist's side. Generally, however, only the opening phrase of the antiphon was sung at the beginning, the soloist going on with the first half of verse 1, the choir on his side finishing the verse. The complete antiphon followed the canticle, usually with the *neuma** of the mode added. The psalm tone sung for Magnificat agreed in mode with the antiphon; for instance at first Vespers of the Assumption (that is, the Vespers sung on the Eve of the feast) the sixth tone was used because the antiphon 'Ascendit Christus' was in the sixth mode. All tones except the sixth had several alternative endings, the one which would ensure the smoothest transition from the last verse of the canticle to the antiphon being selected.

When polyphony was employed at Magnificat (for the even-numbered verses), the setting chosen would have to match the proper antiphon and the tone sung for the odd-numbered verses; thus, for example, Taverner's four-part Magnificat, which incorporates the sixth tone, could go with the antiphon 'Ascendit Christus' at first Vespers of the Assumption. The first and eighth modes are most common for Magnificat antiphons on important occasions, and most polyphonic settings are designed accordingly. Those in the Eton choirbook by Nesbet, Horwood, Kellyk and Lambe all require the eighth tone first ending for the plainsong verses, and so were available on such occasions as the Epiphany (both Vespers), Low Sunday (first Vespers), the Eve of the Nativity and the Assumption (second Vespers), and at Vespers of St Stephen and St John Evangelist. We know that these four settings were performed in alternation with the eighth tone first ending not from any written direction in the manuscript source, but because in each case some polyphonic verses incorporate a melody derived from this tone which is known as its 'faburden' (see Chapter 7, section on the Pepys manuscript).

A hymn formed part of each Office, except from Maundy Thursday to the Saturday after Easter. Its opening line was sung by one or more soloists, the number depending on the rank of the day. The first verse was continued by the choir on the soloists' side, and then the two sides of the choir took alternate verses, except that the doxology was sung by all. Since it is verse 2 and the other even-numbered stanzas which are treated in vocal polyphony, the work cannot be fully identified and correctly titled until the first verse has been traced in the Breviary; thus the piece by Tallis beginning 'Haec Deum coeli' turns out to be a setting of the hymn at first Vespers of the Purification 'Quod chorus vatum'. A few exceptions to the rule of even-numbered verses being treated are found in the Pepys and Ritson manuscripts. In Pepys the

---

* To each mode there belonged a special piece of vocalised melody, which was used at the final vowel of some chants.

first verse only is set of 'Iste confessor', and in both manuscripts all three verses of 'O lux beata Trinitas' are set.

Of the 117 hymns listed in the Sarum Breviary, over forty were set in our period, the majority for Vespers and Compline. Only about half of the forty survive in vocal settings, the remainder, plus nine of the texts treated vocally, being organ settings (of the odd-numbered verses). The organ was used mainly, but not exclusively, for occasions of only moderate importance, when presumably a polyphonic choir was often not available. Hymns represent the bulk of the surviving organ music for the Office.

Te Deum laudamus, of which three vocal and three organ settings survive, is nowadays referred to as a hymn, despite its non-metrical text; before the Reformation it was termed 'psalmus' or 'canticum'. It was sung, with the two sides of the choir taking alternate verses, at the end of Matins on Sundays and most feasts, except in Advent and Lent. But there are records of its use outside the Office on occasions of general rejoicing such as the receptions at York Minster of Richard III in 1483 and Henry VII in 1486.[21]

A respond (or responsory as it is sometimes called) was a chant which followed a lesson, often commenting on it in some way. At Matins the responds were always the same in number as the lessons: that is, nine on most important feasts, three at other times. On many days, including most double feasts, the *Capitulum* or short lesson at Vespers had a respond. The Compline lesson was followed by one only in Lent.

Every respond consisted of two main parts, the 'response'[22] (begun by a soloist or small group of soloists, and continued by the choir) and the verse or verses (solo throughout). At its simplest the pattern was response, verse, latter part of response repeated, as in some Matins responds including the widely set 'Audivi vocem':

Response:	Audivi	sung by soloists
	vocem de coelo venientem . . . sapientissimae. Oleum recondite . . . advenerit.	choir
Verse:	Media nocte clamor factus est. Ecce sponsus venit.	soloists
R. from	Oleum recondite . . .	choir.

The third, sixth and ninth responds at Matins, and those at Vespers normally had the first part of the Gloria Patri as a second verse sung to the same melody as the first, after the repeat of the response; this was followed by a second, often shorter repeat—as for instance in 'Dum transisset sabbatum', the widely set third respond at Easter Matins. 'In pace', the respond at Compline for the four weeks beginning with the first Sunday in Lent, had Gloria Patri leading on to a complete repeat of the response. From Passion Sunday to Maundy Thursday the Gloria Patri verse was not sung; accordingly the arrangement of 'In manus tuas', the Compline respond for this period, was response, verse, partial repeat of response, complete repeat of response.

The earliest settings of responds, as of Alleluias, had polyphony for the solo sections. Choral treatment began much later than in the case of Alleluias, in Taverner's day; and in fact all four responds set in the Pepys manuscript ('Audivi vocem', 'Hodie nobis coelorum rex', 'In pace' and 'In manus tuas') received solo treatment even by composers younger than Taverner. These four responds were the only ones English composers set in our period until the choral respond was introduced; quite clearly they were chosen for repeated polyphonic treatment because each had some special ritual interest.

'Audivi vocem' was the eighth respond at Matins of All Saints' Day, the feast when the normal order of lesson readers (from lowest in rank to highest) was largely reversed, as was the order of those who began responds. The eighth lesson, read by a boy, was part of Bede's exposition of the parable of the five wise virgins. After it 'Audivi vocem' was begun by five boys who stood at the choir-step facing the altar with lighted candles to represent the wise virgins whose lamps were burning. The boys turned towards the choir at the words 'Ecce sponsus' ('Behold the Bridegroom'), and a break was often made in polyphonic settings before these words to emphasise the movement. Some settings, for example Taverner's, are for boys' voices only, in accordance with the rubrics.

'Hodie nobis coelorum rex', the first respond at Matins of Christmas Day, was begun by two men, but the verse 'Gloria in excelsis Deo' was sung by five boys who stood holding lighted candles in a high place above the altar to represent the angels who gave the news of Christ's birth to the shepherds. Normally only the verse was set, appropriately for boys' voices, but Tallis sets the opening word 'Hodie' as well in a piece probably for four men's voices.

'In pace' and 'In manus' were of special interest as the only responds ever sung at Compline. In the Gyffard partbooks only the first of

Sheppard's three 'In manus' settings treats the solo parts. The other two, appropriately labelled 'In manus corus Mr Sheparde', adopt the alternative scheme, setting only the choir's words 'Domine commendo spiritum meum', with a clear break in the music after 'Domine' to permit repetition from 'commendo' after the verse 'redemisti me'. This novel treatment of a hitherto solo respond clearly reflects the growing influence of the new repertory of choral responds.

It is almost certain that Taverner's *Dum transisset* I and II are the first choral responds; but Tallis and Sheppard made the major contributions to the type, treating sixteen new texts between them. The choral respond may to some extent have superseded the votive antiphon after about the mid 1530s as the major vehicle of musical expression and devotion in the evening worship, since most responds treated chorally are taken from Vespers; hymns, which seem also to have been increasingly in favour from about the same time, may also have acquired something of the same function. Both hymns (vocal settings) and responds come mainly from important feasts.

EXTRA-LITURGICAL DEVOTIONS: VOTIVE ANTIPHONS

The Marian antiphon used to conclude Compline in the Roman rite and in most English monastic liturgies is not mentioned in the Sarum books. But the Statutes of many foundations indicate that an antiphon was widely sung, most commonly after Compline, as a separate and very important devotional act.[23] The mode of performance of such 'votive' antiphons varied, but the singers often assembled before an altar or image. Polyphonic settings were widely made, many of them from between 175 and 275 bars being on an even grander scale than individual movements from larger Masses. Most votive antiphons were addressed to the Virgin, but not all: for instance, the Statutes of Cardinal College, Oxford (1525) required antiphons to the Trinity and to St William of York after Compline as well as the customary Marian piece. A Jesus-antiphon 'Sancte Deus, sancte fortis' was also to be sung in the course of additional devotions later in the evening.[24] We have a number of other Jesus-antiphons, including Ludford's *Domine Jesu Christe* and Taverner's *O splendor gloriae*. A few texts were addressed to more than one Saint: Fayrfax's *Aeterne laudis lilium* honours both Mary and St Elizabeth, as more obviously does Banester's *O Maria et Elizabeth*.

The text to be used as a votive antiphon is sometimes specified in Statutes, but more frequently it is left to choice. A few texts were borrowed from the liturgy, notably 'Salve regina', a processional antiphon, and 'Nesciens mater', a psalm-antiphon; these were widely favoured before 1500, much less so afterwards. Passages from the Song of Solomon, popular with composers of Dunstable's time, were used scarcely at all in our period. The devotional material generally preferred may be verse or prose. Some texts are known only from the polyphonic works based on them. A number existed independently, sometimes as antiphons or prayers in books of Hours; for example 'Ave Dei Patris filia', a text set by Fayrfax, Taverner and several other composers, appears in a book of 1513 printed by Richard Pynson of London.[25] Robert Wylkynson's *O virgo prudentissima* uses a text entitled 'Hymnus' written by Angelo Poliziano of the Court of Lorenzo il Magnifico in 1493 and printed in Venice in 1498[26] — a surprising choice in view of the general insularity of English music at this time.

Very many verse texts are in the same form and metre as the later medieval sequence, with paired three-line stanzas, notably 'Gaude flore virginali' on the Seven Heavenly Joys of the Virgin, which appears eleven times in the Eton choirbook. While the Eton manuscript has settings of only three non-metrical texts, by Taverner's time this type was pre-eminent. The longer prose texts, which tend to be very effusive, sometimes lack form and shape, an obvious example being 'Salve intemerata' as set by Tallis. Their Latin is frequently very undistinguished, as indeed is that of some verse texts.

Only a minority of antiphons, consisting mainly of pieces written before 1500, employs cantus firmus construction. Works with liturgical texts use their proper melodies, while others normally appropriate chants from the Office, and may therefore have been performed in the first place on the festivals from which their melodies came, as we have supposed cantus-firmus Masses were.

The growing hostility to veneration of the Saints in the latter part of Henry VIII's reign led to a decline in the popularity of the votive antiphon (see Chapter 10, section on Latin church music and the Reformation). As suggested above, the choral respond and the hymn probably attracted some of the attention formerly paid to it. Settings of psalms, the first of which probably date from Henry's reign, could have been substitutes or successors of a more obvious kind: they were clearly designed for use outside the Office itself, since the Gloria Patri is ignored, *alternatim* treatment is avoided, and some of the antiphon's formal characteristics are often adopted.

3

Some Performance Problems

If anyone today were asked to sing from a fifteenth- or sixteenth-century manuscript he would be likely at best to make numerous mistakes and at worst to be completely baffled, for the performer of old music is used to modern editions in which everything is presented in a familiar, up-to-date way. In the present Chapter we shall talk about some of the main problems which confront editors—and choir-masters—in their efforts to make the music of our period performable, and performable in as historically accurate a way as possible in changed social and religious circumstances. These problems concern the nature of the old notation, tempo, the types of voices used, pitch, the handling of accidentals (especially leading-notes at cadences), and text underlay. (The completion of *alternatim* works, necessary because manuscript copyists normally record only the polyphonic sections, is done in accordance with the patterns described in Chapter 2, and is not discussed here.)

We begin by examining the character of the sources of our music, because it is these which both pose the problems of performance practice and give or suggest solutions.

CHOIRBOOKS AND PARTBOOKS

The manuscript sources are of two types: choirbooks, large volumes containing music for all sections of the choir, and partbooks with single voices and complete only in sets (normally of four, five or six).

In a choirbook the parts are laid out successively, not aligned in the form of a score (except sometimes in the Pepys and Ritson manuscripts where the score arrangement recalls early fifteenth-century practice). Although a few short two- or three-part pieces fit onto a single page, one normally finds one or more complete openings occupied, with some parts on the left-hand page(s), the others on the right. (Plate 2 shows a left-hand page.) A choirbook was put on a lectern at which the choir assembled,[1] boys in the front, men behind. Because of this one would expect to find the music for the boys at the foot of the page; yet it comes almost invariably at the top (as the highest part had done since the earliest times both in score format and in choirbook layout). The apparent awkwardness of this arrangement might mean that the surviving choirbooks were library copies rather than 'performing editions'; and indeed the few signs of actual use would seem to re-inforce this. But on the other hand boys may have sung from memory if it was difficult for them to see their parts. The lack of usage may mean that rougher copies (perhaps in the cheaper and more manageable partbook form) sufficed for learning and rehearsal work, the times when handling is likely to have been least careful.

The three most important choirbooks are those now belonging to Eton College, Lambeth Palace Library and Gonville and Caius College, Cambridge.

The Eton choirbook (Eton College MS. 178), the leading source of late fifteenth-century English music, is a splendid production with fine illuminated initial letters and an attractive use of red ink for coloration (a notational device defined in the second section of this Chapter) and the text of solo sections.[2] It measures 23½ by 17 inches, each stave being about three-quarters of an inch high; thus it is eminently practicable for a sizeable group to sing from. It fits the description of 'a grete ledger of prick song ii folio tum cuncta' in an Eton College inventory of 1531, because the second folio does begin with '-tum Cuncta' (from 'luctum/ Cunctaque peccamina', words used in Browne's *O Maria salvatoris mater*).[3] It is unique among manuscripts of its period in still being preserved in its original home.

An index at the end lists sixty-one antiphons, and this undoubtedly marks completion of the manuscript's first layer. In the body of the manuscript the antiphons are grouped according to the number of voices used: those with most parts come first. About one third are now missing or seriously incomplete. All the survivors are in one hand, and must have been copied mainly, if not entirely, in the 1490s: we can deduce from an inscription at the end of the piece that Davy's *O Domine coeli terraeque creator* was composed between 1490 and 1492 (see Chapter 6, section on Richard Davy); yet the illuminated 'O' in the mean part of the same work contains the arms of Henry Bost, Provost of Eton, who died in 1502.

An index at the beginning includes five more antiphons (two of which have survived fragmentarily), twenty-four Magnificats (four of them complete, four imperfectly preserved), and Davy's Passion (seriously incomplete). The works of this group are in the same hand as those of the first layer, and were probably copied only shortly after them. Wylkynson's nine-part *Salve regina* and his thirteen-part round *Jesus autem transiens/Credo in unum Deum*, which appear in neither index and are written in a later, less elegant hand (perhaps Wylkynson's own), were almost certainly inserted between 1500 and 1515 when their composer was master of the choristers at Eton.

Although there are serious losses from the manuscript, the remains are sufficient to give a good picture of the large-scale votive antiphon and the *alternatim* Magnificat in the last twenty or thirty years of the fifteenth century. Without them we should know nothing of the work of that truly great composer John Browne, have no complete composition by Richard Davy, and only two pieces by Walter Lambe.

The Caius choirbook (Cambridge, Gonville and Caius College MS. 667), an important source for the Masses of Fayrfax and Ludford, is even larger than the Eton book at 28¼ by 19 inches. The illuminations are often of a humorous character and include a mermaid, a grass-hopper, and a fox with a friar's hood labelled 'fryer foxe'; but in general they are not so well done as the less fanciful ones of the Eton manuscript. An inscription ('Ex dono et opere Edwardi Higgons huius ecclesie canonici') indicates that the Caius choirbook was the gift and work of Edward Higgons, and suggests that it was connected with St Stephen's, Westminster where Higgons was a canon from 1518 until his death in 1538 (and where Ludford served and almost certainly wrote the sixth item, the Mass *Lapidaverunt Stephanum*). Geoffrey Chew argues in favour of Salisbury Cathedral, where Higgons held a canonry from 1507 to 1538, and arrives at a date at least in the late 1520s for some of the illuminations.[4] The repertory itself suggests an earlier date (perhaps the 1510s)—unless we have the preservation of a slightly out-of-date repertory—for in the late 1520s it is very likely that works by Taverner would have begun to appear.

Only slightly smaller than the Caius manuscript is the Lambeth choirbook (London, Lambeth Palace MS. 1). The handwriting and the motifs used in illuminations are sufficiently similar for it to be possible that this also is the work of Higgons, and is of roughly the same date; but the two sources appear to be textually independent. In production Lambeth is slightly inferior to Caius. Chew seems inclined to accept that Higgons was the copyist of Lambeth, and associates the manuscript with Westminster rather than Salisbury. The fact that only four of the nineteen pieces bear a composer's name seems to support the connection with St Stephen's, for 'ascriptions (particularly of Ludford's works) would not have been necessary: the musicians at Westminster would have known well enough who the composers of the works were, especially with both Higgons and Ludford in residence'.[5] Only two works are known as Ludford's, the Masses *Lapidaverunt Stephanum* and *Benedicta* (from their preservation in Caius); but there may be other compositions of his among the seven items for which concordances have not yet been traced.

The late fifteenth-century Pepys and Ritson manuscripts (described more fully in Chapter 7) are very much smaller and less elaborate than Eton, Lambeth and Caius; they contain shorter and rather simpler pieces, presumably for smaller and less able choirs.

In the early sixteenth century choirbooks gradually passed out of use in favour of partbooks. (At least for a time some choirs seem to have preferred one type of manuscript, some the other, for in 1524 all the polyphonic music at Magdalen College, Oxford was contained in choirbooks, nine of which had been bought between 1518 and 1524,[6] while in 1529 King's College, Cambridge relied almost entirely on partbooks).[7] Partbooks with small paper leaves were undoubtedly cheaper to produce than large elaborately bound choirbooks of parchment. They were also easier to handle, and probably more convenient for a large number of singers to read from. The choir would no longer gather round a lectern, but would presumably sing from the choir-stalls, except in votive antiphons performed before images, where, unless singing from memory was the practice, each book must have been held by one or more singers for all of those on that part to see.

The number of partbooks surviving is quite considerable, but complete sets are very few. These few include the important Forrest-Heyther and Gyffard sets and the source of Ludford's Lady Masses, British Museum Royal Appendix MSS. 45–48 (described in Chapter 8, section on Nicholas Ludford). The Peterhouse and Christ Church sets both lack their tenor books; reconstruction is easy where proper plain-songs in equal notes are involved, but at other times it is an awkward task.

The Forrest-Heyther partbooks (Oxford, Bodleian Library MSS. Mus. Sch. e. 376–81)[8] are a major source of large-scale Masses. In 1530 they belonged to a petty-canon of Cardinal College, Oxford, William Forrest, for an inscription in MS. 378 reads: 'William Forrest hunc librum jurae possidet cum quinque alijs eidem pertinentibus, 1530'. Taverner, first choirmaster at the new College from 1526 to 1530.

had almost certainly supervised their compilation—or, to be precise, the compilation of the first layer of eleven Masses. His six-part *Gloria tibi Trinitas* heads the collection, very impressively, since nine of the ten Masses following are for five voices, and fittingly, because it is built upon an antiphon of the Trinity, to whom the College was dedicated. The other Masses of the first layer include four by Fayrfax, and John Marbeck's *Per arma justitiae*. Possibly on Taverner's departure in 1530 it was decided that less ambitious music should be used, and Forrest rescued the six partbooks from destruction: exactly why or how else he should be able to lay personal claim to them at this time is uncertain, for one would expect them to be the property of the College, not of an individual.

The second layer, dating from the mid sixteenth century, is probably in Forrest's own hand (except for the last part of the sixth ('sextus') book, which was copied by John Baldwin very much later). It begins with four items perhaps included in the original plan of the manuscript (Taverner's *Corona spinea* and *O Michael*, Ashewell's *Ave Maria* and Aston's *Videte manus meas*); but the last three Masses (Tye's *Euge bone*, Sheppard's *Cantate* and Alwood's *Praise Him Praiseworthy*) are clearly much later works. When Baldwin completed the sextus book, and possibly even when the rest of the second layer was added, the books had become (as some later manuscripts were from their inception) of primarily musical and antiquarian interest, rather than part of a living liturgical tradition.

The Gyffard partbooks (British Museum Additional MSS. 17802–5) are an invaluable source for smaller-scale works for the Sarum rite by Taverner, Tye, Tallis and Sheppard in particular: concordances have been traced for only three out of ninety-four pieces. The basic arrangement is: music for the Lady Mass, including Kyries and Alleluias; works for the Office in liturgical sequence from All Saints to Whit Sunday; the Proper of the Jesus Mass, and the three Masses *Apon the square*; Magnificats; and votive antiphons.

The books were copied in the middle years of the sixteenth century. Work on them may have begun 'as early as the 1540s',[9] but much or most of it was probably done during the Marian reaction of 1553–8, by which time William Mundy and Robert Whyte (b. *c.* 1530) could have been composing. It would be easy to assume that the manuscripts were still incomplete when Mary died, for the name of 'mr birde' appears. But in fact the man who composed *In exitu Israel* jointly with Sheppard and William Mundy is probably not the great William Byrd (b. 1543), but Thomas Byrd, Gentleman of the Chapel Royal 1546–8, or the William Byrd who was a chorister at Westminster Abbey when William Mundy was head of the choristers there in 1543–4.[10] Similarly it seems rather improbable that the John Mundy who composed a Kyrie was William Mundy's son John who died in 1630; possibly William had a brother John, or possibly the Christian name is wrong. The Gyffard partbooks show no sign of use, and contain many uncorrected scribal errors. But if designed for liturgical use under Mary, the brevity of their 'working life' might be sufficient reason for this.

Despite the loss of the tenor, the Peterhouse partbooks (Cambridge University Library, Peterhouse MSS. 40, 41, 31, 32) are a most important and informative source.[11] They contain five-part music by Fayrfax, Ludford, Taverner, Tye and Tallis, and various minor contemporaries, some of whom are known only from this source. A date of 1540–7 is generally accepted, and certainly nothing later could reasonably stand, because the reference to Henry VIII in Taverner's *Christe Jesu* has not been modernised. Paul Doe sees the partbooks, with their large body of votive antiphons and festal Masses at so late a date, as 'a provincial and slightly retrospective anthology, perhaps compiled by a former monastic musician living in retirement just after the dissolution, and . . . not representative of musical composition in and around London during the last ten or twelve years of Henry VIII's reign.'[12] This would account for the manuscript's obvious lack of use—uncorrected copyist's errors are common; and would make it the earliest one surviving to have been compiled for musical or antiquarian reasons, rather than for actual liturgical usage.

The partbooks Oxford, Christ Church MSS. 979–83 were copied between about 1580 and 1600[13] by John Baldwin, who had a hand in completing the Forrest-Heyther manuscripts and who kept a fascinating musical commonplace-book sometimes known as the Baldwin manuscript (British Museum, Royal Music Library MS. R.M. 24 d. 2). The Christ Church books are beautifully neat, and have been used little if at all; they probably formed a kind of private musical treasury. Today they are the leading source for compositions written in the last years of the Sarum rite (especially for numerous responds and hymns by Sheppard and Tallis), and an important one for Latin works composed under Elizabeth. It is interesting to note that some works by Fayrfax and Taverner are still included, as indeed they are in other late sixteenth-century manuscripts.

The one printed source of Latin church music is *Cantiones quae ab argumento sacrae vocantur* which Tallis and Byrd published in 1575 and dedicated to the Queen shortly after she had granted them a monopoly

in the printing of music.[14] Music printing in England had begun with
the *XX Songes* of 1530, pieces for a secular market by Taverner and
others which ranged from the bawdy to the devotional. Subsequent
publications had favoured Protestant devotional material,[15] and had
contained nothing of special musical value. On the other hand the
Cantiones has seventeen important pieces by Tallis and seventeen
already quite impressive ones by Byrd, who was some forty years
Tallis's junior; and one gathers from introductory Latin verses that the
publication was intended to bring the achievements of English music
to the attention of the world at large—a world which had seen all the
major sixteenth-century Continental composers in print. The standard
of printing in the *Cantiones* is very high; many later publications are
much less attractive and less clear. The source is also particularly
authoritative musically, since Tallis and Byrd supervised the presentation of their own music.

NOTATION AND TRANSCRIPTION

   Modern transcriptions involve a change from choirbook or partbook
layout to score format and the addition of bar-lines. Almost invariably
they use shorter notes than the manuscript sources: this gives the singer
familiar values instead of a very 'white' score with many breves, semibreves and minims, which would be less easy to read and might well
have a depressing effect on tempi. The original notes are usually
quartered in late fifteenth- and early sixteenth-century music, because
in this the semibreve generally occupied roughly the place in the scale
of values now held by the crotchet. But in the mid sixteenth century
breves became much less common and the minim assumed greater
importance, and so from then onwards halving is generally preferred.
(However, for reasons given in the Preface, even the later musical
examples in this book employ quartering.)
   In the earlier part of our period manuscript copyists, like modern
editors, had to choose between one notation that was predominantly
black and another predominantly white. But in their case both types
of notation were identical in meaning, for our present white notes were
black until the gradual change to 'modern' practice in the fifteenth
century. The change was almost certainly linked with the increasing
use of paper instead of parchment in making manuscripts; for while
parchment was suitable for filled-in note-heads, the rougher surface
of paper (hand-made!) meant that quill nibs tended to splutter when

splayed out to make the old black lozenge shape.[16] Black notation persisted in England rather later than elsewhere—notably in the Eton, Lambeth and Caius choirbooks, which are in parchment. Black notes may also have been preferred here, rather as a modern editor prefers crotchets and quavers to semibreves and minims, for ease of reading: when a large group assembled round a choirbook the notes had to be clearly visible from several feet away. All surviving Tudor partbooks are of paper, with white notation.

Black and white notations worked on the same principles; these differ considerably from those of our own notation, and only a few main points can be touched on here.[17] While each note today is worth two of the next lower value (except where triplets are used), the old system employs subdivision by three ('perfect' mensuration) as well as by two ('imperfect'), mainly for breves and semibreves. The signature O shows that the breve has three semibreves, the semibreve two minims, while under C all mensuration is imperfect. The more widely used signatures Ø and ₵ in practice (but not in theory) meant the same as O and C. In transcriptions with quartered note-values $\frac{3}{4}$ is substituted for Ø and O, and $\frac{4}{4}$ normally replaces ₵ and C. The signature ₵, with three minims to the semibreve and two semibreves to the breve, corresponds to our $\frac{6}{8}$. It is simplest to think of $\frac{\varnothing}{3}$ as ₵ with doubled values; it is commonly transcribed as $\frac{6}{8}$ with original values divided by eight. Both the white and black forms of notation employ 'coloration'; that is, the value of a note may be reduced, usually by one third, by having its colour changed from white to black or from black to white or red. This is essential in some circumstances for writing imperfect breves in Ø, and for notating triplets (for example in the Eton choirbook, where the minim is normally a black note, triplet minims are always written red). Two or more notes each worth a semibreve or more are frequently joined in 'ligatures' (see for instance the beginning of the music in Plate 4: compare the transcription with quartered note-values in 9.Ex. 8.). However many notes a ligature has, only one syllable is normally provided. The usual editorial sign for a ligature is a square bracket ⌐——¬ over the linked notes; coloration is indicated thus: ⌐ ¬ .

TEMPO

As well as indicating mensuration, time-signatures give some information about tempo, particularly changes of tempo, in the complete absence of verbal directions. But since there is some considerable conflict between the theory of the subject and what can be observed from practical sources, modern performers will have to experiment with tempi, judging the natural pace of the music and taking into account the acoustics of the building in which they are singing.

Theorists from the late fifteenth century onwards speak of a *tactus*, or basic beat, which they imply was constant from section to section and from one piece to another. However, not all pieces can sensibly be taken at the same speed, and there is evidence pointing to variations within single works.

The most important issue concerns changes from Ø to ₵ (or the synonomous O to C change). After changing from Ø to ₵ many late fifteenth- and early sixteenth-century works employ more long notes and less very short ones, so that if the semibreve beat were constant less movement would result and rhythmic impetus would be lost. One answer worth considering in some cases can be deduced from the length relationships discussed in Chapter 4. Since in many sections and works the number of 'bars' of three semibreves each under Ø balances the number of those with four semibreves under ₵, it is possible that the two types of bar may have taken a similar time in performance. This would mean speeding up the semibreve by about one third when the signature changes—although obviously the original singers are unlikely to have achieved (or even aimed for) metronomic precision. This limited difference between semibreves under triple and duple signatures was part of a long development from a situation obtaining in the mid fifteenth century (where the change of signature indicated a move from a semibreve to a breve beat) to a point reached by the mid sixteenth century where there is no noticeable difference in values between Ø and ₵, and hence probably no difference in the speed of the semibreve beat). In a few works by the older Eton composers the mid fifteenth-century situation still persists: in Banester's *O Maria et Elizabeth* and Horwood's *Salve regina*, for example, the shift in note-values from Ø to ₵ is so pronounced that the semibreve under one and the breve under the other are not very different in 'weight' and importance—just as in some works by Dufay the semibreve under O and the breve under ₵ seem to be approximately equivalent. (In Dufay's works the stroke of the ₵ signature indicates a genuine 'diminution', with the beat being on the breve instead of on the semibreve. Later composers and scribes were often extremely casual in their use of the stroke, so that, as we have already seen, ₵ and C, Ø and O were interchangeable.)

Some works by Taverner and his successors have a change of signature from ₵ to $\frac{\emptyset}{3}$ (or the synonomous $\frac{\emptyset}{3.1}$ or $\frac{O}{3.1}$) and a shift to much longer values for short sections, normally concluding ones. This change, although strictly indicating *tripla* (diminution in the ratio 3 to 1, with the beat moving from the semibreve to the dotted breve), apparently implies a *sesquialtera* relationship with three semibreves in $\frac{\emptyset}{3}$ equivalent to *two* in ₵. In Taverner's *Gloria tibi Trinitas* both signatures occur simultaneously in the third Agnus in this relationship. At the end of the fifteenth century composers on the Continent began to use short triple-time sections (often signed simply '3') which it is easy to prove demand a *sesquialtera* interpretation; such sections, although more often intermediate than final, may have suggested the use (and set the mode of performance) of $\frac{\emptyset}{3}$ passages in England.

In a few works, notably some of Sheppard's hymns and canticles, the signature changes from ₵ to 𝄵. 𝄵, like $\frac{\emptyset}{3}$, is a sign of diminution, so one would expect the beat to be shifted (in this case from the semibreve to the breve) and longer values to be used, if there were not to be an absurdly marked increase in speed. But in fact the notation under 𝄵 and ₵ is very similar: in the first setting of *Deus tuorum militum* verses 2 and 4 are actually the same musically except for the change of time-signature. Obviously then, 𝄵 shows a change in the speed of the semibreve beat, not a change from a semibreve to a breve beat; since it is a sign of *diminution*, this change would be an acceleration. In *Deus tuorum militum* it lets the music get quicker and more exciting towards the end of the piece; but in the Magnificat and Te Deum it is used part-way through, and is followed by a return to ₵.

VOCAL SCORING, PITCH AND TRANSPOSITION

It may be safely assumed that the music we are considering was intended for unaccompanied voices. As Frank Harrison points out, some motets and Mass movements 'composed in motet-fashion' before *c.* 1450 had been performed in the pulpitum with a small organ taking part; but after this style of composition had died out we have no reason to think that organs, or any other instruments, accompanied vocal polyphony. They would have served no useful purpose here, their proper place being in *alternatim* works.[18]

Most fully polyphonic pieces have some sections scored for the full number of voice-parts, others for smaller groups. Full sections were obviously taken by the complete body of singers; reduced passages were almost certainly for soloists or possibly sometimes semi-chorus. In some early fifteenth-century manuscripts each part in a duet section is labelled 'unus' (indicating one voice to a part) or the whole duet is marked 'duo', while the full three- or four-part sections are marked 'chorus'.[19] Such labelling did not survive the first half of the century, but the use of red ink for the words of reduced passages and black elsewhere, clearly to imply the solo-chorus distinction, is still found in the Eton choirbook. But reduced and full writing are often sufficiently different in style to suggest the solo-chorus contrast in any case. There may have been occasionally two singers to a line throughout reduced sections, notably in those few where a part divides for the final chord (as in the bass at '(fili)-um' in Lambe's *Salve regina*). But a second singer may have entered for the 'extra' note only; there are after all several cases where additional parts come in for the last syllable of a solo passage before taking part in a full section (for instance at '(glorificamus) te/Gratias' in the Gloria of Taverner's Mass *Corona spinea*).

Changes from reduced to full texture would be pronounced, but by no means overwhelming because pre-Reformation choirs were not large by modern standards. At Eton College the choir in 1476 numbered seven men and ten boys. Perhaps this body was sometimes joined by fellows and chaplains who could sing polyphonic music, as Harrison suggests;[20] if not, there would have been only one singer to some of the men's parts in the few largest antiphons from the College's choirbook such as Browne's *O Maria salvatoris mater* in eight parts. The boys, who sang the top two parts in the majority of pieces, were in good supply, but the larger number of their weaker voices was necessary to maintain balance, particularly since some boys would always be new and inexperienced. Taverner's choir at Tattershall Collegiate Church had six men and six boys;[21] without additional help this would mean two singers apiece for the three men's parts of a five-part work. The size of his other choir, at Wolsey's Cardinal College, Oxford, with twelve clerks and sixteen choristers, clearly reflected the Cardinal's general desire for magnificence.[22]

Parts in a manuscript source may have either no names or names which clearly do not indicate what types of voices are required. To know who should perform a piece the editor must examine the written ranges and the clefs. Pieces with some combinations of clefs—all are among those without a bass clef in the lowest part—have abnormal or unworkable compasses and should clearly be transposed to bring them into line with normal practice. But most works have the bass clef for the lowest voice and a total written range where high boys' voices are used of F or G to f'' or g'', the accepted compass of much music of later times, and thus are often presented untransposed in modern editions. Yet there is evidence that choir pitch was formerly almost a minor third higher than present-day pitch; so that the effect the composer intended can today best be had only by singing such pieces a minor third higher than written. The level of choir pitch has been determined principally from comments about the Worcester Cathedral organ of 1614 in a letter written by Nathaniel Tomkins in 1665.[23] The two open diapasons on the Great organ had 10-foot pipes for their lowest notes, which gave C on the keyboard and F, in terms of choir pitch. According to the modern standard a 10-foot pipe yields a note fractionally lower than A, flat, and hence about a minor third above seventeenth-century choir pitch. Choir pitch may be assumed to have been the same in early Tudor days as a century later; the standard of organ pitch mentioned above was apparently stable over a long period, because a contract of 1519 for the organ of All Hallows, Barking mentions pipe lengths of 10 feet for the diapason at C.[24]

Five very basic vocal ranges may be isolated: these must correspond with the types of voices mentioned in the records of the household chapel of Henry Percy, fifth Earl of Northumberland, who died in 1527,[25] and by Charles Butler in 1636 in *The Principles of Musik*,[26] namely trebles, means (both boys' voices), countertenors, tenors and basses. The treble uses all or most of the interval d' to g'' (in terms of modern pitch approximately f' to b'' flat); the mean will cover some eight, nine or ten notes between f and d'' (*a flat* and f''); the countertenor works between c and g' (*e flat* and *b' flat*); the tenor between A and d' (*c* and f'); the bass between F and *b flat* (*A flat* and *d' flat*).

The total range of about three octaves covered by these five types of voices was much larger than the compass available in the first half of the fifteenth century (usually about two octaves), and a little greater than that of late fifteenth- and early sixteenth-century Continental music. In all countries there had been an extension downwards after about 1440, so that the lowest part was now in the bass rather than tenor register, giving new weight and body to the texture; but it was in England that the greatest upward extension was made, the high treble parts, which reach a'' *flat* or b'' *flat* in present-day pitch, lending a unique brilliance to much of the music of our period. The practicality of the treble's surprisingly high top notes need not be doubted: it has been excellently demonstrated in some modern performances.[27]

The full upward extension of the treble is made in much of the Eton music, but a few works show an apparently intermediate stage where only written *e″* (sounding *g″*) is reached. One such is *Gaude flore virginali* by William Horwood, who was among the older composers represented in the manuscript; this work, like some others with low treble, also keeps the second and third parts a little lower than normal.

Horwood's second part is pitched mainly in the octave *g* to *g′*, with a total range *f* to *a′* (sounding today *a flat* to *c″*). Browne's *O Maria salvatoris mater* has this type of low mean (*f* to *a′*) and a mean of more usual range (*g* to *c″*, with a very limited use of notes below *c′*). The mean regularly reached written *d″* when in the mid sixteenth century it frequently served as the highest voice. The reasons for the treble's decline is unclear, but it is worth noticing that it is something of a rarity in English church music, and also (particularly since Continental influence was stronger in the mid sixteenth century than previously) that it was not cultivated abroad.

Horwood's third part descends no further than the (written) *c* which is pretty consistently the countertenor's lowest note in later works, but uses the highest notes available to it very sparingly. It touches written *f′* only three times, and is chiefly confined to the ninth *c* to *d′*, although in most countertenor parts from the Eton book *e′* and *f′* are quite common. The note *g′*, never found in Eton, became increasingly common for countertenors from Taverner's time onwards. Composers tended to lose interest in the countertenor's three or four lowest notes and concentrate on the top eight or nine, with consequently an increased interest in the head register or 'falsetto' voice. Some mid sixteenth-century countertenor lines already cover much the same ground as a Purcell alto solo such as *'Tis Nature's Voice*, if we agree that a change in pitch to something like the modern standard took place in the late seventeenth century.[28]

Many works have a tenor with a range of about *A* or *c* to *d′*. But especially in the earliest years of our period, the countertenor and tenor ranges were not entirely distinct. It is worth remembering that in the first half of the fifteenth century (before the bass register was in use) the middle and lowest parts in three-part pieces had most frequently been roughly equal; and where they had shared the tenor clef the main range was *c* to *d′*, with some *e′*s and *f′*s, especially perhaps in the middle part. In Horwood's *Gaude flore virginali* the third and fourth parts (both with tenor clefs) still work within the same basic interval of a ninth, the former with its few *e′*s and *f′*s, the latter with one *e′ flat*. In Banester's five-part *O Maria et Elizabeth* the same clefs and general ranges apply, the third voice rising to *e′* several times and *f'* once, the fourth never going above *d'*. Later these small differences in range between the third and fourth voices of five-part groupings became more marked until one really can speak of distinct countertenor and tenor parts in a work like Taverner's *Gloria tibi Trinitas.*

The bass was particularly consistent in range throughout our period from written *F* to *b flat*. It may seem odd that it went down only to *A flat* at modern pitch, but this avoided the lack of clarity which might attend notes lower than these and would have been serious in unaccompanied singing. Unusually low notes do occasionally occur when basses divide to give an octave for the final chord of a section: in Taverner's *Gloria tibi Trinitas* written *D* appears with *d* several times; Cornysh's Magnificat ends with *C* and *c*. Sheppard sometimes uses *D* or *E* independently, not as octave doublings, usually at phrase endings where they are easiest to sing.

Works without a bass clef in the lowest voice do not on paper have the basic written ranges listed above, and were intended to be transposed (except in the case of some smaller-scale pieces, as mentioned a little later). Today they need a double transposition: that originally intended, plus the 'standard' upward shift of a minor third to reflect the change in pitch. By leaving the 'original' transpositions to the performers, the composer avoids notating the numerous flats and (particularly) sharps which would often be necessary in written-out transpositions, and thus preserves a greater measure of his much valued 'modal purity' on paper.

A comprehensive scheme of transpositions for sixteenth-century vocal music has been worked out by David Wulstan, mainly from scraps of informations given by theoretical writers and from comparison of sources which use different clefs (and therefore different written ranges) for the same work.[29] This scheme appears to be capable of application even to the music of the Eton choirbook. (There are certain exceptions however—almost all in two- and three-part works from the Ritson and Pepys manuscripts and in Ludford's Lady Masses. Here there is good reason to suppose that a *tenor* clef at the bottom still means what it seems to have meant in Dunstable's time, namely that the lowest voice is a tenor or countertenor, and that no transposition is required (that is, in fifteenth- and sixteenth-century terms)).

In works requiring transpositions of the 'original' kind one most frequently encounters the C clef on the fifth line in the lowest part and abnormally high ranges. Transposition down a perfect fourth often gives the 'normal' written compasses, especially in works such as Davy's *In honore summae matris* and Taverner's *O splendor gloriae* where the top part has a G clef on the first line; here, remembering the minor third pitch-change since the sixteenth century, the modern transposition is down a tone. Some pieces, including Taverner's *Gaude plurimum*, Fayrfax's Mass *Albanus* and Browne's *O regina mundi clara*, seem originally to have demanded transposition by a third. Here Wulstan assumes a shift of a minor third (which is now cancelled out by the change of pitch-standard); but a major third sometimes seems to produce the 'best' ranges. Of course we do not know how much flexibility there was: the modern performer must adopt the solution which he thinks most convincing. Wulstan interprets use of a tenor clef for the bass part (as in Tallis's *Dum transisset*) as having implied the shift of a fifth down.

Some clefs indicate that the written pitches are too low. The rare 'gamut' clef, as in Sheppard's *Gaude virgo christipera* and *Judica me Deus*, means an original transposition of a fourth, a minor sixth today. An F clef on the top line sometimes means the same (in Taverner's five-part Magnificat and Marbeck's *Domine Jesu Christe* for instance), but elsewhere, as in Taverner's *Ave Dei Patris filia* and Tallis's *Salve intemerata*, it must indicate movements in old and new terms respectively of a fourth and major second.

ACCIDENTALS

No question of performance practice is so vexed as the handling of accidentals. The problem is whether those accidentals given in the manuscripts are sufficient (allowing for errors) or whether considerable additions need to be made, particularly of sharps outside the normal scales or 'hexachords' termed *musica ficta*. The most pressing point concerns the 'leading-notes' at minor and Mixolydian cadences: should they be left flat, as they most frequently are in sources from our period, or be editorially sharpened?

The evidence for sharpened leading-notes is largely knowledge of earlier and later practice. Thomas Morley observes that 'every cadence is sharp', condemning a 'flat cadence' as a 'thing against nature'.[30] The *Cantiones* of 1575, and Byrd's 1589 and 1591 publications, all particularly authoritative sources, regularly insert such accidentals. Some later English adaptations of motets from these collections give far fewer accidentals, which almost certainly means that a tradition of adding accidentals did exist.[31] In 1597 William Bathe complained in his *Brief Introduction to the Skill of Song* that one had often to infer the use of flats and sharps from 'the course of the song', because of the carelessness and ignorance of scribes who did not notate them.[32]

Very much earlier, theorists such as Johannes de Muris (c. 1325)[33] and Ugolino d'Orvieto (c. 1400)[34] had given rules for intervallic progressions which involve chromatic alteration. Accidentals are applied freely in some fourteenth-century manuscripts, for example in Landini's music. But in the fifteenth century they are much fewer. This may mean that the singers could now be trusted to add their own accidentals, and at first it probably does. But Paul Doe points out that in the fifteenth century, with the decline in the 'secular' aesthetic hitherto prevailing vocal lines in church music

> appear to move much closer to the melodic and rhythmic ideals of plainsong. In melodic terms, this would imply a more rigorously 'diatonic' idiom—for plainsong, although it used flats in certain situations, did not (so far as is known) employ *musica ficta* sharps. It is also possible in Ockeghem's generation to visualize a conscious cultivation of 'purity' in realising the melodic and harmonic implications of the modes, and an awareness of modal structure which, in a work like Ockeghem's own *Missa cuiusvis toni*, is seriously impaired by the wholesale application of *musica ficta*, at cadences or anywhere else.[35]

When dealing with English music of the late fifteenth and early sixteenth centuries—even though there are limits to modal 'purity' especially before 1500 (see Chapter 5, section on Sonority and harmony) —similar restraint is very wise. It is worth remembering also that those who sang from the manuscripts of that age were not reading from scores, from which the *harmonic* implications of what they were singing could always be followed; even the most 'stock' cadential formulae could be used in non-cadential contexts where use of a *musica ficta* sharp might result in a very crude clash.[36] Admittedly such problems could be resolved in rehearsal, but scribes are sufficiently careful in dealing with other much simpler situations to make their silence on leading-notes worthy of respect.

The final chord of a cadence is almost always major, the third being marked with an accidental where necessary. Some of the exceptions may be the result of an omitted accidental; but some are clearly not: for example the final chord of 'O clemens' from John Sutton's *Salve regina* would require four different parts to remember to add F sharps if the chord were to be major.

The eventual adoption of sharpened leading-notes is probably best seen as part of the major stylistic change which music underwent in the mid sixteenth century. The expansive 'plainsong' aesthetic was progressively rejected in favour of a more concise expression which would suggest or require the more pointed tonal definition of sharpened leading-notes.

In the 1575 *Cantiones* there are some semitonal clashes or false relations where one part has a sharpened leading-note while another employs the same note unsharpened. This idiom, which is far more logical and controlled than the crude clashes sometimes obtained in earlier music by the indiscriminate sharpening of leading-notes, can rarely have been cultivated before Tallis, not least because composers earlier had not often doubled the leading-note.

TEXT UNDERLAY

In the earlier part of our period the relationship between words and music was often a somewhat distant and casual one (see in particular Chapter 5, section on Words and music). It is not surprising therefore that there is sometimes a lack of clarity in scribes' alignment of syllables and notes. Especially in passages where notes are many but syllables are few, precision may not always have been considered very important in any case; for two sources of a work sometimes vary quite considerably.

The most troublesome textual question concerns the very inadequate underlay of a few cantus firmus parts: this is discussed in Chapter 4, section on Cantus firmus treatment. Here the singers apparently had to play some part in fitting words and music together. They also had to do this where verbal repetition (a device adopted in the second quarter of the sixteenth century) is indicated simply by 'ij' or some other conventional sign (see for instance Plate 8, third stave).

4

Musical Form and Structure

In most *alternatim* works the musical form and structure cannot be distinguished from the liturgical, since the composer simply adds voice-parts to (or replaces) certain sections of the proper plainsong. The sectional divisions of other types of work are also to some extent dictated by those of the text, but the composer often does have very important decisions to make, an understanding of which is necessary before we look at the style and technique of the music of our period.

Most pieces, except some short ones, are made to fall into two principal parts (which we shall term 'major sections'), the point of division, most commonly at or near the middle, being marked by a double-bar and often a change of time-signature. This basic bi-sectional plan is the framework within which other formal techniques to be described in this Chapter often operate: namely textural schemes founded on an alternation between passages for the maximum number of voice-parts and others for various reduced groupings, precise relationships in length between various sections, and the arrangement of cantus firmus statements. Settings of Magnificat, although *alternatim*, apply some of the formal methods of fully polyphonic works.

The techniques just outlined take for granted the very passive role which the listeners would play in the worship of the unreformed church generally: length relationships for example are usually of a kind that no listener could possibly grasp, and the disposition of a cantus firmus is clear only on detailed inspection of the score. Some of these techniques (notably the contrasts between full and reduced textures and the intermediate change of time-signature) also give expression on a large scale to that principle of differentiation which often meant very marked rhythmic and melodic variety at the level of the single section or phrase. In the middle of the sixteenth century, when the desire for greater musical unity really took hold, block textural contrasts became weaker and finally disappeared. Imitation, the principal means of unifying the single phrase or section, was often so powerful that the

38

succession of sets of entries in itself almost constitutes a formal structure. Repetition of phrases and brief sections came to be employed with some frequency, whereas earlier (outside *alternatim* works) it had been virtually restricted to the head-motif technique of having a common opening for all the movements of a Mass.

MAJOR SECTIONS

Many Mass movements and votive antiphons and some psalm-motets, including almost all large-scale pieces, fall very obviously into two 'major sections' by having a change at or near the middle from triple time with signature Ø or O to duple (₵ or C). The point of division is invariably marked with a double-bar, and is sometimes the only really complete internal break in the music. The triple section almost always ends with a passage for full choir, while a reduced group of voices begins the second major section. All this can be traced back at least to early tenor Masses such as Dufay's *Caput* of *c.* 1440–50.

Except for some brief ones, works without change of signature still have the same bi-sectional construction. Some pieces beginning in duple time end with a passage in Ø or (from Taverner's day onwards) $\frac{\emptyset}{3}$; and some with the intermediate change from triple to duple conclude with a return to triple. Such concluding passages are usually short by comparison with the whole work's length, and do not represent third major sections. Walter Lambe's *O Maria plena gratia* for example has a major section of 140 bars in Ø, 141 bars to balance this in ₵, and then a final 26 in Ø which make up a kind of 'coda'. Triple-duple-triple structure had been common in the first half of the fifteenth century, and a Gloria by Dunstable and a Credo by Richard Markham had the same pattern which Lambe adopts (except that their textural plans were different, with *reduced* texture concluding the opening triple section and *full* texture beginning the duple one).

In Magnificats the plainsong–polyphony alternation is the main formal principle, but the six polyphonic verses are virtually always grouped in three pairs, the first and third in triple time, the second in duple. This does not represent a basically bi-sectional plan—the third pair of verses is not a 'coda', because it is normally as long as each of the other pairs if not actually longer. Moroever the first triple section almost invariably ends with reduced texture, the duple section starting with the full choir, which contradicts normal practice in our period, even if it does seem to recall the layout of the Dunstable Gloria and Markham Credo mentioned above.

TEXTURAL SCHEMES

Until the last years of our period all fully polyphonic works except a few very short ones have some passages scored for the full number of parts available, the rest for various reduced groupings (and sung by soloists or possibly sometimes semi-chorus). The resulting contrasts of sonority are a very important and effective means of articulating the structure, because they occur for the most part fairly infrequently. Variations in scoring had been employed in a very limited way before 1450: duets preceded full sections with cantus firmus in Masses and motets, and sometimes provided 'relief' in the middle of a work. Interest in varying the scoring grew in the latter half of the fifteenth century, the choice and balance of the different reduced groupings in particular being most imaginative. This differentiation of weight and sonority was the perfect complement of the rhythmically and melodically differentiated style of counterpoint. Towards the middle of the sixteenth century, as composers increasingly sought *unity*, interest in varied scoring waned: changes of grouping, in the longer pieces especially, tended to become more infrequent, with reduced textures being used less, until in some works by Tallis, Whyte and Mundy continuous full texture was adopted.

It is hardly an exaggeration to say that no two Masses or antiphons with the reduced–full contrast have quite the same textural scheme. But certain basic patterns are standard. Every piece ends with a passage for the full choir; almost without exception full-choir writing concludes the first major section. Most works begin with reduced texture, which virtually always comes at the head of the second major section as well, and there is a change from reduced to full texture at least once in each major section.

Movements from reduced to full (or in the reverse direction) are more important formally than changes from one reduced grouping to another, because they help define the major sections and involve more conspicuous shifts in weight and musical style. Most major sections have either reduced writing plus a full section or (more frequently) the pattern reduced, full, reduced, full. The second (troped) part of a 'Salve regina' setting normally has three changes from reduced to full, because there is a 'verse' (for which liturgical sources demand solo performance) preceding each of the (choral) exclamations 'O clemens', 'O pia' and 'O dulcis Maria, salve'. In other works exclamations such as 'Salve' and names, especially Christ's, are frequently set off from surrounding reduced textures by brief full-choir treatment sometimes involving block chords. Works beginning with such exclamations include Robert Wylkynson's nine-part *Salve (regina)* and Browne's *O Maria (salvatoris mater)*.

Occasionally elsewhere textural changes provide examples of that 'pictorialism' and musical underlining of key words mentioned in Chapter 5, section on Words and music. For instance Tallis in *Gaude gloriosa* chooses the words '*omnia* serviunt' to bring in *all* the voices. And it is presumably Browne's intention to emphasise the highly-charged words 'Et pro nobis flagellato, / Spinis puncto' in his second *Salve regina* when he briefly introduces the full choir, even though these words come in a verse which other composers without exception assign wholly to soloists.

The customary use of solo groups for the mystery and solemnity of the 'Et incarnatus' and 'Crucifixus' sections of the Mass Credo, and the robust sound of all the voices for the triumph and rejoicing of 'Et resurrexit', seems to us today a fitting arrangement. Fifteenth- and sixteenth-century composers may have thought so too, but may simply have been applying one of the numerous textural conventions of Mass composition, which seem to have operated independently of verbal sense. The main conventions, most of which originated in the first half of the fifteenth century, are as follows (almost all are deviated from at least occasionally): full choir is used at 'Gratias agimus' and 'Qui sedes' in the Gloria, at 'Et in unum Dominum' or 'Et ex Patre' and 'Et resurrexit' or 'Et iterum venturus' in the Credo, at 'Dominus Deus Sabaoth' and both Osannas in the Sanctus, and in the Agnus Dei at the first 'miserere nobis' and for all or some of the third invocation; reduced writing is employed for all or some of the text preceding the first full-choir entry of each movement, at 'Qui tollis' in the Gloria, 'Et incarnatus' in the Credo and 'Benedictus' in the Sanctus, and for all or part of the second Agnus.

The textural plan of a Magnificat is again largely a matter of convention. As far as the fourth polyphonic verse at least, it is based on an alternation between full and reduced verses. The first and third polyphonic verses are regularly for full choir, often with a short passage for soloists after the colon. The second and fourth verses are both for reduced groups, with a change of scoring at the colon in each case. The fifth verse often begins with solo writing and ends with full, a pattern generally adopted in the sixth. Introducing the full choir at the beginning was perhaps considered liturgically necessary or desirable since polyphony was alternating with *choral* not solo plainchant, the solo verses later being a measure of latitude allowed in less conspicuous places.

Although the contrast between full and solo textures is the principal means of formal articulation and variety in sonority, composers were interested (some of the earlier ones particularly keenly) in contrasts of vocal colour, register, and weight between different reduced groupings. A major section generally begins with at least two well differentiated solo passages—the number tending to decrease in the sixteenth century so that more than two becomes uncommon and a single passage ceases to be exceptional.

In our period a reduced grouping can be defined as having any combination of voice-parts fewer than the total number available. (Before 1450 almost all reduced sections had been duets, even in four-part works.) After the adoption of five voices as the 'standard' number in the late fifteenth century, reduced writing in three parts is the most widely found; two-part sections are the next most numerous. Four-voice sections were not very widely favoured at first, but enjoyed some popularity towards the middle of the sixteenth century: the growing fondness for full textures presumably prompted this near approach to them in the solo sections. Works for six or more voices give a particularly wide choice of reduced groupings, but sections for more than four parts are rare, most examples dating from the middle decades of the sixteenth century. The division of parts, which again increases the number of solo combinations available, is not uncommon. It seems to occur most frequently in the second major section of a work, and usually involves trebles or means. In the second Agnus of *Corona spinea* Taverner divides both boys' parts—a wonderful sound—with a supporting bass entering half-way through. Subsequently a minor vogue for divided trebles and means developed: Tallis for example employs them in *Gaude gloriosa*, Sheppard in *Gaude gaude gaude Maria*, and their use actually enables Whyte (at a time when use of the reduced–full contrast was declining) to have a *five*-part 'reduced' section in the five-part *Justus es*, and his contemporary Mundy to depart still further from traditional practice by using six-part 'reduced(!)' sections in his five-part *Noli aemulari* and *Memor esto*.

Contrast between solo groups is often obtained by juxtaposing high and low voices, commonly with boys 'versus' men. These and other groups of adjacent voices were the types preferred latterly, but for much of our period composers liked also to set off closely-spaced groups and those with voices far apart. Lambe for example begins his *Salve regina* with the three middle voices, moves to the outer two (treble and bass), and then back to the middle three. As in this instance, the number of parts sometimes varies between reduced sections, so that weight and density are changed as well as colour and register. In the *Stabat mater* by John Browne, whose feeling for textural colour and contrast is exceptionally keen, the entry of the treble and mean at 'Color erat', after a passage for the men, owes something of its magical clarity and lightness to the sudden reduction from four parts to two. It is quite common for an extra voice to be added somewhere after the beginning of a section, usually to turn a duet into a trio. Very occasionally the process of addition is carried further. The most striking instance is the increase from two to seven parts in Browne's *O Maria salvatoris mater* after the initial eight-part section; there is also a build-up from three voices to five at 'Eja mater . . . In amando Christum Deum' in his *Stabat mater*. On both occasions the following full-choir entry is heard as the climax to which the addition of voices has been leading. In *O Maria*, however, a very brief reduction to three voices at '(peccami)-na' provides a most telling moment of relaxation between the seven-part writing and the consummation of the eight-part entry.

Parallelism between the textural schemes of the different movements of a Mass can help to unify them. Fayrfax gives the Gloria and Credo of *O quam glorifica* almost identical schemes; in the Sanctus and Agnus he employs the same reduced groupings as in the other movements, and in the same order, but places them differently in relation to the full sections. Such parallelism between movements underlies Fayrfax's other Masses, but is not worked out so thoroughly in them.[1] The method, largely abandoned by later composers, is occasionally found before 1450; Dunstable, for example, used it in the paired four-part Gloria and Credo.

LENGTH RELATIONSHIPS

Next in importance to the basic bi-sectional structure and the textural scheme is the establishment of relationships in length between various sections of a work—often quite complex ones forming 'secret' structures discernible only on very close examination of the score. Such length relationships had been widely employed in and before the first half of the fifteenth century, most notably as a fundamental aspect of isorhythmic technique. Thus the three statements of an isorhythmic tenor by Dunstable are always presented in progressive diminution, for example in the ratio 3:2:1, as in *Veni sancte Spiritus / Veni creator* and several other motets.

Perhaps today we are inclined to dismiss this kind of construction as having more to do with mathematics than with music. But to the medieval mind music and mathematics were vitally connected. Boethius, the Roman philosopher (*c.* 470–525), whose writings on music were standard texts throughout the Middle Ages, thought of music as 'number made audible'. According to him, as Albert Seay puts it,

> all things that are beautiful are subject to the power of number and can be explained by it. . . . All . . . beauties may . . . be expressed as forms of numerical ratio, ratio that has been made easily sensed by the ear in music. Thus it is that music stands as a way of depicting the beauty and perfection of God and his creations, the world and man. It is here that music achieves its real place in medieval philosophy, for, as a microcosm in the macrocosm, it can duplicate on a small scale the power of number inherent in the otherwise incomprehensible grand expanse about us.[2]

'Ratio' in Boethius refers to musical intervals, not to the formal methods of polyphonic music, which were devised centuries after the philosopher's death; but the men who developed these methods must have been conscious of their speculative implications.

Length relationships persisted until the mid sixteenth century, the latest examples so far traced being in Tallis's *Gaude gloriosa* and Whyte's Magnificat; but probably for some considerable time before this composers had ceased to be interested—or perhaps even to realise—their speculative implications, and had regarded them simply as structural conventions. Many relationships quoted below are not absolutely exact in the way that isorhythmic ones were. In some cases the count given may be slightly imprecise (for instance, it is sometimes difficult to see *exactly* where a full section ends and a solo one begins if the two overlap very slightly; but composers may no longer have felt complete exactitude necessary.[3]

Successive statements of isorhythmic tenors employed simple ratios such as 2:1, 3:2, and 4:3—the same ratios as, respectively, the 'perfect' intervals, the octave, fifth and fourth. But Dunstable sometimes also made the number of semibreves in the second and third sections of a motet together equivalent to the number in the first section. This equality between sections, which was also present in some non-isorhythmic pieces before 1450, underlies almost all length relationships in our period. The actual numbers used in these relationships do not, so far as one can see at present, appear to have any particular symbolic or numerological significance of themselves—except in Taverner's *Playn Song* Mass. Here there is 'virtual identity between the number of syllables and breve beats in both the Gloria and the Credo (i.e. Gloria, 188 breves, 186 syllables . . .; Credo, 266 breves, 264 syllables . . .)'.[4]

In a Mass the most important relationships affect the work as a whole, thus demonstrating the essential unity between movements, but some do concern individual movements or pairs of movements.

Although few of these length relationships have been noticed in the past, it has often been remarked that the movements of a Mass are generally similar in length. Curiously this most obvious type of relationship is the least close, involving as a rule no more than a broad similarity. Taverner's *Western Wynde* is the only Mass in which all four movements balance (with 100 bars each in the Gloria, Credo and Agnus, and 97 in the Sanctus). Many works do, however, have two movements that match; Fayrfax's *Regali* for instance has 166 bars in the Gloria, 163 in the Credo, but 187 in the Sanctus and 145 in the Agnus. It is not unusual to find the Gloria and Credo closely related; these were after all the movements most commonly paired in the early fifteenth century before the four- and five-movement cyclic Mass had fully evolved, and in the York manuscript of *c.* 1490–1520. A further type of pairing is sometimes found: in *Regali* for example Fayrfax makes the Gloria and Credo together 329 bars, the Sanctus and Agnus 332, thus giving his entire Mass two equal sections in a way comparable to his establishment of two equal major sections in a single movement or antiphon.

Since the movements of a Mass form a unity, it is not surprising that the first major sections of all of them together should sometimes be made to balance all the second major sections. In *Corona spinea* Taverner makes the four first sections come to 381 bars, the second sections to 386. His Mass *Small Devotion* sets 150 bars against 152.

In some Masses length relationships are linked to the textural scheme. Sometimes there is equality between the full-choir passages in a major section or movement and the reduced ones, sometimes between the full (or reduced) writing in the two sections of a movement. But one even finds cases where the first major sections are balanced by the full texture. Thus in Taverner's *Mater Christi* we have

all four first major sections	143 bars;
full-choir passages in all four movements	145 bars

and therefore

all four second major sections	196;
reduced passages in all four movements	194.

Fayrfax's *Tecum principium* has a similar arrangement:

first major sections	481 bars;
full texture	476
second sections	342;
reduced texture	347.

The origin of this can probably be traced to the isorhythmic motet. In Dunstable's *Salve schema sanctitatis* sections in four parts total 540 semibreves, the same as the first and second sections, while the third section and all the duets throughout the work equal 108.

In *Salve schema sanctitatis* the full sections and those with the cantus firmus are the same in extent, as therefore are the duets and passages without the cantus firmus. But in later music a borrowed plainsong sometimes penetrates a few solo sections, and a fresh set of relationships may occur between music with cantus firmus and music without it. Thus in Fayrfax's *Regali* sections in duple time (that is, all the second major sections minus the triple-time Benedictus Osanna) balance all the music with cantus firmus (288 and 289 bars). Cantus firmus statements are occasionally related: the two in the Credo of Taverner's *Corona spinea* for example come to 52 and 50 bars.

Some votive antiphons have no more than a broad similarity between major sections, some not even this; but Horwood's *Gaude flore virginali* is one of several works to show a relationship between major sections and types of texture:

first section	107 bars;
full texture	105
second section	90;
reduced texture	92.

Although Tallis's *Gaude gloriosa* was written probably seventy or eighty years after Horwood's piece, and was one of the last antiphons composed, it still has exactly the same kind of arrangement.

In Magnificat settings verses and pairs of verses may be related, while some arrangements concern groups of verses and full or reduced textures. Both anonymous settings from the Lambeth choirbook have the number of semibreves in the four triple-time verses corresponding with the number in reduced sections throughout the work (and thus the duple verses balancing the full texture). Taverner in his five-part setting has

verses 1–4	376 semibreves;
reduced texture	376

verses 5–6   261;
full texture   261

and a somewhat similar arrangement in the six-part one with the first
and second polyphonic verses balancing the full sections. Magnificat
verses usually have a break at the colon, and some composers (Lambe,
Kellyk, Horwood and Prentyce) even establish a relationship between
the six first halves of verses and all the full textures, the second halves
and the reduced writing.

CANTUS FIRMUS TREATMENT

A cantus firmus is a melody with a prior existence—most commonly
it is plainsong—which is incorporated into a polyphonic composition;
it may receive little or no elaboration and provide a foundation part
(the method predominant in our period and discussed here) or be treated
more freely as something of melodic as well as structural interest (instances of this are mentioned in later Chapters, especially Chapter 7, as
they arise).

The inclusion of a plainsong from a particular feast may serve to
relate a polyphonic work to that feast. In addition the melody, with its
hallowed associations, may be to some extent the reference to authority
and tradition so dear to medieval man; in which case the weakened
status of the cantus firmus in the fifteenth century (as described below)
and later its less frequent use can be seen as mirroring the decline of
medieval culture and its eventual passing. The waning influence of the
cantus firmus in the sixteenth century is connected more obviously
with the rising emphasis on textural equality and integration at that
time, for this new emphasis would naturally discourage use of a foundation part aloof from its neighbours—although proper plainsongs in
equal notes, less distinct from the surrounding voices than other cantus
firmi with their mostly longer mixed values, were much used in
alternatim works for the Office.

The cantus firmus in mixed values is a descendant of the early Mass
tenor, which is itself a successor of the isorhythmic tenor. The isorhythmic tenor, with its recurring rhythmic patterns and strict diminutions, controlled the structure and length of a motet almost absolutely.
In some early Masses there was rhythmic patterning of a weaker kind:
thus Power's *Alma redemptoris mater*, Dufay's *Caput* and Frye's *Summae
Trinitati* have the same rhythmic layout in the tenor in all movements,

but without any system of diminutions. After the decline of isorhythm, reduced sections without cantus firmus begin to occupy much more of a work, and length relationships become increasingly independent of the cantus firmus. In fact by the late fifteenth century it often appears that the cantus firmus is tailored to the bi-sectional plan rather than actually shaping the piece.

One statement per major section appears to be the basic cantus firmus arrangement, but there are many departures from this, and in comparatively few antiphons and Mass movements are composers content to have one complete statement in *each* section. Variations are generally within fairly narrow limits however, and most pieces have one, two or three statements. It must be remembered that English cantus firmus treatment is on the whole less varied and enterprising than Continental[5]—although one should not forget when saying this the experiments in double cantus firmus construction mentioned in Chapter 6, in the sections on Walter Lambe, Richard Davy and Robert Wylkynson.

A few masses have considerably more than the normal maximum of three statements per movement. The most interesting of these, discussed in detail elsewhere, are *Albanus* by Fayrfax, which is built on a frequently re-iterated nine-note phrase; Alwood's *Praise Him Praise-worthy*, another 'ostinato' Mass; and Masses by Taverner, Tye and Sheppard which are essentially sets of variations on the secular tune 'Western Wynde'. These latter show most powerfully a sixteenth-century tendency for the cantus firmus to be present in solo sections instead of being restricted to full sections as it was in the isorhythmic motet, early tenor Masses, and generally in the Eton antiphons.

The *Western Wynde* Masses present their tune very clearly, so that it would be immediately recognisable to those who know it; but this is unusual, for cantus firmus treatment in most Masses and antiphons deliberately goes against the character of the melody as melody. Thus there is the rhythmic disguise of very mixed note-values, the distortion of tempo in the choice of mostly long notes, with the breve as a kind of basic unit, and sometimes dislocation of the original phrase structure. Such treatment, inherited from the isorhythmic tenor, which applied it far more rigorously, was not considered a violation of the cantus firmus or an undermining of its 'authority', for to the medieval mind, with its ability to trace such 'hidden' layers of meaning as the allegorical and anagogical, the chant's surface identity alone would have been of limited importance. Melodic dislocation, predictably, is most acute before 1500. The first cantus firmus statement of

(1.Ex. 4.)

Browne's *O regina mundi clara* (*1.Ex. 4.*) is an extreme case—and one whose effect we can appreciate particularly easily because the plainsong is a well-known one, that shared by the hymns 'Pange lingua gloriosi proelium certaminis' (Holy Week) and 'Pange lingua gloriosi corporis mysterium' (Corpus Christi). After 1500 there is some use of a simple equal-note cantus firmus layout, and a melody's phrase structure is generally honoured.

The use as cantus firmi of only parts of liturgical melodies was fairly common in the fifteenth century, particularly in the first half with many isorhythmic compositions. Composers of these works often paid no more attention to the melodic phrase structure when selecting cantus firmi than when disposing them: for instance the tenor of Dunstable's *Veni sancte Spiritus | Veni creator* consisted of lines 2 and 3 of 'Veni creator' minus the last two notes, but preceded by the final note of line 1. Later composers choose parts of melodies which have rather more right to separate existence. Richard Hygons builds his *Salve regina* on the long 'Caput' melisma from the Maundy Thursday antiphon 'Venit ad Petrum' which had also formed the tenors of Masses by Dufay, Ockeghem and Obrecht.[6] Taverner quotes verses 1, 2, 5, 14 and 29 of the Te Deum melody, plus the *neuma* of the fourth mode, in *Ave Dei Patris filia*; and in the Mass *Albanus* Fayrfax takes simply the nine-note phrase for the name 'Albanus' from the antiphon 'Primus in Anglorum'.

In a few works one statement of a cantus firmus is incomplete, despite full quotation of the melody elsewhere. (There is occasionally a very brief reference to a plainsong at the head of a Mass movement or antiphon, but we refer now to something much weightier and not necessarily at the beginning of a piece.) In *O Maria salvatoris mater* Browne uses the first eleven notes of his cantus firmus in the opening eight-part section, and the first statement proper does not begin until 'Cunctaque peccamina' (bar 48). The latter has *f* as its first note, but the 'false start' is on *c'*, as if to mark it off from the complete statements. Browne uses an anticipatory cantus firmus fragment in several other works; in *O regina mundi clara* it comes at 'Consortes nos facere' before the second statement, where, because the tenor is resting, it is in the 'wrong' part as well as at the 'wrong' pitch. The second statements in the Gloria and Sanctus of Taverner's *Gloria tibi Trinitas* also have anticipatory fragments (at the 'correct' pitch, but in the 'wrong' voice). Davy's *In honore summae matris* has a single statement of the long respond melody 'Justi in perpetuum', but the Amen includes a partial re-statement which ends at 'Dominum' in the middle of a phrase.

A cantus firmus does not always have exactly the same number of notes as the melody in its original form. Extra repetitions are sometimes made, especially where a long text demands it; for example there may be three Cs in a cantus firmus where the plainsong original had only two. Repeated notes in the plainsong may be omitted, usually of course in sections with few words. In the last section of John Sutton's *Salve regina* ('O dulcis Maria, salve') each note of the chant 'Libera nos' normally becomes a semibreve, but repeated notes are combined as breves, thus slightly 'disguising' a basically equal-note layout. In some early sixteenth-century works there is an undisguised form of equal-note presentation, with notes repeated whether or not there are syllables to go with them; this happens for example in several sections of Taverner's *Gloria tibi Trinitas*.

In a number of works, chiefly Ludford's Lady Masses, some of the Forrest-Heyther Masses and Eton antiphons, a borrowed melody and its new text appear to fit even less well; for instance *1.Ex. 4.* shows the complete omission of words and phrases on the one hand and the placing of several syllables beneath a single note or ligature on the other. The composer (or copyist) presumably left some of the arranging to the singer. It is clear at any rate from remarks made on the Continent in the sixteenth century by Adrian Petit Coclico, Josquin's pupil, and by Zarlino, that part of a singer's training was the fitting of text to music[7]—and although neither writer enlarges on what he means, the kinds of situations discussed below may have been catered for. Instrumental performance is not implied by the incomplete texting of the soloist's part of Ludford's Lady Masses, because the text actually provided is more than would be necessary to cue an instrumentalist, and is underlaid with care as if for a singer. In other works incompleteness of underlay is so limited and sporadic that it constitutes no argument at all against vocal performance.

In Ludford's Masses the soloist's sections of an *alternatim* Gloria or Credo normally employ parts of the 'square' presented earlier in the Kyrie; but whereas in the Kyrie full text is supplied and most notes are in ligature, in the Gloria and Credo some ligatures are broken and only the opening words of a section are underlaid. Some ligatures are broken to accommodate the given fragments of text; other broken ligatures invite the addition of missing words. With the longest sections however, all the missing text can be inserted only if further ligatures are broken and some single notes are sub-divided (*2.Ex. 4.*). These techniques would be straightforward enough for an experienced singer to whom the words of the Mass were familiar.

Outside Ludford's Lady Masses textual omissions and irregularities pose greater problems. In Browne's *O regina mundi clara* for example, the phrase beginning at bar 26 of *1.Ex. 4.* is completely without text. This is clearly not an accidental omission, because it is only one of a number of textual irregularities in Browne's tenor and because there

are several similar cases in other works (always in cantus firmus parts), as at bars 63–70 in Browne's O Maria salvatoris mater and in the Gloria and Credo of Ashewell's Mass Jesu Christe. Presumably the missing words had to be supplied—from memory, even though the O regina mundi clara text was not a familiar one like the Mass Gloria and Credo. Browne's textless phrase is partly in a full-choir section, as other problematic phrases are wholly; one would expect there to be two or more singers to a part in such places, and so unless the singers were very well prepared and singing almost from memory, there would be a great danger of disagreement when sub-divisions of notes and similar amendments had to be made.

Occasionally parts of a cantus firmus are texted incompletely even though all the notes given are underlaid. Taverner's Gloria tibi Trinitas shows this peculiarity from time to time.[8] Near the beginning of the Credo for example, there is a four-note phrase in the cantus firmus part which has only the words 'Et ex Patre', although other voices sing 'Et ex Patre natum ante omnia saecula' while it is in progress; presumably the given notes were sub-divided in performance and the 'missing' words supplied. In some parts of Gloria tibi Trinitas the notes given are not enough for the text provided, sub-division again being the only reasonable answer; for example there are only two notes for 'bonae voluntatis' in the Gloria (see Plate 5).

With Gloria tibi Trinitas the copyist seems concerned to retain the same number of notes in the cantus firmus as there was in the plain song. On the other hand the Eton scribe, in O regina mundi clara and to a lesser extent in several other works, tries to avoid all repeated notes in his tenor whether or not the plainsong has them, admitting them only where a rest intervenes or (once or twice) where it is impossible in his system of notation to express a particular duration by a single note-symbol.

The techniques just described give the tenor a distinctive character, even a distinctive appearance on paper, which underlines its special function as foundation part and the voice of authority and tradition. Occasionally cantus firmus parts are further differentiated from the surrounding voices by the employment of unusual or awkward notational devices. For instance in *1.Ex. 4.* (bar 30) one has a change of time-signature and five-minim values (five-*quaver* ones in transcription) mostly expressed by notes which are partly black and partly red. The main source of notational puzzles in a tenor is the early sixteenth-century Mass *O quam suavis* by John Lloyd,[9] where the composer devises numerous very thorny problems within the accepted notational system, and also indulges in some trick notation whose solution lies in cryptic clues or 'canons'. The trick notation could not possibly have been interpreted correctly at sight even in Lloyd's time; the singers must have solved the riddles at their leisure, and then memorised their part—unless the sole copy of the Mass which now survives was merely some kind of presentation copy, and another existed in which the tenor was notated normally.

One of the most fascinating riddles comes at 'Et vitam venturi saeculi, Amen' in the Credo: 'Hic tenor cantatur in proportione geo-metrica, harmonica, arithmetica, sed tantum in numero'. This is accompanied by a series of nine semibreves, which will not fit the other parts. By trial and error H. B. Collins discovered that the nine notes should be grouped in threes, with one group for each of the numerical progressions demanded by the canon. The values in the first group should be (in semibreves) four, six, nine (a geometrical progres-sion); in the second group two, three, six (a harmonic progression); in the third four, six, eight (an arithmetical progression)—a novel expres-sion indeed of the Boethian concept of 'number made audible'. How-ever, Collins explains that the phrase 'sed tantum in numero' is probably 'a warning to the singers that they are not intended to sing like mere mathematicians . . . Having made sure of the notes, they were not to forget to meditate on 'the life of the world to come'.[10]

SHARING OF MATERIAL BETWEEN MASS MOVE-MENTS AND BETWEEN SEPARATE WORKS

Repetition of sections is fundamental to many musical forms such as the *da capo* aria, but it has no place in the structure of the single Mass movement, antiphon or Magnificat. We do of course find the re-statement of part of the response in a choral respond, but this is done for liturgical not musical reasons (although it may have helped encourage the adoption of a similar 'A B B' form in the early English anthem and in a few Elizabethan motets). But for most of our period the re-statement of polyphonic material was restricted to the linking of separate works (occasionally) and the unifying of Mass movements into genuine cycles (often).

In the latter case it normally takes the form of a 'head-motif', that is, a short polyphonic segment which appears at the beginning of every movement, usually recurring exactly except for alterations made to accommodate new words. Although the head-motif and the recurring cantus firmus were first used independently, in our period they often came to be employed together, with the head-motif supplying a clearly audible relationship between movements, the cantus firmus a more subtle internal unity. Occasionally, as in Fayrfax's *Tecum principium*, the first few notes of the first cantus firmus statement are anticipated in the head-motif, a neat way of combining the two unifying methods.

A few Masses without cantus firmus have a common ending to the movements and/or some internal correspondence as well as the head-motif. In Taverner's 'parody' Mass *Mater Christi* the parallelism between movements is explicable first and foremost as parallelism between the parent antiphon and each individual movement (further, see below). In Taverner's *Meane Mass* and Tallis's four-part Mass (see Chapters 9 and 11 respectively) the special interest in audible structural unity matches the very considerable concern for textural unity through imitation and chordal writing.

There are several Masses which are related to antiphons or Magnificats by common polyphonic material and sometimes a common cantus firmus as well. The extent of the music shared varies widely. Hugh Aston's Mass and antiphon *Te Deum*, for example, correspond very briefly indeed at the beginning to give an audible link, and draw upon parts of the same 'Te Deum laudamus' melody, while Tallis's Mass and antiphon *Salve intemerata* are very extensively connected. Limited relationships, as between Fayrfax's Mass, antiphon and Magnificat *O bone Jesu*, or Ludford's Mass and Magnificat *Benedicta* (see Chapter 8) are probably a kind of extension of the unifying links between Mass movements. Since linked Mass movements are all associated with one service, related *works* may originally have been designed for performance on the same day—or, in the case of Fayrfax's *Albanus* and *Regali* sets, connections with particular places may have been intended.

The two most extensive sharings of polyphony, between Taverner's *Mater Christi* and his Mass 'apon the antyme Mater Christi' (as the Peterhouse partbooks call it), and between Tallis's antiphon and Mass *Salve intemerata*, may just be particularly wide extensions of the limited linkages mentioned above, or may be something more. Their practice invites comparison with, and is possibly related to, the method usually referred to as 'parody', which was very widely employed on the Continent particularly in and after the second quarter of the sixteenth century. The term 'parody' indicates the re-use, normally on a fairly large scale, of polyphonic material from a motet, chanson or madrigal in the composition of a Mass; no connection with the literary meaning of the word is implied. In a parody Mass the Continental composer very frequently borrowed from someone else's music, but he was not guilty of plagiarism because he normally altered what he borrowed, notably by re-working imitations or adding extra voice-parts. In writing a parody Mass a composer was paying tribute to a fellow craftsman, and subjecting himself to an exacting test of skill, for the 'new' version would inevitably be compared with the original.

Taverner and Tallis, on the other hand, re-used their own work, and did not as a rule change the borrowed music much beyond what was necessary to accommodate the new words; consequently their practice appears to be largely independent of Continental parody method. A parallel might be seen with *contrafactum* technique where a piece has a new text substituted for the original yet suffers no significant alteration musically (Walter Frye's motet *O sacrum convivium* for example started life as the ballade *Alas Alas*).[11] But the comparison is of limited use, because while a *contrafactum* and its original have the same number of sections and use them in the same order, the Masses *Mater Christi* and *Salve intemerata* have some material not found in their parent works and do not necessarily incorporate borrowed sections in the 'correct' order.

In both *Mater Christi* and *Salve intemerata* two main considerations weighed when the composers borrowed from their antiphons: paralleling the structure of the antiphon in the Mass, and placing the transferred material where its scoring would accord with the normal textural conventions of the Mass.

With *Mater Christi* the parent antiphon is divided into short passages of a few bars each; all are transferred once, those which produce structural parallelism, and a few others, several times.[12] The opening of the antiphon is quoted at the head of each movement, its ending at the conclusion of each except the Sanctus. 'Unica spes nostra ... filium', which occurs before the first double-bar of the antiphon, is similarly placed in the Gloria ('Domine Deus rex coelestis ... omnipotens'), while a closing fragment from this passage recurs at the same point in the Credo and Agnus. Since the antiphon is quite short, many sections of the Mass, extending to about two-thirds of its length, are freely composed. In particular the Sanctus embodies very little borrowed material. This is partly because Taverner wanted to include more reduced writing than elsewhere, while there are few extended passages for soloists in the antiphon. The Sanctus is also predominantly free because of its melismatic text-treatment; if material from the antiphon, which employs a syllabic style most of the time, were used much for sparsely-texted sections, there would be a risk of stylistic discrepancy, because melismatic sections are often more florid in manner than syllabic ones. When parallelism between the original piece and a Mass movement is desired, the risk may have to be ignored: for example the head-motif, syllabic in the parent work, has melismatic word-setting in both the Sanctus and Agnus; but it undergoes slight ornamentation

to give a more typically melismatic style (*3.Ex. 4.*). Almost all departures from the original nature of the antiphon material are due to ornamentation, not genuine re-working. The phrase 'vitalis cibus', which re-appears several times in the Mass, retains its original harmonic basis, but has simply various decorations and re-distributions of the upper voices, except at 'Osanna' (Benedictus) where the bass part of the original is developed imitatively.

Mater Christi has one or two short underived passages from the Gloria repeated in later movements; such repetition occurs at the most odd moments, for the ending of '(Qui sedes ad dexteram Pa)-tris' suddenly re-appears part-way through the Sanctus Osanna. At '(miserere) nobis' in the first Agnus there is a most extraordinary patch-work effect: Taverner begins by bringing back a passage first heard at 'filius Patris' in the Gloria, and then leads straight on to a transference of 'rigantes fida pectora' from the antiphon, an inexact reference to the cadence of 'corpora' (antiphon), and the last bar or so of 'rogare audemus filium' (antiphon).

The Mass as a whole could be considered a little disappointing in that it fails to show the borrowed material in any significant new light, and destroys the 'flow' of the original by quoting from it chiefly in very short units. But there is no lack of continuity between 'old' and 'new'; and judged on its own merits *Mater Christi* is a worthy partner for Taverner's other five-part Masses.

Most sections from Tallis's antiphon *Salve intemerata* have been included in his Mass of that name, material being transferred in much larger blocks than in *Mater Christi*. Each section of the antiphon, except that used as head-motif, is transferred once only; but because the anti-phon is a long one and the Mass comparatively short, not a very great deal of free material (only about one quarter of the work) has to be supplied. The guiding principle is a kind of parallelism between parent work and Mass; for as Harrison has shown, the derived passages within each movement come (with one exception) in the order they appear in the antiphon.[13] The original piece has mostly syllabic word-setting, but Tallis, unlike Taverner, makes substantial borrowings in the Sanctus and Agnus; he manages this without the kind of stylistic dis-crepancy which Taverner was anxious to avoid because now melisma is strictly limited in these movements through frequent verbal repeti-tion (further, see Chapter 11).

5

The Style of the Eton Music

The Eton choirbook is by far the most important of the few English sources surviving from the first part of our period: in fact it is unquestionably one of the greatest monuments of English music in any age. After discussing its style in fairly general terms in the present Chapter, we investigate the work of its leading composers more closely in Chapter 6.

In the 1490s the Eton manuscript cannot but have represented the summit of English musical endeavour; yet it cannot on the other hand have been quite the isolated achievement which it now appears to be. Its composers belonged to a wide variety of major choral institutions,[1] and the kind of large-scale pieces which Eton contains must have been sung, composed and copied in many or all of these; and although we have no other large choirbooks before the Lambeth and Caius manuscripts of 1510 or later, we do have several fragmentary survivals of 'Eton-style' music. British Museum Additional MS. 54324, which consists of three bifolia from a small choirbook copied in about 1475,[2] has, among some considerably earlier music by Plummer, Dunstable and Dufay (*Caput* Kyrie), sizeable fragments from a five-part *Gaude flore virginali* which has much in common with the earlier Eton music. The ten leaves which constitute Bodleian Library MS. Mus. e. 21 formed the original covers of the late sixteenth-century Sadler partbooks (Mus. e. 1–5).[3] They were cut for this purpose from five folios of a choirbook which dated from the late fifteenth century (or possibly a little later). The leaves contain fragments of the Gloria and Credo of a six-part Mass[4] which seems to be based on the 'Veni creator' melody (or the identical 'Salvator mundi') transposed down a second. The Bodleian Library also has two complete folios (MS. Lat. liturg. a. 9) from a choirbook of *c.* 1490 which was similar in size and character to the Eton choirbook. The fragment contains the ending of Fayrfax's Magnificat *Regali* and the beginning of another (unidentified) Magnificat.[5]

Works such as the Eton antiphons and Magnificats would have been beyond the smaller, less proficient choirs; some of these presumably used the kind of music preserved in lesser sources, the Pepys, Ritson and York manuscripts. These latter, with very varied contents dating from about 1460 to 1510 and few direct links with the Eton repertory, are dealt with in Chapter 7.

The most outstanding traits of the Eton music are a richness and brilliance of sonority not found in earlier music or as a rule in contemporary Continental work (see section on Sonority and harmony) and outstanding rhythmic vitality and melodic variety (section on Rhythm and melody). The usually rather distant relationship between words and music is considered in the first main section of this Chapter.

The origin and early history of the magnificent Eton style are obscure, because of the paucity of late fifteenth-century sources and the lack of precise chronological data about individual works or composers' lives and movements. The existence of some broad parallelism between the stylistic developments of Continental and English music after Dunstable, particularly in the adoption of the harmonic bass part and in greater complexity of rhythm and phrase structure, suggests that there was *some* cross-Channel exchanging of ideas until about 1450 or even a little later; such men as John Plummer (d. *c.* 1462) and Walter Frye (d. 1474) are indeed known from both English and Continental sources. But it is clear from the distinctive character of the Eton style that by the 1470s at the latest (given William Horwood's death in 1484) English music was developing more or less in isolation from the 'mainstream' of activity in France and the Netherlands. Indeed it is noticeable that neither the Eton choirbook nor the minor sources discussed in Chapter 7 contain Continental music, thus ignoring completely such men as Ockeghem, Obrecht and Josquin. The latest pieces of foreign church music which have been traced in England are the fragments from Dufay's *Caput* Mass of *c.* 1440–50 in B.M. Add. MS. 54324 and in two fly-leaves from the Coventry Leet Book of *c.* 1450.[6] By 1500 when the choirbook was virtually complete, English music was decidedly insular and conservative; on the Continent Josquin, pioneer of pervasive imitation, was already in middle age.

WORDS AND MUSIC

The connection between words and music in the Eton choirbook is often a very loose one, much of the logic, character and structure of the music being independent of the text rather than allied to it. The Eton composers did not see their work as a form of preaching or teaching in which the message of the words was pre-eminent as mid sixteenth-century composers of Protestant church music often did, or were intended to do—its language alone would be a barrier to that—although as we saw in Chapter 1 they certainly recognised the power of music itself to express and aid devotion.

Because of their limited interest in text treatment composers often allowed the complex rhythmic interplay between voices to obscure the words, and they regularly employed extensive melisma which might run to six, eight, ten or even more bars, so long in fact that a listener would probably forget what word was being sung before it was finished. Such melisma is inevitable in the larger-scale works, since there is none of that verbal repetition which later became customary; but it may have been positively valued too: the *jubilus* of the plainsong Alleluia certainly was, being seen by medieval writers as 'an over-whelming expression of the ecstasy of the spirit, a joy that could not be restricted to words' and as carrying 'implications of catharsis, a cleansing of the soul'.[7]

Melisma usually comes on the penultimate syllable of each little segment of text (which may be a line, short phrase of even a single word) after basically syllabic treatment. Syllabic treatment, in spite of the often loose connection between words and music, sometimes reveals a close regard for matching the musical rhythm with the metre of the words through use of longer or metrically stronger notes for accented syllables than for weak ones. Limited use of dotted rhythms and repeated notes aid clear projection, as in our quotation from Davy's *In honore summae matris* (1.Ex. 5.). Even melodic shape is linked with the verbal stress patterns here, with the highest notes generally coinciding with important accented syllables.

(1.Ex. 5.)   *MB*, xi.105.

The syllabic writing of the Eton composers is a very considerable advance on most early fifteenth-century practice; in Dunstable for example, although strict syllabic writing—one note to one syllable—was sometimes used, close observation of verbal stresses was rare. The growing care for verbal accentuation is best seen, as John Stevens believes, as an example of 'that passion for natural detail which is a general characteristic of late medieval art in the north of Europe'; it certainly does not represent any 'humanist desire to achieve the ideal union, known to the ancients, between words and music', and is not, as we already know, born of any Reformatory 'zeal for the mere supremacy of the words'.[8]

This love of 'natural detail' would seem to explain most of the few links we can be sure of between verbal sense and musical content, for these are small examples of 'word-painting' or pictorialism. Notable ones are the speeding up of the music with a rush of crotchets (semiquavers in modern transcriptions) at 'citius' in Fawkyner's *Gaude virgo salutata*; the use of crotchets in Banester's *O Maria et Elizabeth* to suggest the miraculous flowering of Aaron's rod ('ut arida virga Aaron miro ordine *florida*'); the odd *stand*still, with semibreves in both parts, on the first syllable of 'Stabas' in Browne's six-part *Stabat virgo mater Christi*; the choice of an unusually high phrase for the first mean at 'coelum' in Sturton's *Gaude virgo mater Christi*; and Fawkyner's depiction of the serpent in the undulating phrase at bars 91–94 of *Gaude rosa sine spina*. At 'mortem pati' in Sturton's antiphon and 'Crucifixo vulnerato' in Browne's first *Salve regina* the introduction of accidentals seems to be a kind of musical underlining of highly-charged words, as does Browne's introduction of the full choir at 'Et pro nobis flagellato' in his second *Salve regina* (see Chapter 4, section on Textural schemes).

SONORITY AND HARMONY

The characteristic Eton sonority owes much to the frequent use of five- and six-part writing, with a uniquely wide total compass. This contrasts with the earlier preference for three voices and the contemporary bias abroad in favour of four. Love of a very 'big' sound was not altogether new in England, for there are such precedents as the thirteenth-century rota *Sumer is Icumen in*, the first known example of six-part writing, and several five-part works in the Old Hall manuscript—although these employ a much narrower total compass than late fifteenth-century pieces.

The basic Eton grouping is for five voices, with a treble, mean and three men's voices of which the lowest was a bass. This can be seen as the end-product of a development in several stages from the 'chanson-type' scoring of the early fifteenth century which had two frequently crossing parts (labelled 'contratenor' and 'tenor') in the same clef with the same (tenorish) range, and a third part pitched about a fifth higher (see *8.Ex. 5.* below). After about 1440 a fourth voice was often added below the 'contratenor' and 'tenor' in a region of its own as a true harmonic bass; Dufay is credited with this extremely important innovation, and it is already seen in his *Caput* Mass. The English could have learned it from him, for at the very least they knew his *Caput* Mass. Walter Frye used the same scoring in his *Flos regalis* as Dufay in *Caput*, and there is broad stylistic similarity. Although Frye's work is preserved in Continental manuscripts, it may possibly have been written in England: it lacks the Kyrie, and has been tentatively linked with Ely Cathedral.[9] The Eton composers employed a very high boy's voice at the top of the Dufay–Frye type of four-part scoring; but the full upward range of this apparently did not develop all at once (see Chapter 3, section on Vocal scoring, pitch and transposition).

The harmony in the full-choir writing of the Eton choirbook is based on complete triads in five-three and six-three position, usually with almost the minimum of dissonance; the use of five or more parts often allows the special richness of doubled or even trebled thirds. 'Bare' fifths are not common in three-part writing as they had been in earlier music, and there are far fewer of the prominent fourths between the upper voices which had also tended formerly to give a bare effect. Contrary to contemporary foreign practice a work's last chord nearly always includes a third. It is fitting that this final emancipation of the third was English, since much earlier the English had played the leading part through their descant style in asserting the claims of the third and sixth at the expense of the perfect consonances.

There is a considerable preference for five-three chords over six-threes, most especially in full sections where the strength of the former is particularly appropriate as a firm and steady background for the wealth of complex rhythmic and melodic detail. The succession of chords is not generally subject to the kind of logic and discipline essential to later systems of tonality, for there is not the clear hierarchy of triads based on the primacy of tonic, dominant and subdominant, often no regularity of harmonic rhythm and, although harmonic variety may be obtained by having some important cadences on degrees other than the final of the mode, there is in no sense a tonal scheme. Where a cantus firmus is present, the choice of chords is closely bound up with the progress of this, since each note of it offers certain possibilities and precludes others. Both in cantus-firmus and 'free' textures movement between triads a fourth apart, the 'strongest' kind of progression, is particularly liked.

The Eton composers did not use the major and minor scales of later centuries; their music must be understood in terms of the eight ecclesiastical modes (the first two of which are today often termed Dorian and Hypo-dorian, the third and fourth Phrygian and Hypo-phrygian, the fifth and sixth Lydian and Hypo-lydian, the seventh and eighth Mixolydian and Hypo-mixolydian). None of these modes contains any sharps or flats. Modes 1 and 2 have D as their final (or 'key-note' as we inevitably tend to think of it); the former 'authentic' mode has its main compass between one final and another (that is, it runs from D to D using only the white notes of the keyboard); the latter 'plagal' mode has the final in the middle of its range and works mainly within the octave A to A. The third and fourth modes have E as final, the fifth and sixth F, the seventh and eighth G; the first of each pair is authentic, the second plagal.

Strictly speaking no polyphonic work is simply in the first or second mode, because some parts will have a 'plagal' compass foreign to the former, some an 'authentic' compass foreign to the latter; to speak of 'Dorian' modality is often more helpful. The situation is often complicated by the mixing of elements from unrelated modes, and one comparatively rarely has a completely 'pure' Dorian, Lydian or Mixolydian modality in a polyphonic work. To avoid the Phrygian, which the Eton composers never used, presumably on account of its harmonic difficulties (chord V is diminished), Browne transposes the third-mode plainsong he chose for O regina mundi clara to A with a key-signature of one flat and makes the overall modality Dorian with the addition of numerous B flats. Whatever the mode composers usually flatten the note B in the bass[10]—where a cantus firmus has f a B has to be flat or a diminished fifth will result; in non-cantus firmus writing a flat is again essential if a five-three chord is to be formed over a B: one cannot have f sharp above a B natural, because the note f sharp is found only as the third of a chord. B flats often have to be added in higher voices to avoid semitonal clashes with the bass, but many false relations still occur, especially in Mixolydian pieces: the quite frequent use of different key-signatures in different parts is a concomitant of this. In Lydian works B flats are sometimes incorporated so freely (as they are in some plainsong melodies) that we should describe the music as being in F major, or in the Ionian mode transposed up a fourth. (The untransposed Ionian and Hypo-ionian modes (numbers 11 and 12) on C were first 'officially' recognised by the Swiss theorist Glareanus in his *Dodecachordon* of 1547).[11] Lambe's *Stella coeli* is almost 'pure' Lydian; his *Ascendit Christus* has B flats in all parts throughout—a pure F major. Consistent addition of B flats to works whose final is D gives (transposed) Aeolian modality, the closest relative of our minor scale; the Aeolian and Hypo-aeolian modes on A without flats were numbered 9 and 10 by Glareanus. There are as yet few advances towards Aeolian modality in the Eton choirbook—not least because about three-quarters of the Eton works use *major* (Lydian and Mixolydian) modes.[12]

The Eton composers far more often than not avoid written transpositions of the modes, even where this results in impracticable pitch-ranges on paper; for such problems are solved by the performers in accordance with the 'clef code'. Failure to transpose on paper was due to a wish to preserve as high a level of modal purity as possible, by not admitting too numerous flats and (above all) sharps. The written transpositions which one does find normally involve one-flat signatures, but occasionally there are two-flat signatures in single parts or even in several parts at once.

The handling of cadences in the Eton manuscript shows great variety and enterprise; in full sections particularly each cadence seems to have some piece of decoration or trick of part-writing that makes it unique. There are two principal categories of cadence—in modern terms V–I (the perfect cadence) and VIIb–I. The former is preferred in sections for four or more voices, the latter for duets; in three-part writing both are quite common.

The crucial feature or 'core' of many cadences, both V–I and VIIb–I, is the fall of a second in the lowest or next-to-lowest part from 'supertonic' to 'tonic' (to use anachronistic but very convenient terms). This 'tenor fall' was inherited from earlier music, and is least frequently abandoned in the work of the older composers and Lambe. Where it is abandoned one quite often has a supertonic in the middle of three voices *rising* to the mediant to give a third to the final chord. Sometimes, outside the work of Lambe and the older men, and mainly at important full-choir cadences, the tenor fall forms part of neither a V–I nor a VIIb–I progression, but has some chord other than V at the end of its supertonic and a plagal cadence on its tonic. *2.Ex. 5.* is from the end of *Virgo templum Trinitatis* by Davy, who is more fond of this type of cadence than anyone else; as in some other examples of the cadence, including that shown in *7.Ex. 6.* below, the second note of the

(2.Ex. 5.)

MB, xi.104.

tenor fall is stated twice. The second note has therefore become considerably more important than formerly, because it carries two chords
instead of one and is sometimes prolonged through repetition: in fact
it acts as a very short tonic pedal, as it might also be said to do in those
many places where the final chord of a V–I cadence is ornamented instead of having all parts reaching their final notes at the same time in
the manner of earlier music. The tenor's last note (whether or not it
belongs to the traditional stepwise fall) tends to become even more important in much of the music discussed in Chapter 8 and later Chapters.
Sometimes it has several changes of chord (as already happens in a

(3.Ex. 5.)

MB, xi.161.

passage from Eton by Fawkyner (*3.Ex. 5.*)); normally chord I comes at
the beginning, but the plagal cadence type shown in *2.Ex. 5.* is still
occasionally found in the sixteenth century (see *14.Ex. 11.* below).
The new cadential developments give greater weight to important
closes than there had often been in the past.

Most of the fairly few cadences which end with a bare eight-five chord are of the 'octave-leap' type from which in three-part writing at least the third is almost bound to be absent. The octave-leap cadence was evolved in the early fifteenth century; it occurred when the middle of three voices jumped an octave from a fifth below the first note of the tenor's stepwise fall to a fifth above its second: this produced a perfect cadence at a time when the VIIb–I type was almost universal, but still permitted the tenor to sound the lowest note at the end as it traditionally had. A more 'modern' form of perfect cadence developed a little later as the new Dufay-style bass parts came in with their rise of a fourth or fall of a fifth to a unison or octave with the tenor. But the old octave-leap cadence lingered on for a very long time in England, its wayward character being not out of place in the Eton music. There are isolated occurrences in the sixteenth century, even in Tallis, Tye and Sheppard. In Eton it most commonly seems to come at the end of a reduced section which precedes a full-choir entry; possibly its bareness was thought to give added point to the very rich sound following it. In a couple of places we even find the bass rising a sixth instead of an octave to supply a third to the final chord: there are a few sixteenth-century instances of this, as in Tallis's *Sancte Deus*.

The Eton sound owes a great deal to the lack of an active interest in dissonance. Short unaccented passing-notes are naturally very common in the little scalic figures which are so widely used, and auxiliaries appear from time to time, notably in the decorative resolutions of suspensions; but accented dissonance is never prominent. Suspensions are fairly frequently used, chiefly at cadences, but the dissonant effect is often minimised by some decorative formula which anticipates the note of resolution.

This distrust of dissonance was not something new, because Dunstable's music had been imitated abroad partly on account of its remarkably euphonious character. The French poet Martin le Franc refers to the 'frisque concordance' which Dufay and Binchois had learned from the English master;[13] and Tinctoris, in commending Dunstable, contrasted his work with that written earlier in which 'there were more dissonances than consonances'.[14] The Eton composers, except for a few of the older ones, took refinement of sound still further than Dunstable in that they virtually eliminated short échappées and cambiata dissonances. Music with so limited a place for dissonance could sound featureless and insipid. But there is no danger of this with the Eton music because of its extraordinary rhythmic vitality.

RHYTHM AND MELODY

Rhythmic and melodic variety are of essential importance to the Eton composers. Chordal writing and very simple textures are avoided almost completely in favour of a vigorous contrapuntal style in which the repetition of imitative patterns has a very limited place. The individual melodic line is marked by irregular phrasing and a generally unpredictable, one might almost say irrational, progress; sequential patterning, naturally rare, generally involves the fairly unobtrusive repetition of some small detail.

Imitation is not only rather infrequent (especially in full textures and in the work of the older composers), it is used on the whole incidentally, rather than structurally as in mid sixteenth-century music. Important types of imitation include that without stretto, where entries do not overlap but are placed 'end to end' or separate (as at 'Vidit mori' in Browne's *Stabat juxta Christi crucem*); the kind where three or more entries are equally spaced (as at '(O dulcis) Maria' in Cornysh's *Salve regina* where each statement begins four semibreves later than the one before it); and the 'static' type in which the entries, usually of a triadic shape, are projected against an unchanging harmonic background (see the first two entries in bars 11–13 of 4.Ex. 5. below). Imitation is most commonly at the octave or unison, but may be at the fourth or fifth. As one would expect, there are very few instances of imitation being maintained strictly for any considerable time in canonic or near-canonic fashion. These few come mainly in the Magnificats by Nesbett and Horwood, two of the earliest pieces in the choirbook; like the canonic essays in Pepys (ff. 124v. and 127) and York (a Kyrie described in Chapter 7), they stand perhaps as last reminders of the canonic tradition of the Old Hall manuscript. At 'et sanctum nomen' in Nesbett's Magnificat two equal voices move in virtually exact canon for about nine bars over a free lower part before imitating slightly less strictly (see 3.Ex. 6. below).

Textures as melodically varied as those in Eton would be complex enough if fairly simple rhythms were used. But late fifteenth-century composers employed many rhythms which are anything but simple: in fact the working of syncopations against the basic metrical structure is one of their chief joys. Naturally we find the 'easy' kinds of syncopations which were still in favour in the mid sixteenth century—notably the placing of semibreves on weak minims, and the beginning of dotted minim/crotchet groups on weak minims—but other more

'difficult' effects used little or not at all by the end of our period are
also important. There are those in which a dotted semibreve is followed
by some note other than a minim or two crotchets (see bars 2, 3 and 5

(4. Ex. 5.)   *MB*, x.124 : Browne, *Salve Regina* I.

of *4.Ex. 5.* below, remembering that the original values are quartered there). There are those where a long, very heavy note begins at a very weak point (for instance a breve may start on a weak minim—see bar 13 of *4.Ex. 5.* (quartered values)); in the mid sixteenth century a breve on a weak *semibreve* was normal enough, but not a breve on a weak *minim*. Other syncopations in the Eton music involve very short notes (for instance in bars 4, 5, 6 and 8 of *6.Ex. 5.* below). A part is often quite seriously 'unbalanced' by having several syncopations consecutively or within a very short space (as happens in the second highest

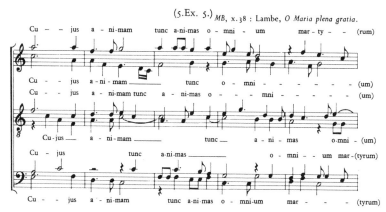

(5.Ex. 5.) *MB*, x.38 : Lambe, *O Maria plena gratia.*

part of *6.Ex. 5.* from bar 3 onwards). The kind of complexity which is more or less standard in five-part melismatic writing may be seen from the beginning of *4.Ex. 5.*; *5.Ex. 5.* indicates the less fluid manner associated with syllabic word-setting. *6.Ex. 5.*, from Browne's *O regina mundi clara*, is an extreme situation.

A major feature of the Eton style is the frequent use of more marked contrasts in pace than one generally finds in mid sixteenth-century styles. These contrasts, sometimes quite extreme, come within a section both in the single voice-part and between one voice and another, and they come between different phrases or passages. The range of note-values regularly used is very wide—to take a very simple example, there are thirteen different note-values in the section quoted as *4.Ex. 5.*, while in the whole of many mid sixteenth-century pieces there are about six, seven or eight. Variations of pace between sections or distinct segments of the same section are frequently tied to changes in text-treatment, notably where movement quickens as a predominantly syllabic style gives way to melisma. The most marked increases in activity of this kind are found as some important cadences are ap-

(6.Ex. 5.)

proached, the so–called 'drive to the cadence';[15] this 'drive' is seen very strongly in the final sections of Fawkyner's two complete antiphons. Movement in reduced sections tends to be more rapid than in the full ones because the smaller number of parts means less risk of congestion, and since the few most highly-trained singers would perform them. Amazing extremes of florid display are sometimes cultivated, especially by Davy from whose music 7.Ex. 5. is taken; such passages are without parallel in the choral music of other ages.

As well as variations in note-values within single pieces there are some inconsistencies between separate works in addition to those resulting from a greater use of florid display in some works than in others. To avoid excessive length, pieces with very extended texts such as Davy's *Virgo templum Trinitatis* use the small values more in syllabic sections than others do. There seems to have been a growth in spaciousness as the Eton style developed: some of the earliest works, notably Horwood's *Salve regina* and *Gaude flore virginali*, tend to show less diversity of values than usual, with notes longer than the dotted semibreve appearing abnormally little under Ø. In the smaller-scale music dis-

(7.Ex. 5.)

MB, x.113. Davy, *Salve regina* : xi.106 : *In honore summae matris*

cussed in Chapter 7, where there is naturally no great sense of spaciousness, the longest notes are also generally avoided.

Now it is of course very right to emphasise the variety and complexity of the Eton music, especially by comparison with mid sixteenth-
century polyphony. But there are limits to them. In particular these
relate to the functional differentiation of parts: that is to say rhythmic
activity and melodic interest are shared less unevenly between voices

(8.Ex. 5.)   MB, viii.115.

than in much early fifteenth-century music where the top part often dominates the others by its quicker pace and greater melodic interest. This will be appreciated if one contrasts the opening of Browne's *Salve regina* (*4.Ex. 5.* above) with the beginning of Dunstable's setting (*8.Ex. 5.*). The new functional homogeneity was beginning to develop everywhere about 1450, but was cultivated most assiduously by Ockeghem, in whose work there is often almost an equalisation of the voices. The Eton composers were more cautious, particularly in full textures. With them the bass retained an independent character for much of the time, with a rather slower pace than the other parts and more disjunct movement, because of its special harmonic function. A tenor cantus firmus often stands very much apart from the other voices; indeed even in works where no borrowed plainsong is to be found, the tenor sometimes behaves as a foundation part (for example in Kellyk's *Gaude flore virginali* at 'Gaude sponsa cara Dei' and in Davy's *Salve regina* at the final 'Salve'). Inner voices from time to time are obvious filling-in parts designed to complement more important and more elegant rhythmic-melodic shapes; but no part is regularly assigned this role in the way that the early fifteenth-century contratenor frequently was.

Melodic lines tend to move somewhat more boldly within wider pitch-limits than in earlier styles. Almost gone are the nervous little anticipatory notes (consonant and dissonant) and échappée-type figures which helped to point up strong beats in the more strongly metrical melodies of earlier times (see for instance the last notes of bars 1, 3, 4, 6 and 7 of the top part of *8.Ex. 5.* above). Extended scalic motion is sometimes found, especially in display passages, as in *7.Ex. 5.* above. In lines where melodic interest is high (those other than angular filling-in parts and some bass lines) the perfect fourth is more important than formerly and fifths are admitted a little more freely. Nevertheless seconds and thirds are still predominant, and many lines are character-ised first and foremost by rhythmic energy rather than immediately arresting or memorable melodic profiles.

Since each lower part can now have genuine melodic interest, its phrase structure need no longer coincide with that of the top voice, as broadly speaking happened in the old treble-dominated style, but can be to some extent independent. This new complex phrase structure means greater continuity and drive: points of repose within sections are less complete, with cadences often side-stepped or left vague and in-conclusive, and occasionally there is some dovetailing of sections. While Dunstable in *8.Ex. 5.* has three very clear cadence points in thirteen bars, Browne in the three-part section of 4.*Ex. 5.* has an indefinite cadence whose conclusion is interrupted by the mean's imitative entry (bars 10–11), a very weak kind of perfect cadence (bar 14), and an interrupted cadence (bar 17) which gives no rest but propels us forward to the vigorous phrase that follows. In addition, the five-part ending (bars 20–22) with its magical shift to the minor, is welded on to the perfect cadence at bars 19–20 before movement is impeded.

Occasionally a section will end with a kind of surprise cadence which does not resolve the tension of what goes before, but leaves the listener poised, normally on the subdominant, for what follows. For instance at the end of the first major section of *O Maria salvatoris mater* Browne decides that the final chord of the F major cadence to which he has been clearly moving for some time shall serve in turn as

(9.Ex. 5.)

MB, x.7.

chord V of another cadence, on B flat (9.*Ex. 5.*). Something rather similar happens at the end of the first major section of his *O mater venerabilis*, at 'O pia' in Wylkynson's five-part *Salve regina*, occasionally elsewhere in Eton outside the work of Lambe and the older composers, and in early sixteenth-century music.

6

The Eton Composers

Twenty-five composers' names appear in the Eton choirbook. The largest and finest contributions are by John Browne, Walter Lambe and Richard Davy. Next in importance are William Cornysh, Robert Wylkynson, Robert Fayrfax (known chiefly from other sources and discussed in Chapter 8), and Horwood. Most composers have only one or two pieces to their credit.

THE OLDER COMPOSERS

The oldest composer named in the manuscript is Dunstable, but the five-part *Gaude flore virginali* ascribed to him has been lost. The index tells us that his piece had a range of twenty-one notes, three octaves minus a note, much wider than any of Dunstable's known works or than other music from the first half of the fifteenth century. It is accordingly possible if not probable that the ascription is wrong— although the ascriptions in general seem to be accurate, for where several works are attributed to the same composer there is normally the unity of manner which confirms common authorship.

The following seem to be the oldest composers by whom at least one work has survived: Horwood, Gilbert Banester (represented in the Pepys manuscript), Nesbett (presumably the J. Nesbet of the same manuscript). Richard Hygons (vicar choral at Wells from 1459 until about 1509),[1] Edmund Turges (joined the Fraternity of St Nicholas, the London Guild of Parish Clerks in 1469),[2] and Hugh Kellyk.

Horwood, whose Christian name is not recorded, must be the William Horwood who was a vicar choral at Lincoln in 1476 and choirmaster from 1477 until 1484 (obviously the year of his death because it was then that the administration of his goods was given to one of the other vicars).[3] John Horwood, a chorister of King's, Cambridge from 1480 to 1483 and a student there in 1489,[4] was born too late to be

74

our Horwood, whose music is stylistically as old-fashioned as any in the choirbook.

One of the first old-fashioned features that one notes about Horwood's work is that his *Salve regina* has two frequently crossing voices of equal range at the bottom (labelled 'tenor' and 'bassus'), unlike all

(1.Ex. 6.)

MB, x.107

other five-part works in the manuscript (*1.Ex. 6.*). It seems likely that five-part writing was only beginning to be standard in Horwood's day, because it comes a little less easily and naturally to him than to most other Eton composers—particularly in the *Salve regina*. There are various rough dissonances not typical of most Eton music, and one notes a greater incidence of old-fashioned échappées, cambiatas and anticipations (as in bars 4 and 5 of *1.Ex. 6.*); suspension dissonances are not so frequently abbreviated by decorative resolutions as later. Consecutive fifths and octaves are unusually noticeable; subsequently they are almost, but not completely, outlawed. Cadence practice in Horwood shows none of the more progressive tendencies noted in Eton: several three-part VIIb–I cadences still end with a bare fifth; there are no plagal cadences or concluding tonic pedals of the kinds shown in *2.Ex. 5.* above and *7.Ex. 6.* below. Away from cadences Horwood is a little less careful than Eton composers normally are to avoid bare sounds: notice for example the prominent fourths and fifths between the top

(2.Ex. 6.)

MB, xi.133.

and middle voices in the passage from *Gaude flore virginali* quoted as *2.Ex. 6*. Further early characteristics of Horwood's work are scarcity of imitation even by Eton standards, and the very marked shift to longer note-values where the signature changes from triple to duple.

We know of five works by Horwood, four of them in Eton, one in the York manuscript. Two of these are incomplete, a Kyrie (York) and *Gaude virgo mater Christi*, whose text on five corporal Joys of the Virgin, the Annunciation, Nativity, Resurrection, Ascension and Assumption, was also used by Sturton, Wylkynson and one or two later composers. In common with Horwood's two other antiphons, *Gaude virgo* has no cantus firmus. In fact Hygons's *Salve regina* is the only antiphon mentioned in the present section which does have one. The cantus firmus was favoured by Lambe and Browne, declined a little with Davy, and was rarely used *in antiphons* by Fayrfax, Cornysh and composers younger than they. Both Horwood's *Gaude virgo mater Christi* and *Gaude flore virginali* employ the standard five-part grouping with genuine bass line, and are more compelling works than the *Salve regina*. The Magnificat stands a little apart from the antiphons as Horwood's only work with the maximum Eton compass of twenty-three notes and in using imitation (some of it of the quasi-canonic type) a little more.

Gilbert Banester's only work in the Eton choirbook is the antiphon *O Maria et Elizabeth*. This is similar in many ways to Horwood's music, but a compact, consistently syllabic style is employed very much more widely because the text is exceptionally long. As in only two other Eton antiphons, the text is in prose; this choice of form is all the more remarkable since there are two poems ascribed to Banester, the *Miracle of St Thomas* (1467) and the first known version of Boccaccio in English (*c.* 1450).[5] *O Maria et Elizabeth* is partly about the motherhood of the Virgin and of St Elizabeth, but ends with a prayer for king, church and people. The king's name is omitted, and unfortunately the three notes provided for it could fit 'Henricum', 'Edwardum', or even 'Ricardum'. In view of the allusions earlier to St Elizabeth, it is possible that the piece was composed for the marriage of Henry VII and Elizabeth of York on 17 January, 1486.[6] The tenor, in place of a regular cantus firmus, twice quotes the opening phrase from 'Benedicam te Domine', third antiphon at Lauds for the Sunday before the wedding, the first after the Octave of the Epiphany (bars 45 and 255). But in spite of this it is perhaps possible that Banester's piece was written during Elizabeth's pregnancy,[7] or after the birth of Prince Arthur in September 1486. Why should the king's name be omitted? Was the king in fact Edward (IV), whose order in the 1460s that the Eton treasures be handed over to his own St George's, Windsor could well have discouraged the scribe from perpetuating his name? The Elizabeth would then have been Edward's queen and Henry VII's mother-in-law, Elizabeth Wydeville. Banester after all appears in records as the 'king's servant' in 1471, received corrodies at two Abbeys from Edward, became a Gentleman of the Chapel Royal in 1475 and master of the choristers in 1478;[8] he had ample reason to pray for Edward's success.

Nesbett is represented in Eton only by a Magnificat, one of the most attractive settings surviving. As in Horwood's Magnificat there is some quasi-canonic writing; this sounds decidedly archaic when compared with most of the Eton music (3.Ex. 6.).

(3.Ex. 6.)

MB, xii.64.

Richard Hygons's *Salve regina* is interesting primarily because its tenor is the 'Caput' melisma which Dufay had used in his Mass of that name. While Ockeghem and Obrecht in their *Caput* Masses maintained the same rhythmic layout as Dufay, Hygons's scheme is his own, apart from occasional correspondences with Dufay's.[9] Choice of cantus firmus and knowledge that he was active in 1459 prompt us to group Hygons with the older Eton composers; his style argues less definitely in this direction.

Edmund Turges is now known from two settings of *Gaude flore virginali* in Eton, a very florid Magnificat in the Caius choirbook, and presumably the Kyrie and Gloria ascribed to Sturges in the Ritson manuscript. A very great deal by him has been lost—three four-part Magnificats from Eton, and the eight six-part pieces listed in the 1529 King's College Inventory. The style of his music in Eton and Caius does not always argue very decidedly for an early date; but the three-part Ritson piece does have frequently crossing lower parts in the old-fashioned way.

Nothing at all is known of Hugh Kellyk, but his five-part Magnificat and his cleverly managed seven-part *Gaude flore virginali* appear to be among the earlier Eton pieces.

WALTER LAMBE

We take Walter Lambe first of the three leading Eton composers because his music has a little more in common with that of such older composers as Horwood and Banester than has Browne's or Davy's: there is often a very limited use of imitation, cadence practice is a little more old-fashioned, and once or twice there are very old-fashioned sonorities as at 'peperisti' in *Nesciens mater* with its prominent open fifths. Lambe's music is remarkable for showing several correspondences with that lesser tradition of the late fifteenth century discussed in Chapter 7.

A Walter Lambe from Salisbury, clearly the composer, was elected King's scholar at Eton in 1467; he was aged fifteen the year before, and so was born in 1450 or 1451. Lambe was installed as a clerk at St George's, Windsor in 1479, and held the post of master of the choristers jointly until 1480 and on his own from 1482 to 1484. He then probably sought further advancement elsewhere, because his name does not appear in the records again until 1492. After that year the records are very incomplete, but he was still a clerk in 1499.[10]

Table 1: Walter Lambe

Votive Antiphons
à6: O Maria plena gratia, O regina coelestis gloriae†
à5: Nesciens mater, Salve regina
à4: Ascendit Christus, Gaude flore virginali, Stella coeli

Magnificat
à5: one setting

Lost

Votive antiphons à5: Gaude flore virginali, O regina coelestis gloriae, Virgo gaude gloriosa; a4: O virgo virginum praeclara.‡ Nunc dimittis.§

Lambe's work is published in *MB*, x and xii.

†Fragmentary (reconstruction difficult or impossible).
‡All lost from the Eton choirbook.
§Mentioned in a King's College inventory of 1529 (see Harrison, *MMB*, pp. 432-3).

Lambe's music shows an imagination and technical mastery exceeded only by Browne's. His achievement is very diverse; for example, he wrote the longest antiphon in Eton, *O Maria plena gratia*, and one of the shortest, *Nesciens mater*. There is great variety in cantus firmus treatment, including use of double cantus firmus and a very free handling of proper plainsongs. *O Maria plena gratia* has the orthodox treatment in long notes of a borrowed melody, 'O sacrum convivium', the Magnificat antiphon at second Vespers of Corpus Christi. The melody of *Gaude flore virginali*, similarly presented, has not been identified, but is almost certainly not plainsong. Two plainsongs were used simultaneously in the now fragmentary *O regina coelestis gloriae*. To draw attention to this feat, each of the cantus firmus-bearing parts is labelled with the name of its melody, one having 'Hodie in Jordane' (seventh respond at Matins of the Epiphany), the other 'Magi videntes stellam' (antiphon to Magnificat at first Vespers of the same feast, for which, incidentally, the work's text seems particularly appropriate). Other examples of double cantus firmus are almost certainly to be found in imperfectly-preserved works by Davy and Wylkynson, as detailed in the sections on these composers. A few Continental pieces also use two or more plainsongs simultaneously, notably Obrecht's Mass *Sub tuum praesidium* and Regis's *Ecce ancilla Domini*; such examples are probably unlikely to have been known to Lambe, however.

Nesciens mater, *Salve regina* and *Ascendit Christus* incorporate plainsong material proper to their texts. In *Nesciens mater* the phrases belonging to the words of the full sections appear in these sections in the second-to-lowest voice, the solo writing being free except for a brief opening reference to the plainsong; thus the technique is not far removed from that of works based on borrowed melodies. But in *Salve regina* and *Ascendit Christus* phrases from the proper plainsongs are used very freely, appearing in various voices sometimes in decorated form. The cantus firmus treatment here is one of the closest points of contact between the Eton repertory and the music described in Chapter 7.

In the *Salve regina* both full and reduced sections incorporate plainsong material, but there is no systematic treatment, and some passages (notably the last forty bars or so) appear to be completely free. The five-part 'O pia' has the plainsong in long notes in the tenor in 'normal' cantus firmus fashion. The full passages 'Vita dulcedo' and 'Ad te suspiramus' begin in this way, but incorporate one or two decorative notes; both end with the plainsong in the bass, the second having been free for some time before this. The section 'Nobis post hoc ostende' is freely composed, and 'O clemens' has only three borrowed notes at the beginning in the mean. Some reduced passages begin by quoting from the chant, sometimes in the middle part, sometimes in the lowest

(4.Ex. 6.), but at 'ecclesiae / Aeterna porta' the chant is at the top in longer notes than usual and without the limited ornamentation generally employed.

In *Ascendit Christus* the plainsong quotations almost all come in the two full-choir sections. These sections run parallel in that the melody comes first in the tenor, then moves elsewhere, then returns, before finally disappearing in mainly melismatic writing. In the first section treatment is initially in fairly short notes, lightly decorated, then, after the first migration which is downwards to the bass, in 'normal' cantus firmus fashion; in the second section treatment becomes freer instead of stricter, and presumably to illustrate the words 'ad aetherium' the melody moves upwards to the top part.

Lambe's most impressive achievement is *O Maria plena gratia*. The text, in prose, is a kind of meditation on the Litany. The writer hails Mary as most full of grace because she makes manifest the Holy of Holies and all the Saints of the Litany; when he thinks of her he can see and contemplate the whole host of heaven. He develops this idea at great length, with the various sections (about the Trinity, the Angels, patriarchs and prophets, apostles, martyrs, confessors, virgins) corresponding in order to the petitions of the Sarum Litany. Even with very limited melisma and much very brisk declamation, the piece runs to just over 300 bars. Imitation is used rather more widely than in Lambe's other works, but still less often and less flexibly than by Browne. As usual it comes mainly in solo sections.

Nesciens mater is not much more than a quarter as long as *O Maria plena gratia*. Yet its text is so short that the musical treatment is predominantly melismatic—the word 'angelorum' for instance having an eleven-bar section to itself. The formal structure is particularly neat, with two major sections of the same length, in both of which two roughly equal passages for complementary solo groupings together balance a passage for full choir. The major sections are dovetailed instead of being separated by a double-bar. This is exceptional for the Eton choirbook, although common enough in small-scale fifteenth-century antiphons, including a number from the Ritson book. *Nesciens mater* is also the only Eton work which is in triple metre throughout; this is a rather old-fashioned trait, for although plenty of triple-time pieces were written before 1450, few are found after this, apart from some in the Pepys manuscript, the carols from the roughly contemporary first layer of the Ritson book and the *Ave regina* which appears with them. Use of *duple* time only, found in many short pieces in Pepys and Ritson, became increasingly common in the sixteenth century. But apart from Cornysh's *Stabat mater*, Lambe's *Salve regina* is the only large-scale Eton piece treated in this way.

Salve regina employs a more elaborate style than *O Maria plena gratia* or *Nesciens mater*, and singers have to cope with some very tricky rhythms in a few solo sections. In *Gaude flore virginali* this type of display is exploited very widely. The cantus firmus is in augmentation throughout; that is, the note-values given must be doubled to correspond with those of the other parts—so in a modern transcription where one normally quarters notes, one must *halve* the values of the cantus firmus part. This augmentation is of no practical value, but just a notational trick, a show of erudition. Similarly 'unnecessary' are some of the proportional signs preceding groups of triplet quavers: passages in other works make it clear that the coloration at for instance 'Dignitate numerum' would be sufficient without the sign $\frac{3}{2}$. The most complex passages come in the last quarter of the work at 'poli sedem' (bars 94–99), where the free parts have signs of triple diminution which indicate that the dotted breve equals the preceding semibreve; 'Quia sola . . .' (bars 103–5), with diminution in the ratio 3:2; and virtually at the end at 'saecula' (5.Ex. 6.), where the effect is similar to that at 'poli sedem' but notated in *proportio sesquialtera* (3:2) instead of *tripla* (3:1). But *Gaude flore virginali* is not simply a *tour de force*. There

(5. Ex. 6.)

are moments of great beauty, as at 'Mater Christi', so clear and simple with its repeated notes in all parts. Less active material such as this is interpolated between complex passages in several other places to prevent excessive intricacy.

JOHN BROWNE

John Browne is first among the composers of the Eton choirbook both in size of contribution and excellence of achievement. Harrison justly considers him to be 'among the greatest composers of his age' and 'perhaps the greatest English composer between Dunstable and Taverner'.[11] It is astonishing that work of such exceptional interest should be known to us only from the Eton choirbook, even given the paucity of late fifteenth- and early sixteenth-century sources; works by Lambe and Davy are after all found elsewhere. Carols ascribed simply to 'Browne' are preserved in the early sixteenth-century Fayr-fax Book (British Museum, Additional MS. 5465), but it is possible that they were composed by William Browne, Gentleman of the Chapel Royal from 1503 to 1511.[12]

Nothing is known for certain about Browne's life. A John Browne

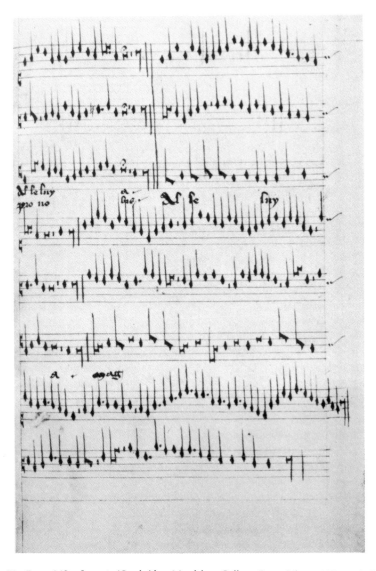

The Pepys MS. of *c.* 1460 (Cambridge, Magdalene College, Pepys Library MS. 1236), f. 32, showing score format in an Alleluia *Post partum* . . . pro nobis, and (minus the end of the lowest part) in an Alleluia *Virtutes coeli* . . . magna.

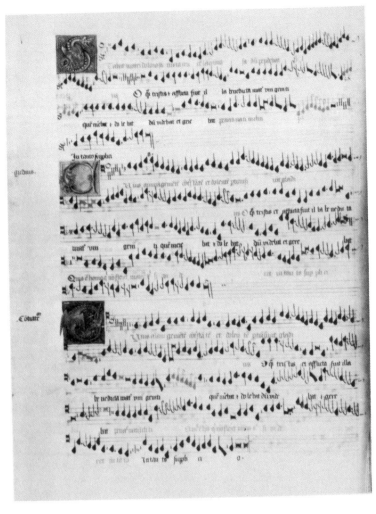

The Eton choirbook (Eton College MS. 178), f. 15 v. First page of John Browne's *Stabat mater.*

Eton College Chapel.

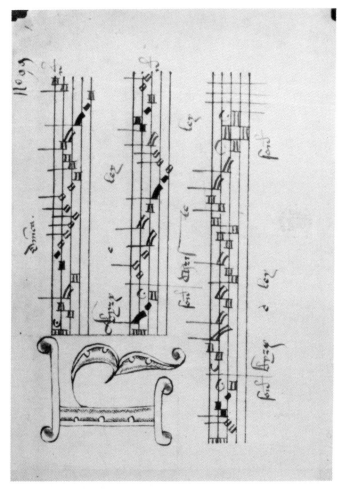

British Museum, Royal Appendix MS. 48, f. 1. The beginning of the soloist's part of Ludford's Sunday Lady Mass.

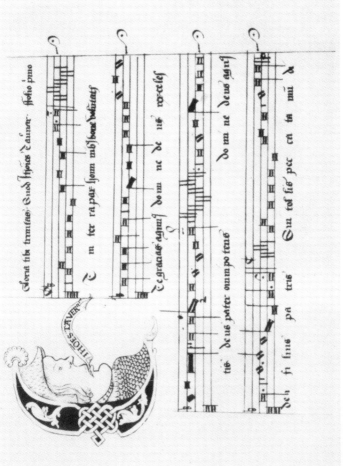

Oxford, Bodleian Library MS. Mus. Sch. e. 377 (one of the Forrest-Heyther partbooks), f. 4. The beginning of the mean (cantus firmus) part of Taverner's *Gloria tibi Trinitas*, with supposed sketch of the composer.

Christ Church Cathedral, Oxford, formerly the Chapel of Cardinal College, where Taverner was master of the choristers from 1526 to 1530.

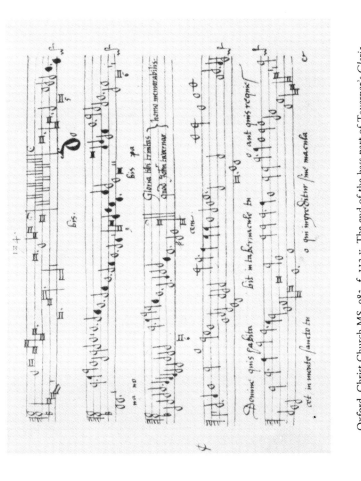

Oxford, Christ Church MS. 983, f. 112 v. The end of the bass part of Taverner's *Gloria tibi Trinitas* and the beginning of Whyte's *Domine quis habitabit* III.

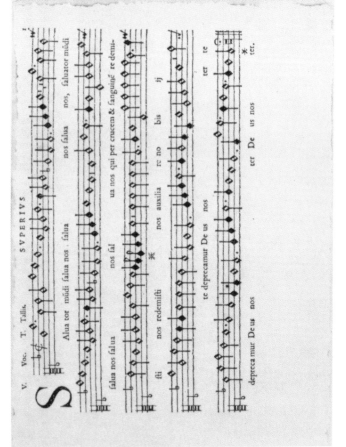

The beginning of the top part of Tallis's *Salvator mundi* I from the 1575 *Cantiones*.

Table 2: John Browne

Votive Antiphons

à8: O Maria salvatoris mater
à6: O regina mundi clara, Stabat juxta Christi crucem, Stabat mater, Stabat virgo mater Christi*
à5: O mater venerabilis,* Salve regina I, Salve regina II
à4: Stabat virgo mater Christi

Magnificat

à5: one setting†

Lost

Votive antiphons à5: Ave lux totius mundi, Gaude flore virginali. Magnificats à7, à5, à4.‡

Browne's work is published in MB, x–xii.

*Imperfectly preserved (a reconstruction exists, or is possible).
†Fragmentary.
‡All lost from the Eton choirbook.

from Berkshire, born in 1425 and scholar successively of Eton and the sister College of King's, Cambridge in the 1440s, is almost certainly too old to be our man: for musical reasons we should expect Browne the composer to have been born at about the same time as Lambe, or a little later, rather than a quarter of a century earlier. Therefore it is extremely likely that the composer was the John Browne from Coventry elected scholar of Eton in July 1467 at exactly the same time as Lambe, and aged 14 in December of that year (which would make him just a year or two Lambe's junior). The John Browne (d. c. 1498) who was Rector of West Tilbury and canon of St Stephen's, Westminster had important legal and civil service connections and is almost certainly not the composer.[13]

John Browne stands apart from the other Eton composers in his exceptionally varied choice of vocal forces—no two surviving works employ exactly the same—and in some predilection for very sombre texts. He stands apart from Lambe and the older composers in his greater liking for imitation and his somewhat less rigid handling of it (with for example more entries at intervals other than the unison or octave, notably at the fifth). Like Davy he is less inclined to use the old 'under-third' or 'Landini sixth' progression at a cadence (with leading-note falling by step before rising to its tonic) so beloved of Dunstable and Dufay. Like Davy also he sometimes uses the 'new' type of plagal cadence shown in 2.Ex. 5. above.

But despite the very varied scoring Browne's work is in some respects not nearly so diverse as Lambe's. There are not the extremes of scale: instead of works ranging from about 80 to 300 bars, all are between 180 and 250. All Browne's pieces begin in triple metre and end in duple, whereas Lambe also employs duple time only, triple only, and triple-duple-triple structure. Browne's adherence to triple-duple structure in both *Salve regina* settings is the more remarkable because all the other Eton settings except Lambe's and John Hampton's end with a return to triple metre. While Lambe's cantus firmus treatment is very varied, Browne uses a tenor cantus firmus predominantly in long notes in all his antiphons except *O mater venerabilis* whose tenor probably had no prior existence. In five antiphons, *O regina mundi clara*, the two *Salve regina*s and the two settings of *Stabat virgo mater Christi*, he presents a borrowed plainsong twice, in three cases with a 'redundant' quotation of its opening phrase. *O Maria salvatoris mater* also uses two statements plus redundant opening phrase, but the cantus firmus here is perhaps not plainsong. The tenors of *Stabat mater* and *Stabat juxta Christi crucem* are much more obviously not plainsong; perhaps they were specially composed by Browne, or just possibly they came originally from some earlier polyphonic context, as squares did.[14]

Browne's varied choice of vocal forces may to some extent reflect changing practical requirements and limitations, but a genuine interest in exploiting new groupings must have existed. There is some fondness for groups of low voices, but this now appears more pronounced than it really was because no less than five works with trebles have been lost. Only one surviving work, the first *Salve regina*, has the standard five-part scoring for two boys' and three men's voices.

One of Browne's special attributes is his love for very sombre texts relating to Mary's grief at the time of Christ's Passion. (Incidentally this does not appear to be very closely connected with the fondness of low vocal groupings—see further below.) The best known of the sombre texts, also set by several of Browne's contemporaries, is that of the *Stabat mater*; this was based on verses 1–6 and 9–10 of the well-known thirteenth-century poem, plus six independent verses which have four instead of three lines each. The text of *Stabat juxta Christi crucem* consists of eight verses (numbers 1–4 and 9–12) from a Marian sequence of York Use[15] which, in English translation, had enjoyed extra-liturgical performance as early as the thirteenth century.[16] *O mater venerabilis* is an account of Christ's betrayal, trial and crucifixion seen from Mary's point of view; its words are not known from any other source. Another poem not traced outside the Eton manuscript, 'Stabat virgo mater Christi', tells of Mary's anguish at the foot of the Cross, and is ad-

dressed in parts to the Jews who crucified Christ. It is difficult to follow
in places, and it is very likely that in both Browne's settings three lines
are missing (the third of verse 9 and the first two of the following
verse, line 3 of this latter verse being wrongly employed as the third of
verse 9).[17] This would imply an astonishingly casual attitude towards
the words, and perhaps even an imperfect understanding of them on
the part of the composer, or the person who supplied him with the
text, or both; it should remind us not to look for the positive expressive response which the words of the 'Stabat' pieces would suggest to
many later composers. In fact both *Stabat virgo mater Christi* settings are
in *major* modes and are clearly free of musical sorrow. But such
features of the *Stabat mater* as its minor modality, the semitonal movement D-E flat-D or G-A flat-G in the opening section at 'dolorosa' and

(6.Ex. 6.)

'pendebat' (*6.Ex. 6.*), and the unusual number of falling themes in the
'Eja mater' section do inevitably seem to us today to underline Mary's
grief; yet in view of what we know of the Eton music generally it
would be rash to claim that Browne deliberately intended them
to do so. The unusually low six-part scoring of *Stabat juxta Christi
crucem* (described and discussed further below) may again strike us as an
apt matching of dark sounds with dark words; but the textures of
Sturton's *Gaude virgo mater Christi* and Browne's second *Salve regina*,
works with very different texts, are only a little lighter: so in general
there is no clear relationship between scoring and textual character.
    The *Stabat mater* is almost certainly both Browne's masterpiece and

the finest work in the Eton choirbook. There is an unusual flexibility of scoring, with the full choir being brought in no less than eight times, and sections for different groupings being dovetailed with great subtlety. The melodic lines have exceptional interest, balance and shapeliness. Tiny decorative features are worked in with consummate skill, with the occasional use of triplet figures contributing considerably to the general rhythmic flexibility. Almost every section is remarkable in some way, but here it must be sufficient to mention only the very powerful full-choir writing with its rapid scales at 'Plebs nunc canit clamorosa "Crucifige!"', a 'naturalistic' depiction of the violent energy of the mob at Jesus's trial, and the magnificently managed complexity of the Amen.

The splendid *O Maria salvatoris mater*, given pride of place in the choirbook, is the only work for eight voices. The words are mostly of praise and prayer to the Virgin, but verse 10 refers to three other Saints: 'Rogamus et Frideswidam, / Magdalenam, Catherinam / Doctam philosophiae'. Mention of Frideswide offers the possibility that the work, and therefore its composer, had some connection with Oxford, since Frideswide is best known as patron Saint of the Abbey there which Wolsey later suppressed in founding his Cardinal College. In 1458 Mary Magdalene had been honoured in Wayneflete's foundation of Magdalen College, Oxford.

O Maria salvatoris mater is scored for treble, two means, a countertenor, two voices of countertenor/tenor range (c to e', but rarely going above d'), the higher of which has the cantus firmus, and two basses. The two basses are of virtually identical compass and frequently cross. This looks at first like an old-fashioned trait, but contrary to the practice of Dunstable or even Horwood in his *Salve regina*, neither of the crossing parts is the tenor or in any sense a foundation part; one has instead the function of the harmonic bass given alternately to two voices which also take turns at being free inner voices. A similar doubling of the bass part is found in two of Browne's other works where the standard five-part scoring is exceeded, in Wylkynson's nine-part *Salve regina*, and in a few sixteenth-century works. The textural scheme of *O Maria salvatoris mater* is second in interest only to that of *Stabat mater*, the most striking features being the contrast between the initial eight-part section and the following duet and the build-up step by step from two to seven voices which follows this. The eight-part passages, which Browne handles with apparently just the same ease as writing for five or six voices, are very carefully distributed to give as much weight and strength as possible without overwhelming the listener.

The most extended one, 'His jam sanctis', twenty-one bars long, is appropriately placed at the end.

The six-part *Stabat virgo mater Christi* is one of the other works with two bass parts. The cantus firmus is 'Exulat vir optimus', fifth antiphon at Matins of St Thomas of Canterbury. This is treated unusually freely, especially in the first statement: at 'Vide tute' it moves abnormally quickly; an independent phrase is inserted at 'Visi mirabiliter'; and bars 125–8, also free, end on *c'* instead of the plainsong's *f* to permit the desired C cadence. The first fifteen notes of the melody are not present in all that survives of the first full-choir section (bars 38–58) namely the tenor, second bass and mean, and Harrison has not succeeded in working them into any of his reconstructed parts in any form.[18] Possibly their being 'banished' in this way was intended to match the words which belonged to them—'Exulat vir optimus', 'The excellent man [St Thomas] is banished'. At the beginning of the final section the plainsong is moved to the countertenor, but fades out before the end to permit another cadence on C instead of F. At 'Mundum hunc' the plainsong is the subject of imitation, something which only very rarely happens in the Eton music.

The scoring of Browne's remaining work with two basses, *Stabat juxta Christi crucem*, is altogether most unusual, with the six voices covering a total range of only fourteen notes (*F* to *e'*). In addition to the basses there are two tenors (*A* to *c'*), the cantus firmus-bearing part (*B flat* to *d'*) and a lowish countertenor (*c* to *e'*). While it was common enough to have such a limited total compass in four-part pieces such as Browne's second *Stabat virgo mater Christi*, the only comparable works among the larger ones are Browne's own *O regina mundi clara* and *Salve regina* II and Sturton's *Gaude virgo mater Christi*. The first and last of these have six parts within a range of fifteen notes, the second has five parts within this compass; but all have scoring which is a little lighter than that of *Stabat juxta Christi crucem*. As mentioned above, the singularly dark scoring of *Stabat juxta* seems to us to accord well with this work's many explicit references to the extreme sufferings of Christ on the Cross. The darkness is particularly intense because full sections are unusually long: the passage beginning 'Vidit corpus flagellatum' runs to forty bars, with only one brief reduction in density at 'crudelibus'; the final section of forty-four bars is the longest without change of scoring anywhere in Browne's music. So Browne clearly did not feel restricted by having six voices moving in a compass of only fourteen notes; indeed he positively revelled in the many subtle variations of spacing and shifts of emphasis from one part

(7.Ex. 6.)

MB, x.68.

to another which are possible where lines cross so constantly (7.Ex. 6.). Bars 1 and 3 of our quotation show an exceptionally close working of very brief imitative points at the unison or octave against a static harmonic background. This device is favoured particularly in *O regina mundi clara* (as in the first two bars of 6.Ex. 5. above). The textural scheme of *O regina mundi clara* is more varied than that of *Stabat juxta Christi crucem*: full sections are considerably shorter, and the choice of reduced groupings is wider, with an exceptional flexibility even for Browne at 'Solvas oro . . . Omniumque vitia' and 'Nunquam cessa . . . Diei miseriae'.

In the second *Salve regina* the full sections again have a very restricted compass, but there is one less part for the composer to deal with, and the work has neither the extreme intricacy of *O regina* nor the gloom of *Stabat juxta*. There is a greater sense of continuity in the second half than in most 'Salve regina' settings; for as in Browne's other *Salve regina* and in John Hampton's setting, some neat dovetailing of sections avoids several of the double-bars which normally separate the full-choir exclamations from the solo verses, and which sometimes come in mid-verse as well.

The plainsong cantus firmus of *Salve regina* II is 'Venit dilectus meus', sixth antiphon at Matins of the Assumption. Since Eton was dedicated to the Assumption, this choice could conceivably mean that the piece was written at or for the College (as could the choice of 'Regali ex progenie' for cantus firmus in the second *Stabat virgo mater Christi*, for reasons explained in our comments on Fayrfax's *Regali* pieces (see Chapter 8)). Two other works in the choirbook, both by composers associated with the College, are linked with the feast of the Assumption: Lambe's *Ascendit Christus*, whose text comes from the Office of this feast, and Wylkynson's nine-part *Salve regina* on the plainsong 'Assumpta es Maria'.

RICHARD DAVY

All that is known for certain about Richard Davy's life is that he was at Magdalen College, Oxford from 1490 to 1492, first as organist and joint choirmaster, then as choirmaster and one of the organists. But it is very probable that he was the Richard Davy, priest, who was a vicar choral at Exeter Cathedral between 1497 and 1506.[19]

Davy is third among the Eton composers in size of contribution, and probably in excellence of achievement as well. His work shows somewhat less diversity than Browne's or Lambe's, with its preference for the long antiphon in five parts for men and boys, and it has less 'depth'. Instead there is a certain facility which makes quite credible the Eton scribe's note that *O Domine coeli terraeque creator* (Davy's second longest piece at 260-odd bars) was written in one day ('hanc antiphonam composuit Ricardus Davy uno die Collegio Magdalenae Oxoniis'). Short passages of very rapid soloistic display are more prominent than in Browne's music or in Lambe's. At the same time there is an avoidance of the most complex rhythms which, despite a somewhat more limited use of imitation, puts Davy's music a little closer to that of the early sixteenth century than Browne's is. A slight melodic simplification results from a stronger feeling for extended scalic movement (as in 7(*b*).*Ex. 5.* above) and more sequence. Davy's sequential writing is normally based on a very short figure all of whose statements are contained in a single phrase (as at bars 27–29 and 124–5 of *Virgo templum Trinitatis*, and in 7(*a*).*Ex. 5.*).

Virgo templum contains several particularly striking scalic passages. In the most remarkable of these, at '(Speciali gra)-tia' the treble is taken through its entire range. Top G, sounded here for the first time

Table 3: Richard Davy

Votive Antiphons

à6: Gaude flore virginali†
à5: In honore summae matris, O Domine coeli terraeque, Salve Jesu mater vera, Salve regina, Stabat mater, Virgo templum Trinitatis

Magnificat

à4: one setting†

St Matthew Passion

à4: Dominica in Ramis Palmarum: Passio Domini†

Lost

Magnificat à5‡ *A book of canticles, Masses and antiphons bound for Magdalen College, Oxford in 1495–6.*||

Davy's work is published in *MB*, x–xii.

†Fragmentary.
‡Lost from the Eton choirbook.
||Harrison *MMB*, p. 457.

in the work, is reached only once again, in the penultimate bar as a final climactic gesture (*2.Ex. 5.* above). *Salve regina* on the other hand employs *g″* quite frequently. It was obviously designed to impress with the brilliance of its writing for trebles as well as with the floridity of solo sections for the three lower voices. Thus we have not only the opening full passage with its use of divided trebles and the gimel* for two trebles and a mean which balances this at the head of the second major section, but also the trios for men's voices at 'Ad te clamamus', 'Virgo clemens' and 'Exaudi preces' (part of which was quoted in *7(a).Ex. 5.*). Dazzling display is unfortunately a little overdone: the busy movement of the forty-four bars beginning at 'Virgo clemens' palls somewhat before the end, and at times Davy is rather harsh in his demands for the trebles' very highest notes. In other works less is demanded from the boys, but treble parts limited to *e″* as in works by Horwood and Banester, and in Browne's first *Salve regina*, are no longer encountered in Davy.

A far more impressive work than the *Salve regina* is *In honore summae matris*. At almost 300 bars it is second in length to Lambe's *O Maria plena gratia*; but size in its case is much more a matter of deliberate musical choice than the product of a very long text, since the number of words is almost 100 fewer than in Lambe's work. There are some fine florid melismas, particularly at '(Jubilemus) Domino', 'non uritur' (*7(b). Ex. 5.* above) and 'concipere'. The scoring is very interesting. The

* A section in which a voice-part is divided ('gemelli' (Latin)—'twins').

solo sections employ two-part writing to an unusual extent, no less
than nine of the ten such groupings possible being tried. Davy likes
to group several duets together and then introduce the richer sound of a
trio before a full-choir entry comes. The work has several memorable
climactic moments. The first comes at 'castitate'; Harrison notes 'the
astonishing effect of the momentary vision of a new tonal panorama'
which is created by unexpected introduction of chords of B flat and E
flat.[20] Since the text of *In honore summae matris* is about the miraculous
nature of Christ's birth and Mary's chastity, the treatment of 'castitate'
may be intended to underline a key word. Both here and at 'impossibile'

(8.Ex. 6.)

MB, xi.109.

(8.Ex. 6.) the harmonic effect of a surprise chord is emphasised by a
brief reduction in rhythmic activity. Moreover the reduction to three
parts in the middle of our quotation allows an increase in weight and
depth of tone when the vital B flat chord is reached.

Davy's two most important departures from the long antiphon for
five voices are the four-part Passion and the six-part *Gaude flore virginali*.

The Passion, according to St Matthew, is for Mass of Palm Sunday—
the manuscript calls it *Dominica in Ramis Palmarum: Passio Domini*. It is
a setting of those sections assigned in the Sarum Missal to the 'high
voice' ('voce alta'), namely the words of the crowd, other groups, and

individuals other than Christ.[21] The role of Christ and the Evangelist's narrative are sung in plainsong by a low voice and one of medium range respectively. As with earlier settings of the Passion, no plainsong is present in the polyphonic sections. The music of the first eleven choruses is lost altogether, but Harrison has made the work performable by re-using some of the complete ones (numbers 24–42) and reconstructing the parts missing from choruses 12–23. Some choruses begin with reduced scoring, with text in red, but the full choir is in use most of the time. The work as a whole is not the kind of 'functional' setting that each of the Passions in the Egerton manuscript of *c*. 1440 is,[22] but an imaginative and resourceful one with many subtle variations in manner and style. Notable moments include the two 'Crucifigatur'

(9.Ex. 6.)

MB, xii.128,129.

passages (*9.Ex. 6*.), the first entirely chordal and all within the compass of a thirteenth, the second (when the crowd 'cried out the more') contrapuntal in style and covering almost three octaves.

The six-part *Gaude flore virginali*, from which only part of the second major section survives, was Davy's most ambitious piece; it appears to be an example of double cantus firmus. The third lowest voice is labelled 'secundus tenor', and in each full passage has a section from 'Virgo flagellatur', a respond from Matins of St Catherine (bars 50–63, 126–42, 150 to the end). The second-to-lowest part, whose label if any has not survived, is missing from bars 50–63; but in the last two full sections it is clearly a structural tenor, moving with somewhat longer notes than the already fairly restrained 'secundus tenor'. Its melody is unidentified.

On the whole cantus firmus structure is less important for Davy than for Browne or Lambe, with the *Salve regina, Salve Jesu mater vera, Stabat mater* and the Passion free of plainsong. This seems to anticipate the disappearance of cantus firmi from the votive antiphon in the works of Cornysh, Fayrfax and subsequent composers of the genre. Of Davy's three works with cantus firmus, *Virgo templum Trinitatis* uses 'O virum ineffabilem', from Lauds of St Martin, *In honore summae matris* 'Justi in perpetuum', a respond belonging to All Saints' Day, the Common of Confessors and the feast of Relics, while *O Domine coeli terraeque creator* has an unidentified melody. Harrison observes that this is similar to, but not exactly the same as 'Iratus es Saul', one of the antiphons to Magnificat on Saturdays in the Trinity season, and an antiphon of St Martin, 'Beatus Martinus'.[23] Especially as the two statements of the melody differ somewhat more than usual, it is perhaps possible that Davy was *basing* his tenor on one of these melodies rather than quoting it, as a kind of compromise between the plainsong cantus firmi of *Virgo templum* and *In honore* and the invented tenors of other works. 'Iratus es Saul', as a Trinity antiphon, would be an appropriate model, since the first part of Davy's text is largely concerned with Mary's part in making the nature of the Trinity known to men.

WILLIAM CORNYSH

There were two musicians named William Cornysh. One was choirmaster of Westminster Abbey from 1479 to 1491; he died in 1502. The other, perhaps his son, was master of the children of the Chapel Royal from 1509 until the year of his death, 1523. This younger Cornysh was certainly a composer, since the ascription 'William Cornysh, Junior' appears in the Fayrfax book; and it is generally accepted that he was the contributor to the Eton manuscript. He was an accomplished man, active in the field of secular music, and in producing court pageants under Henry VII and Henry VIII. One of his pageants was performed at the Field of the Cloth of Gold in 1520. His writing, in the form of a satire on Sir Richard Empson, had led to his imprisonment in 1504, but a witty poem of protest composed in prison in turn probably hastened his return to favour.[24]

Cornysh shows the boldness and versatility in his sacred music which we should expect from his more widely known part-songs and consort pieces and from what we know of his life. In saying that his talent is 'not remarkable for depth or consistency', Harrison is perhaps a

Table 4: William Cornysh

Votive Antiphons
à6: Gaude flore virginali†
à5: Salve regina, Stabat mater*
à4: Ave Maria mater Dei, Gaude virgo mater Christi Quae te matrem

Magnificat
à5: one setting

Lost

Votive antiphons à5: Ad te purissima virgo, Stabat mater;‡ à?: Altissimi potentia.¶ Magnificat: the setting lost from Eton is probably different from that listed above. Masses à6: one setting; à4: one or more settings.§ Sequences.**

Cornysh's work is published in MB, x–xii.

†Fragmentary.
*Imperfectly preserved.
‡Both lost from the Eton choirbook.
¶Mentioned in a fragment of an index of polyphonic works found in the binding of Oxford, Merton College Printed Book 62, f. 8 (see Hughes, 'An Introduction to Fayrfax', p. 94).
§Harrison, MMB, pp, 432–3.
**Copied at King's College by Sygar in 1508–9 (Harrison, MMB, p. 164).

little harsh, but not altogether unjust.[25] The slight tempering of rhythmic and melodic complexity noted in Davy's work is a mark of Cornysh's as well. But imitation is again used as much as by Browne, with a slightly greater use of it in full textures. Davy's extremes of vocal display are occasionally present in Cornysh, notably in parts of the Magnificat. Cornysh is often very anxious to show off the abilities of his boy singers: in *Stabat mater* the trebles are worked as hard as in Davy's *Salve regina*. Divided trebles are used at 'Crucifige' for some thirty bars, twice touching a'', which under 'normal' clefs is as exceptional for them as is the e'' for the solo mean in the preceding 'Stabat mater rubens rosa' section. The 'Stabat mater rubens rosa' and 'Crucifige' sections contain some of Cornysh's most impressive music. The former, for treble, mean and bass, has some fine imitation and sequence at 'Juxta natum dolorosa' which leads on, with the compass of the voices gradually expanding and excitement mounting, to the energetic passage work at '(Plebs nunc canit) clamorosa' (*10.Ex. 6.*). At 'Crucifige' trebles and means divide, so that, although the full choir does not enter at this word as in Browne's *Stabat mater* or in Davy's, the number of voices still reaches a peak here.

Apart from the *Stabat mater* the most important of Cornysh's works are the *Salve regina* and the Magnificat. The latter, preserved in the

(10.Ex. 6.)   *MB*, x.143.

Caius choirbook, is probably distinct from a lost Eton setting ascribed
to Cornysh; it has a range of twenty-six notes (from *C*, which the bass
touches twice in octave doublings at cadences, to *g''*), while the Eton
work covers twenty-three notes. There are two four-part antiphons:
the fairly brief *Gaude virgo mater Christi*, whose text is different from
that used by Horwood and others, and *Ave Maria mater Dei*, which at
about sixty bars is the shortest piece in the Eton choirbook. The text of
Ave Maria is a very brief prayer in prose asking the Virgin for mercy
and help in avoiding mortal sin; it re-appears in the Peterhouse manuscript in a setting by Hunt.

ROBERT WYLKYNSON

Robert Wylkynson was at Eton from 1496 to 1515, first as parish
clerk and then from 1500 as master of the choristers. His nine-part
Salve regina and his Apostles' Creed are the last entries in the manuscript and possibly were copied by him.[26] Wylkynson's work, like
Cornysh's, has suffered severe losses, for only three of his eight works
survive complete; but what remains shows Wylkynson to have been
an extremely ambitious composer and a more than competent one.

The *Salve regina* is the only work from our period in nine parts. To
some degree it was probably intended to outdo Browne's eight-part
O Maria salvatoris mater. But, more important, the number of voices
corresponds with the number of angelic orders: the initial letter of
each part has the name of one of the heavenly choirs, and there is an

Table 5: Robert Wylkynson

Votive Antiphons
à9: Salve regina
à6: O virgo prudentissima†
à5: Salve decus castitatis,† Salve regina
à4: Gaude virgo mater Christi†

Magnificat
à6: one setting†

Apostles' Creed
à13: Jesus autem transiens/Credo in Deum

Lost
Votive antiphon à6: Gaude flore virginali. Magnificat à5.‡

Wylkynson's work is published in *MB*, x–xii.

†Fragmentary.
‡Both lost from the Eton choirbook.

explanatory Latin inscription at the foot of the second page.[27] The nine-part textures are handled most confidently, but they are less flexible than the full-choir writing in Browne's eight-part work: most immediately one notes that the two basses cross hardly at all except in the second full section. The cantus firmus is an antiphon from the feast of the Assumption, 'Assumpta es Maria'; in view of Wylkynson's position at Eton, it is more than likely that the work was written specifically for the College, perhaps for performance on its patronal festival.

The Apostles' Creed is set as a round for thirteen voices made up of an initial plainsong phrase 'Jesus autem transiens' and a freely composed melody for the twelve clauses of the Creed (each of which has affixed to it the name of the apostle supposed by tradition to be its author). It is quite unlike any other piece of church music from our period; possibly Wylkynson was consciously re-applying and extending the technique of three-part rounds with secular words such as Cornysh's *Ah Robin* and Daggere's *Downberry Down* from British Museum Additional MS. 31922. Each of Wylkynson's thirteen voices has to cover the range of a thirteenth (c to a' with a tenor clef); this is clearly a piece of number symbolism, because a thirteen-note range is exceptionally wide for any voice-part. In fact it is not easy to see how it accords with what we know of the normal vocal ranges of the time. The Apostles' Creed text was used every day at Compline, and Wylkynson may have designed his piece for Compline in Lent when the choir attended, especially since the plainsong phrase 'Jesus autem transiens' comes from an antiphon used at Magnificat on the third Monday in Lent. It is fitting that Wylkynson's Apostles' Creed, unusual in so many ways, should be unique in the matter of concordances; no other Eton work appears in any manuscript later than Henry VIII's reign, but this is included with various other musical 'curiosities' in John Baldwin's commonplace book of *c.* 1600.

In his (now fragmentary) six-part Magnificat Wylkynson probably attempted the double cantus firmus construction used in Lambe's *O regina coelestis gloriae* and apparently in Davy's *Gaude flore virginali*. Harrison has remarked that the faburden of tone 4 is used to begin with, that of the fifth tone later, and has taken this as 'apparently a unique case' of changing from one faburden to another'.[28] But the work now has only three parts surviving as far as 'bonis', the *other* three only from 'Et divites'; so that the voice which carries the fourth tone faburden is not the one which carries the fifth tone faburden. The cantus firmus part may have been changed part-way through; but the voice which has the fourth tone faburden is labelled 'secundus tenor', an appellation found otherwise only in Davy's *Gaude flore virginali*.

SEVERAL LESSER COMPOSERS

The only remaining composer with more than one complete work surviving in Eton is Fawkyner, of whose life we know nothing. He has left us *Gaude virgo salutata* and *Gaude rosa sine spina*, two very long antiphons, both striking works with some exciting florid display.

Composers with a single work in the manuscript are Robert Hacomplaynt or Hacomblene (King's scholar at Eton in 1469, Provost of King's 1509-28[29]—his name is on the King's Chapel lectern), John Hampton (Worcester Priory, 1484-1522),[30] Nicholas Huchyn, William, monk of Stratford, Edmund Sturton, and John Sutton (Fellow of Magdalen, Oxford in 1476 and of Eton in 1477).[31] The first three and the last of these wrote settings of 'Salve regina'. Stratford composed a four-part Magnificat. Sturton, presumably the composer of the six-part *Ave Maria ancilla Trinitatis* in the Lambeth choirbook, wrote the *Gaude virgo mater Christi* whose six voices cover a fifteen-note range.

7

The Pepys, Ritson and York Manuscripts

The music of the Pepys, Ritson and York manuscripts is generally very different from that of the Eton choirbook, and was obviously written for less highly skilled choirs. It is smaller in scale: most pieces are quite short, and three-part writing is the 'norm', with only two excursions into five-part texture being made in Ritson. This music is also easier to manage because there is much less florid elaboration and rhythmic complexity; much of it in any case was written and copied considerably before the Eton style had fully evolved. The contents of the smaller manuscripts together cover a much wider range of liturgical types than the Eton choirbook does.

The clearest links between the music in Eton and that in the 'lesser' sources are to be found between the style and manner of the shortest antiphons of Eton and some of the more elaborate writing of the York manuscript, between the handling of proper plainsong cantus firmi by Lambe and by some Pepys and Ritson composers, and in the appearance of works by the Eton composers Banester and Nesbett in Pepys, Turges in Ritson, and Horwood in York.

The Pepys, Ritson and York manuscripts do not have a great deal in common apart from their differences from Eton—their repertories are totally separate, not a single piece being shared between them. Pepys, begun about 1460 and probably not many years in the making, contains ritual items, chiefly for the Office and Lady Mass Proper. Ritson, compiled in five main stages from the third quarter of the fifteenth century to the earliest part of the sixteenth, has short votive antiphons, several Masses and a few Office works among numerous carols and secular songs. The fragmentary York manuscript (*c.* 1490–1520) has three- and four-part music for the Ordinary of the Mass.

THE PEPYS MANUSCRIPT

Samuel Pepys the diarist numbered among his books a manuscript containing 'monkish music of Edward IV's time'.[1] This, still in an excellent state of preservation, is now MS. 1236 in the Pepys Library at Magdalene College, Cambridge.* It is a small choirbook, $7\frac{1}{4}$ by 5 inches, partly of paper, partly of parchment, not elaborate, but very clearly and accurately written.[2] It contains 121 haphazardly arranged liturgical pieces, only one of which, Inventor rutili, is known from another source. There are alternatim works for the Office (responds and hymns), processional music, settings of Benedicamus (the concluding versicle of each Office and many Masses), and music for the Lady Mass Proper (Alleluias, and a handful of Communions and Graduals), but no votive antiphons or Magnificats. The Mass Ordinary is represented only by a Kyrie with trope 'Deus creator omnium'. Most works are rather short and fairly simple; most are scored for two or three voices, but there are seven in four parts and fifteen one-part pieces. The writing is competent, except in a few rather amateurish pieces and a few which are better than just competent, notably some by John Tuder. All but sixteen pieces are anonymous. Musically the Pepys works are of the following types, of which the first three are the most numerous: settings with proper plainsong decorated in the top part; those based on the faburden of the plainsong; a number composed independently of the plainsong or with only a brief reference to it; works with plainsong presented, mainly undecorated and in equal notes, in the lowest voice; and those in which the plainsong moves from voice to voice ('migrant' cantus firmus).

Samuel Pepys associated his manuscript with the reign of Edward IV (1461–83). There is no serious quarrel with this, but in fact the book was probably begun a year or two earlier, because there is a table near the beginning with the dates of Easter from 1460 to 1519 which would obviously have been intended for use starting in the immediate future. The manuscript was completed some time after 1465: the composer Hawte, knighted in that year, is referred to as 'Knight' and 'Sir William Hawte'. Several of the few composers named are known to have been active by and after the 1460–5 period—particularly in Kent where the manuscript quite possibly originated. The non-musical contents of the manuscript, which include astronomical tables, information on the best days for blood-letting, and a poem on the conduct of boys, have been seen as suggesting monastic connections for the manuscript—one recalls Pepys's reference to 'monkish' music—and in particular as pointing to a school where boys learned music under monastic auspices —although very few pieces could be sung by boys alone. Several texts

* Contents published in CMM, xl.

do specifically relate to boys: the responds 'Audivi vocem' and 'Gloria in excelsis', whose special ritual was for them, each appear several times, the former on one occasion for boys only; a boy Bishop's blessing is given twice, although in a tenor range; and there are six treatments of 'Sospitati dedit aegros', the prose belonging to the ninth respond at Matins of St Nicholas, patron Saint of children.

In many respects the Pepys manuscript looks back to the first half of the fifteenth century rather than forward to the Eton music. In total range the works are usually as narrow as earlier compositions— although a four-part *Salve festa dies* (item 65)* has a written range *d* to *b″* with tenor clefs for the two lowest voices: compare the *c* to *b″ flat* written range and two tenor clefs of Horwood's *Salve regina* in Eton. There is no five-part writing at all. The unfamiliarity with handling even four parts is especially obvious in *Beata viscera Mariae virginis* (93)

(1.Ex. 7.)   *CMM*, x1.134.

(*1.Ex. 7.*), not least because of several prominent consecutive fifths and octaves. The lowest voice is not normally a harmonic bass part either in three- or four-part writing (being either a tenor in the same clef as the part above it or basically the type of 'counter' part found in early fifteenth-century descant style), and the VIIb–I cadence ending with a bare fifth is almost universal. Exceptionally the lowest part in a four-part *Salve festa dies* (17) does show some slight movement towards a

---

* An item number (according to Charles's index in *CMM*, xl, p. xix) is given to aid identification when the manuscript has two or more pieces with the same name.

bass function: we do find perfect cadences at the end of Alleluia *Per te Dei genetrix, Miserere mihi* (*94*) and Tuder's *Gloria laus et honor* (all à3): and there are thirds in the final chords of Benedicamus settings by Nesbett and Hawte. Sixteen pieces retain score notation, which, although long discarded on the Continent, had been very common for simpler works in England in the first half of the fifteenth century. Imitation is very rare. The melodic style recalls earlier practice—particularly where a plainsong is elaborated in a work's highest voice. But alongside all these old-fashioned features there is something new: the quite wide adoption of composition on faburden tenors, one of the important aspects of the manuscript. The Pepys scribe shows no awareness of contemporary developments abroad. The one composer known from Continental sources is Frye, to whom a *Sospitati dedit aegros* is ascribed; but his piece does not stand apart stylistically from the other contents of the manuscript. It could well have been composed in England: it has no Continental concordances, and its text is a characteristically English choice.

Elaboration of a plainsong in the highest voice goes back in England to the first layer of the Old Hall manuscript; the style of melody associated with it was derived from the French chanson of that time. The older descant method had the plainsong most commonly in the middle, with little or no ornamentation and sometimes in equal notes; all three voices had different clefs, did not normally cross, and no part dominated the others as the treble did in chanson style. Works with plainsong elaborated in chanson manner might adopt a chanson's vocal spacing, with tenor and contratenor in the same clef frequently crossing, and with the latter being at times a rather inelegant filling-in part. But sometimes one had a kind of fusion of descant and chanson, as in the simpler pieces from the second layer of Old Hall (*c.* 1410–20) such as Glorias by Sturgeon, Damett and Burrell. Much of the three-part writing in the Egerton manuscript of *c.* 1440 continues this tradition. A few three-part pieces from Pepys are still of a similar kind, notably *Gloria in excelsis* (*36*), *Rex saeculorum* and *Inventor rutili*. The last is actually an abbreviated and slightly simplified version of a piece in Egerton.[3]

That the Pepys scribe felt the need to simplify *Inventor rutili* is not really surprising because a number of his other pieces are in a rather plain functional style, including some with treble cantus firmus such as two settings of *Sospitati dedit aegros* (*15, 51*). Some simpler pieces, *Trinitas sancta* (verse 2 from the Trinity hymn 'O Pater sancte) and *Iste confessor* (verse 1 of a hymn from the Common of a Confessor) in particular, show considerable fondness for that movement in parallel six-three chords which is associated first and foremost with improvised polyphony.

Three terms need to be mentioned in this connection: English descant, faburden and fauxbourdon. English descant[4] refers both to a method of improvising on a plainsong developed by the English in the thirteenth and fourteenth centuries, which is characterised by movement in parallel imperfect consonances (thirds and sixths), and to the application and extension of this principle in written music. Theorists deal principally with improvised descant in two parts, but there is evidence that improvisation in three parts was practised. Presumably this involved parallel motion—any other method is hard to imagine—and we do find extensive parallel motion, often in six-three chords, in composed descant up to the mid fourteenth century. Later composed descant had more independent part-writing: first a part was added below the plainsong to produce perfect and imperfect consonances by contrary motion and similar motion between imperfect consonances, and then a part was added above the plainsong to complete eight-five, five-three and six-three chords.

Faburden and fauxbourdon both usually describe three-part music which moves mainly in six-three chords with eight-fives coming at the beginning and ends of phrases and from time to time elsewhere. Faburden, as described in an anonymous treatise of the mid fifteenth century,[5] had the plainsong in the middle voice. It was of English origin; its links with improvised descant are obvious. Fauxbourdon had the plainsong, transposed up an octave, at the top, and seems to have been a Continental adaptation of the English method. However in the late fifteenth century the distinction was not maintained, for in England the term faburden encompassed the Continental fauxbourdon method of placing the plainsong at the top, and a related English practice of fauxbourdon at pitch, with the plainsong *not* transposed up an octave; while abroad fauxbourdon could signify (English) faburden.

Examples of faburden as it was improvised were not of course normally recorded outside theoretical writings, but several works from Pepys, particularly the hymns *Trinitas sancta* (*2(a).Ex. 7.*) and *Iste confessor* mentioned above, are only slightly irregular forms of the extemporised technique. The Alleluia *Laudate pueri*, except for its opening word, is a stage further removed from the improvised form (*2(b).Ex. 7.*), and the Lady Mass Communion *Vera fides* (*2(c).Ex. 7.*) one further still.

All four pieces just mentioned appear to have an octave trans-

position of the chant in the highest voice, and thus to be strictly speaking Continental fauxbourdon. But Alleluia *Laudate pueri* has the plainsong incipit 'Laudate pueri Dominum' transposed up a fifth in the *middle* voice; it is therefore more accurate to describe this piece as true

English faburden transposed up a fifth, with the top part, by co-incidence, because it moves mainly a fourth above the middle one, being the same as the plainsong at the upper octave and rendering the setting indistinguishable in sound from fauxbourdon. *Vera fides* also has its plainsong incipit transposed up a fifth in the middle voice; and it is possible that *Trinitas sancta* and *Iste confessor* (which have no plain-song incipits) are similarly 'true' faburden transposed. Some Old Hall descant settings had a plainsong in the middle voice transposed up a fifth when, as would have happened with the melodies of *Trinitas sancta*, *Iste confessor* and Alleluia *Laudate pueri* particularly, they were uncomfortably low for a middle part as they stood.

Vera fides is at times quite far removed from the parallel six-three movement of improvised faburden, but this kind of movement is still a major element. In some other pieces six-three movement is used little or almost never, the plainsong is absent or rarely touched upon, and yet we still speak of faburden. For the term 'faburden' applies not only to the three-part improvisation as a whole, but to the tenor or lowest voice of this in particular. Such a 'faburden tenor', often much elabor-ated, was used in its own right as a basis for composition in Pepys and Ritson considerably before this technique appears in organ music by such men as Redford.

The most important application of composition on a faburden tenor is in the Magnificat, for as Harrison has shown,[6] most late fifteenth- and early sixteenth-century settings have a decorated version of the faburden of the tone used for the non-polyphonic verses in the tenor of the polyphonic verses for full choir.

Faburden tenors are sometimes recorded as single lines, that is without polyphonic setting. These may well have been the subjects of improvisation, or they may have been complete as they stand. The most imporatnt in Pepys is Tuder's *O lux beata Trinitas*, which shows an interesting set of length relationships: verse 1 has the same number of dotted breves as there are notes in the plainsong proper to it, verse 2 has the same number of breves, verse 3 of semibreves.[7] But surpris-ingly the chant will not fit against this in equal notes: it can be added only at the expense of slight rhythmic irregularity and melodic decoration, particularly at cadences; this is also the case with *Tu cum virgineo*, *Tu fabricator* and *Adesto nunc propitius* (the second verses respectively of 'O quam glorifica', 'Jesu salvator saeculi Verbum' and 'Salvator mundi').

The monophonic entries in the Pepys manuscript include two in plainsong notation, *Crucis signo* (*49*), the boy Bishop's blessing on the

Feast of the Holy Innocents, and *Benedicat vos Deus* (*50*), a blessing not known from any other source. Both these items appear also in mensural notation with mixed note-values and occasional touches of melodic decoration (*52*, *45*).

The most impressive of the several other monophonic pieces is John Tuder's setting of the Lamentations. Verses from the first and second Chapters of the Lamentations of Jeremiah were read at Tenebrae, Matins of Maundy Thursday, Good Friday and Easter Eve, in each case forming the three lessons of the first nocturn. Every verse was prefixed by a Hebrew letter, and each lesson ended with the sentence 'Jerusalem, Jerusalem, convertere ad Dominum Deum tuum'. Tuder sets the Hebrew letters and the closing formula, but strangely misses out four verses, one from each of four lessons. He takes the simple reading-tone of the Lamentations transposed up a fifth as the basis of his work, and adds much florid detail, some of it using sequence, especially near the ends of phrases and when treating the Hebrew letters.

In a few pieces plainsong cantus firmi in equal notes are used for some or all of the time. Cantus firmi of this kind are found in some of the simpler Old Hall descant settings, but normally appear in the middle voice in breves, whereas in all the Pepys works it is the lowest part which carries the melody in semibreves. Six short Alleluias (*29–34*) begin with equal-note cantus firmus, but include shorter notes at the approach to sectional cadences. All are quite simple, but have little of the note-against-note movement which characterises some of the Old Hall descants. In the Communion *Beata viscera Mariae virginis* (quoted in *1.Ex. 7.*) the plainsong is in equal notes throughout, and the parts above it are a little more rapid than in the Alleluias.

THE RITSON MANUSCRIPT

British Museum Additional MS. 5665, or the Ritson manuscript as it is sometimes called after an eighteenth-century owner, is like Pepys a small choirbook (10½ by 6 inches) of parchment and paper, scarcely any of whose contents are known from other sources.[8] But in many respects it is very different from Pepys. Two-thirds of Ritson's ninety-seven pieces are carols and English part-songs. Of the pieces for church use only about a dozen are the types of ritual item to which Pepys is entirely devoted, the others being votive antiphons and four Masses. There are no concordances with Pepys, and the name of only one composer, Hawte, appears in both manuscripts. Ritson is not the work of a single elegant hand as Pepys is, but has five distinct layers,[9] the last in particular being rather rough in places. The manuscript was compiled over a long period between early in the second half of the fifteenth century and about 1510, apparently in the West Country. Various pieces in the first layer are ascribed to Richard Smert and Trouluffe, who must be respectively a Devonshire priest-musician active between 1428 and 1477 and John Treloff, canon of St Probus in the diocese of Exeter in the 1460s and 70s;[10] the book also includes several documents dated 1510 and 1511 which relate to Devonshire. Not surprisingly there is much greater stylistic diversity in Ritson than in Pepys. Some works are markedly more modern: harmonic bass parts, perfect cadences and thirds in final chords are far from exceptional, and there are two ventures into five-part writing with full Eton compass. The very simplest styles of Pepys are avoided, and there is a tendency to write at greater length.

The manuscript's first layer, probably compiled by Smert and Trouluffe, contains all the carols in the collection and four short votive antiphons. The former are 'similar to the more mature examples in the Egerton collection',[11] and use score notation, unlike any other works in the manuscript. The antiphons comprise three three-part settings of *Nesciens mater*, two by Trouluffe, one ascribed to Trouluffe and Smert jointly, and a four-part *Ave regina coelorum mater regis angelorum*. The *Ave regina* is the concluding work in the first layer of Ritson, and is probably meant to be specially impressive, because it is the only example of four-part writing in that layer apart from a single section in one carol; but in fact it is a rather crude, dissonant production. The two lowest parts are both in the same (bass) clef, but the lower one, unnamed in the manuscript, has something of a genuine bass function, cadencing below the 'tenor' which, although cantus firmus-like in places, is not apparently based on plainsong. The second and third *Nesciens mater* settings (ff. 56v. and 57v.)* both follow the proper plainsong from time to time in the highest and lowest voices, sometimes in decorated form. They have descant-style scoring with a different clef for each part, and end with VIIb–I cadences whose final chords are eight-fives.

The first *Nesciens mater* (f. 54v.) has the plainsong in semibreves in the middle. The middle voice also carries the plainsong in three other works with equal-note cantus firmus, as it did in the equal-note descants

---

* A folio reference is given to aid identification when the manuscript has two or more pieces with the same name.

of Old Hall; only an Alleluia, which is very similar in character to the
Alleluias in Pepys, has the melody in the lowest voice in accordance
with the practice of that manuscript. In Ritson the parts added to equal-
note plainsongs enjoy greater, sometimes much greater, rhythmic
independence than in Pepys; in fact the four works to be mentioned
below constitute a very important link between the simple Old Hall
descants and the works with equal-note cantus firmus by Taverner,
Tallis and Sheppard. *Nesciens mater* is the simplest of the four, with

outer parts surrendering their independence in the last few bars (*3(a*).Ex.
7.). The lowest voice behaves like a bass part rather than the traditional
descant 'counter', and there are several perfect cadences. *3(b*).Ex. 7.
shows the quite lively movement in the outer parts of Richard Mower's
Beata Dei genetrix which, like his very similar *Regina coeli* is among the
sacred works in the manuscript's final layer. In another work from the
final layer, the Compline antiphon *Miserere mihi* by John Norman
(presumably the man who wrote the Mass *Resurrexit Dominus* in the
Forrest-Heyther partbooks) the elaboration of the added parts is taken
very much further than elsewhere by consistently more rapid motion,

and this against breves instead of semibreves in the middle part (minims in transcription: *3(c).Ex. 7.*): one is reminded of the elaborate treatment of slow-moving plainsongs in Taverner's *Audivi vocem* and *Gloria in excelsis* (see *13.Ex. 9.* below).

The second, third and fourth sections of the Ritson book are all numerically small. The second has eight part-songs and an *O lux beata Trinitas* whose lower voice, the faburden, has the same length relationships as the *O lux* in Pepys. The third layer has two Masses; and the fourth contains the only two five-part pieces.

The two Masses are by Thomas Packe, who may be the same man as Thomas Pykke, clerk at Eton from 1454 to 1461.[12] In *Rex summe* Packe treats alternate sections of the Kyrie, Gloria and Credo fairly briefly, but makes complete settings of the Sanctus and Agnus of over 100 bars each. *Gaudete in Domino* demands *alternatim* performance only of the Kyrie, and apart from this movement is about 400 bars long, almost half as long as Fayrfax's longest Mass. The names *Rex summe* and *Gaudete in Domino* are puzzling. In each Mass the title is given in every movement at the entry of the lowest voice as if it were the name of a plainsong melody appearing in that part; yet neither Mass uses a regular cantus firmus, and even the melodic fragments which do recur do not appear to be connected with any 'Rex summe' or 'Gaudete in Domino' melodies. In *Gaudete in Domino* the four notes *d f e d* appear quite frequently in the lowest voice—perhaps a little too frequently for the harmonic interest of some sections; the more extended phrase *d f e d f e d a b c' d' a g f e d* crops up in about half a dozen places, in three cases near the end of a movement. Strangely the four-note figure *d f e d* heads a number of sections in *Rex summe* as well.

Rex summe has a total compass of two octaves and a third (*d* to *f''*), with a different clef and range for each voice. The lowest voice, although written in the tenor range and labelled 'tenor', acts as a harmonic bass much of the time, and almost all three-part sectional cadences are perfect, with the lowest and middle voices falling a fifth and a step respectively, the final chord having neither a fifth nor a third. Packe is not an outstanding composer, but some of his two-part writing in particular compares quite favourably with that in the Eton choirbook. In *Gaudete in Domino* the second and third parts have the same range and same clef, and the sectional cadences are chiefly VIIb–I, ending with a bare fifth; one might suggest from this that *Gaudete in Domino* is the earlier of Packe's Masses.

It was Packe who composed the two five-part items which form the fourth section of the manuscript. He is now referred to in each case as

'*Sir* Thomas Packe'; since his name is not to be found among lists of kinghts, the title was obviously used in its alternative sense, to mean that he was a priest. The first five-part piece is a short setting of the antiphon 'Lumen ad revelationem' plus a section which does duty in turn for the second half of each verse of the canticle Nunc dimittis; it was for use at Mass on the feast of the Purification during a ceremony in which candles were distributed. The five-part writing, which ranges from *F* to *f″*, is a little tentative, and remarkable only because it is an exceptional venture. The proper plainsong of the antiphon comes in the tenor, very slightly decorated. The psalm-tone for the canticle is less clearly presented. The other five-part work, very similar in character, is a setting of the three words 'Te Dominum confitemur' from verse 1 of the Te Deum; this forms part not of an *alternatim* setting of the hymn such as Taverner and Sheppard wrote, but of the burden of an extraordinary carol whose verses, partly in Latin, partly in English, are closely based on the Te Deum.

The final layer of the Ritson manuscript, the second largest and by far the most varied, has thirty-one pieces. Twenty-two of these are for church use. The remaining nine include an instrumental piece and eight part-songs which are in a more modern style than those from the second layer of the manuscript, with genuine bass lines instead of chanson scoring; they include two almost identical versions of *Pastime with good company* ascribed in British Museum Additional MS. 31922 to Henry VIII and here labelled 'the king's ballad'.

Half of the sacred works are three-part votive antiphons. The two by Mower use equal-note cantus firmi, as already mentioned. Other very small-scale pieces include a *Nesciens mater* (f. 123v.) which is quite independent of the plainsong; Packe's *Gaude sancta Magdalena*; and two settings of *Stella coeli*, the first a most neat and attractive work, the other a slightly unpolished one by Sir William Hawte. The 'Stella coeli' text, which is also set by Lambe, is a plea for the Virgin's protection against the plague, with four lines from the Marian sequence 'Ave praeclara' added.

Gaude virgo mater Christi is a much longer work than any of those just mentioned at over 130 bars. It has a bi-sectional triple-duple outline, a full-scale alternation between reduced and full sections instead of predominantly three-part writing broken by the shortest of duet passages in the manner of the shorter pieces, and is a kind of miniature Eton antiphon. The presence of a third in the final chord and the nature of the imitation in the closing section suggest that this is one of the latest works in the manuscript.

The four remaining antiphons are all written in a form of notation derived from plainsong, presumably designed for singers with little experience of polyphonic music. This notation uses only the two symbols ◄ (corresponding to the normal breve) and ◄ (semibreve): compare a *Salve festa dies* (*89*) in Pepys. It is surprising what variety is achieved within such limits. The most interesting work is the *Salve regina*: its three-part sections turn out to be adapted from the setting by Dunstable (or Power)[13]—a piece written probably as early as 1420 or 1430. Ornamental features of the original using short notes are necessarily removed; notes greater than the breve are represented by two or more symbols placed side by side; all rests are eliminated; full text is given in all voices; and because the contratenor is now a vocal rather than an instrumental part, a few of its more angular passages are

smoothed out. *4.Ex. 7.* demonstrates this extraordinary process of 'Dunstable made easy'. The concluding inscription 'Benedictus Deus in donis suis' ('Blessed be God in his gifts') may be the scribe's cryptic acknowledgement of his borrowing; the initials 'W.P.' are presumably his as well. 'W.P.' may have written the duets, in which he reverts to orthodox notation, obviously because soloists better versed in polyphony than the three-part choir would take them; but the style of these duets, if we rule out deliberate archaism, suggests composition earlier than the closing decades of the fifteenth century. *Anima mea liquefacta est*, copied immediately after the *Salve regina*, has the same inscription, and looks very much like another adaptation into plainsong notation of a much earlier work, one with the proper plainsong ornamented in the top part. *Nunc Jesu te petimus* and *Sancta Maria virgo* (whose proper melody is elaborated in the lowest voice) are the two other antiphons in plainsong notation; both are again very old-fashioned in style and one wonders where and in what form *they* originated. The most extended essay in plainsong notation is much more up-to-date, a Mass without Kyrie by Henry Petyr. Since Petyr had studied and practised music for thirty years when he became an Oxford Bachelor of Music in 1516,[14] his Mass dates from about 1485 at the very earliest. Petyr copes well within the severe limitations he sets himself in what is a much longer work than the 'plainsong-style' antiphons: changes of grouping help; there are some well-shaped lines, particularly in some two-part sections (none of which reverts to orthodox notation, by the way); and rhythmic activity is effectively built up towards several of the most important cadences. The other Mass in the final layer of Ritson, which consists of Kyrie and Gloria only, is in normal notation; it is probably a somewhat older work, and is by Edmund (S)turges.

The remaining piece in black plainsong notation is a simple setting on the faburden of *Salve festa dies . . . qua sponso* (f. 122). There is another more elaborate setting of this same text in normal notation, again on the faburden (f. 106v.). Of the few small-scale liturgical works remaining, it is worth noticing a *Benedicamus* (f. 121v.) written entirely in white semibreves and minims, a kind of white plainsong notation; and, by John Cornysh, probably some relative of William Cornysh, a very florid two-part setting of *Dicant nunc Judei*, verse of the antiphon 'Christus resurgens' from the Procession at Mass on Easter Day.

THE YORK MANUSCRIPT

The York manuscript (York, Borthwick Institute of Historical Research MS. Mus. 1) consists of twenty-two folios of paper which were discovered in the 1940s bound into the covers of a volume of Consistory Court Acts in York Diocesan Registry.[15] The manuscript contains music for the Ordinary of the Mass, mostly in four parts (which explains why its pages are larger, at 15 by 10½ inches, than those of Ritson and Pepys where three-part writing predominates). The surviving pages were from a choirbook which originally had forty-six leaves. The notation, the work of several hands, suggests a probable date of 1490–1520; the style does not contradict this, most works suggesting late fifteenth-century origin, while the last Mass may be early sixteenth-century. The choirbook's place of origin is not known, but Lincoln has been very tentatively suggested: the two composers named had or may have had connections with that city, Horwood presumably being the William Horwood of the Eton manuscript who was at Lincoln in the 1470s and 80s, John Cuk possibly the man who was sub-provost of Lincoln in 1520.

We probably still have all or some of each work copied into the original ninety-two-page choirbook. There are four Kyries at the beginning, three of them incomplete, including Horwood's *O rex clemens*. The fourth Kyrie looks incomplete at first sight, but is not: the bass is not written out, but a piece of Latin doggerel indicates that this part has to move in canon with the treble in the first section, with the mean in the Christe and with the countertenor in the final section. Two *alternatim* Gloria-Credo pairs, both still intact, follow the Kyries. Three four-movement Masses come next; these have suffered severe damage. The concluding item is a fully polyphonic Gloria-Credo pair from which only a little has been lost; this is the only work for three voices. The three Gloria-Credo pairs are the only ones from our period, although it was not uncommon for their two texts to be linked in the early fifteenth century.

The York music includes both fairly simple writing, as in the second and fourth Masses, and very florid and complex passages, notably in

(5.Ex. 7.)

the first Mass (*5.Ex. 7.*) and the fifth, which at times would have challenged even the Eton choir. The overwhelming preference for four-part writing (with a genuine harmonic bass line) also brings the York music closer to the Eton repertory than the Pepys or Ritson music is.

The first Mass is perhaps the earliest known work based on a square.

It has the melody which Ludford used in his Tuesday Mass in the tenor of some sections (but not in the reduced passage quoted in 5.*Ex. 7.*). The second and fifth Masses are both fairly free in their treatment of borrowed material: the former quotes a melody derived from the Compline versicle 'Custodi nos' from time to time in the bass or tenor; in the fifth Mass, on 'Venit dilectus meus', John Cuk even omits the plainsong from some full sections and curtails it in others.[16]

8

Robert Fayrfax and Nicholas Ludford

In Chapters 8 and 9 we deal with those composers active partly or wholly after 1500 whose works are represented in manuscripts dating from the first half of the sixteenth century and who died or ceased composing before the introduction of English services in 1549. The three chief composers are Robert Fayrfax (d. 1521), Nicholas Ludford and John Taverner (who probably composed little or nothing after 1530); Hugh Aston is first among the lesser men. The most important manuscripts are the Lambeth and Caius choirbooks and the Forrest-Heyther and Peterhouse partbooks.

Some of the work discussed below shows, sometimes in a very limited way, those changes which first weakened and later destroyed the style seen to perfection in Browne's music. In particular we shall see that Fayrfax rejects extravagent florid display; that Taverner has very little use for extremes of rhythmic complexity; and that with Taverner imitation becomes more important, sometimes much more so. Harmonically we notice a move away from differentiation of the parts, for conflicting key-signatures are now rare, and prominent false relations are less common. There is a closer approach to our major and minor scale-system: pure Lydian modality, used a little in Eton, surrenders almost completely to transposed Ionian; and the regular addition of a one-flat key-signature to a considerable number of works with D as final gives instances of transposed Aeolian. Incidentally there is a greater liking for minor modality now than in Eton, although not so pronounced a one as later—and even the Phrygian mode appears once or twice, as in Taverner's *Ave Dei Patris filia*.

Several of Taverner's smaller-scale pieces are markedly simpler and more direct than anything by Fayrfax and Ludford, and anticipate later music particularly closely. In his *Meane Mass* we find unmistakeable Continental influence, mainly that of Josquin's imitative practice, and one strongly suspects it at a few other points in the shorter pieces. Some of the English secular music of the period, as in British Museum

Additional MS. 31922, is a very simple, direct and syllabic, and may have had some very general fertilising effect, but there are no close parallels between it and church music.

Although Continental music apparently exercised a small influence as yet, more of it seems to have been known in England after about 1500 than before, for a few manuscripts containing it do now survive. But its dissemination was clearly limited: there is no common ground between these 'Continental' manuscripts and the early sixteenth-century sources of native church music; in fact, the latter contain no foreign works apart from two in Peterhouse. All the 'Continental' manuscripts mentioned below were associated with the royal court where musical taste might be expected to be more cosmopolitan than in the cathedrals and colleges which produced the 'English' manuscripts.

The earliest of the sources containing Continental music (Cambridge, Magdalene College, Pepys Library MS. 1760) is a collection of chansons, plus several Marian antiphons, made for Henry VII's elder son Prince Arthur (1486–1502); the Frenchman Antoine de Févin (*c.* 1470–*c.* 1512), a less than outstanding follower of Josquin, is the composer most generously represented; works by Mouton and Richafort are also present.[1] British Museum Additional MS. 31922, which includes numerous part-songs and consort pieces attributed to Henry VIII, has a transcription for instruments of most of the Credo from Isaak's Mass *O praeclara*. There are a few chansons here, and the song *Adieu mes amours* by William Cornysh is 'clearly an imitation of the contemporary French *chanson*'.[2] Between 1519 and 1528 a collection of Continental motets including anonymously Josquin's *Missus est Gabriel* and his setting of Dido's lament *Dulces exuviae* was made for the King (British Museum MS. Royal 8. G. vii).[3] Benedictus de Opitiis, formerly organist at Antwerp, became Henry VIII's court organist in 1516, and contributed to another small manuscript of motets and antiphons now in the British Museum (MS. Royal 11. E. xi). The first work, an elaborate canon, is in honour of Henry: so is *Psallite felices* by the Englishman Richard Sampson, who visited Antwerp and was probably influenced by Benedictus.[4]

ROBERT FAYRFAX

Although Fayrfax was born in 1464,[5] and was therefore little over ten years younger than Browne and Lambe, only three of his surviving works were included in the Eton choirbook (*Salve regina, Regali Magnificat*, and *Ave lumen gratiae*). Three of those preserved in later sources (*Aeterne laudis lilium, O quam glorifica* and *Lauda vivi Alpha et O*)

Table 6: Robert Fayrfax

Masses

à5: Albanus, O bone Jesu, O quam glorifica, Regali, Tecum principium
à4: Sponsus amat sponsam†

Votive antiphons

à5: Aeterne laudis lilium, Ave Dei Patris filia, Ave lumen gratiae,* Gaude flore virginali,†
Lauda vivi Alpha et O,* Maria plena virtute, O bone Jesu,† O Maria Deo grata,†
Salve regina

Magnificats

à5: O bone Jesu, Regali

Faburden

à4: O lux beata Trinitas

Lost

*Votive antiphons à5: Ave cujus conceptio, Quid cantemus innocentes, Stabat mater.‡ Nunc dimittis.§ Sequences.***

Fayrfax's work is published in *CMM*, xvii.

†Fragmentary.
*Imperfectly preserved.
‡All lost from the Eton choirbook.
§Harrison, *MMB*, pp. 432-3.
**Harrison *MMB*, p. 164.

are known to have been composed as well as copied after *c.* 1500; probably a good number more are of similar date since, as we shall see in a moment, Fayrfax was very active musically in the first two decades of the sixteenth century. *Aeterne laudis lilium* is assumed from its words to be the antiphon in honour of the Virgin and St Elizabeth for which Queen Elizabeth of York paid Fayrfax twenty shillings at St Alban's in 1502: there is an obvious compliment to the Queen in the treatment of the name 'Elizabeth', because some voices sing this more than once despite the usual ban on verbal repetition, and because additional parts are specially introduced. The Mass *O quam glorifica* is the 'exercise' Fayrfax wrote for his Cambridge Doctorate of Music in 1504: in the Lambeth choirbook it bears the inscription 'Doctor Fayrfax for his form in proceeding to be Doctor' (f. 8v.). *Lauda vivi Alpha et O* was written in or after 1509 because it ends with a prayer for Henry VIII.[6]
   The first information that we have about Fayrfax's musical career

is that he was a member of the Chapel Royal in 1497. In or before 1502 he became organist of the very rich St Alban's Abbey. In 1501 he graduated Bachelor of Music at Cambridge, three years before he attained his Doctorate. By 1509 his reputation was very considerable, for his name headed the lists of Gentlemen at Henry VII's funeral and Henry VIII's coronation. In 1511 came his final academic honour—the first Doctorate of Music conferred by the University of Oxford. Henry VIII made Fayrfax a Poor Knight of Windsor in 1514 to supplement his existing income, and continued to reward him by paying most handsomely each New Year's Day from 1516 to 1519 for books of music; in 1519 payment was for 'a ballad book limned' (that is, il-luminated, or more probably simply copied), but the other sums for a 'book', 'a book of anthems' and a 'pricksong book' may have been for composition as well as copying. In June 1520, only a year before his death, Fayrfax once more headed the list of Gentlemen of the Chapel Royal when Henry went to France to meet Francis I at the Field of the Cloth of Gold.

Fayrfax's surviving Masses, antiphons and Magnificats show that his reputation was well deserved. They are the work of an extremely thoughtful, discriminating composer who in particular achieved most subtle rhythmic effects very economically, and one who had little time for florid display. Even his scoring and textural schemes show restraint and economy: they are less obviously colourful than those of many Eton works, with for example no use of the gimel; among so many works there is no essay in writing for more than five voices; and the upper region of the treble range is treated cautiously, with virtually no use of g''.

The decline in floridity is very important as one of the first marked signs of the sixteenth-century stylistic revolution. Crotchets are employed less, often much less, than before, and in particular the use of more than two or three in succession is now not common. Quavers, never frequent, appear scarcely at all, and triplet figures are virtually abandoned. There is even a tendency for minims to be used less freely and to attract syllables less often than in earlier music, even in sections with many syllables. All this might seem to imply just a total shift towards longer values and a quicker semibreve beat, but comparison of Fayrfax's notation as a whole with that of earlier men does not confirm this.

Fayrfax's restraint is seen most clearly in the masterly *Aeterne laudis lilium* and *Maria plena virtute; 1.Ex. 8.* shows some syllabic writing from the former, and its most florid melisma. In *Maria plena virtute*,

(1.Ex. 8.)   *CMM*, xvii, vol.2. pp.50,48.

which begins and ends with prayers for Mary's intercession, but is concerned mainly with the Seven Last Words of Christ from the Cross, the generally economical approach seems to explain a (for Fayrfax) unusually wide employment of two-part writing; 'Sicut tuus filius' for treble and countertenor is a particularly fine section in which great rhythmic interest has been achieved with almost the minimum of means, hardly a trace of elaboration being admitted and rests being

(2.Ex. 8.)   *MB*, xi.34.

more and longer than normal for two-part writing. The *Salve regina* on the other hand is as florid as many other pieces in the Eton manuscript. The 'Benedictum fructum' section (*2.Ex. 8.*) is the most ornate, with its unusual preponderance of very short notes and the presence of uncharacteristic rhythms such as the syncopations in bar 4.

The general reduction in florid detail may indeed be seen as a step in the sixteenth-century progress towards stylistic simplification; but it is a very limited step, not generally being accompanied by any loss of interest in the sheer *complexity* of rhythm which, more than floridity, was fundamental to the Eton music. Fayrfax shows a remarkable appreciation for syncopated patterns in which a dotted semibreve is followed by some note other than a minim, something of a favourite being dotted semibreve, semibreve, minim.

Effects such as these are found above all in the Mass *O quam glorifica*, a work whose quite exceptional complication even by Eton standards

(3.Ex. 8.)

CMM, xvii, vol. 1, p.87.

is obviously due to its being an academic exercise. Even the form of notation is remarkable, for two time-signatures are used simultaneously throughout, a duple one in *two* parts (no mere co-incidence?) and a triple one in the other three. As with the augmentation in the cantus firmus of Lambe's *Gaude flore virginali*, no practical purpose is served: this is just a show of 'learning'. But it is important to stress that the special effects are not unduly forced or unmusical, and that the work as a whole is much more than a demonstration of technical cleverness. Triplet groupings, avoided in the rest of Fayrfax's church music, appear in many of the duos and trios of *O quam glorifica*; however they are not generally points of detail as they commonly are in the Eton music, but occur in quite long passages, usually towards the ends of sections. Only one part at a time is involved in the Gloria and Credo, but in some sections of the Sanctus (*3.Ex. 8.*) and Agnus triplets appear in all voices, usually with one part beginning them ahead of the others to establish the new pattern safely and avoid any sudden rhythmic lurch. Chains of dotted notes are a feature of some passages, the dotted minims (quavers in transcription) in the top part of *3.Ex. 8.* representing the most extended use of an extremely rare rhythm. The plainsong tenor (the melody of the hymn at first Vespers of the Assumption)

(4.Ex. 8.)   CMM, xvii, vol. 1, p. 79.

TENOR continues :—

quite often has groups of dotted semibreves (crotchets in our quotation), the most remarkable passage being at 'coelis' in the Credo (*4.Ex. 8.*), with its exceptionally persistent repetition of a *d* without change of syllable. The total rhythmic effect here results largely from the staggering of the various dotted-note rhythms; as often in Fayrfax the pace of the music is significantly quicker than the appearance of each part separately would imply. The use of chains of equal notes and the repetition of tiny rhythmic cells (for instance the minim-semibreve pattern (transcribed as quaver-crotchet) in the middle and lower parts of *3.Ex. 8.*) gives the lines clarity and cohesion, and are particularly valuable since imitation and sequence are used unusually little.

As a rule Fayrfax uses imitation about as frequently as Browne did, and still mainly in solo textures. He shows greatest fondness for it in *Albanus*, *Tecum principium* and *Maria plena virtute*, the last two having several striking instances of its penetrating full-choir sections. Melodic sequence is a little more important than formerly; as in Davy a single phrase often includes several statements of a very brief figure, but, as sometimes in Taverner the archexponent of melodic sequence, we find a weightier figure used, with each statement a separate phrase

(5.Ex. 8.) CMM, xvii, vol.1, p.152 : *Tecum principium.*

(*5.Ex. 8.*). The second part of the Credo of the very fine Mass *Tecum principium* has some of the most exciting imitative and sequential writing. A descending triadic shape with the rhythm dotted semibreve, semibreve, minim is prominent in the upper parts from 'Et resurrexit' to 'Et ascendit', while the bass has a sequence founded on a very striking related figure which spans an octave.

In *Lauda vivi Alpha et O* we find a new type of antiphonal writing which composers younger than Fayrfax, Taverner in particular, were to adopt. In this a phrase for the two boys' voices is repeated an octave lower by men's voices with a third 'free' part added; examples come at 'ancilla praefulgidissima', 'Henrico octavo inclito' and 'nosque tuos pios' (*6.Ex. 8.*).

The words of *Lauda vivi* seem to be modelled on those of a favourite text for sixteenth-century antiphons, 'Ave Dei Patris filia'. In each of

(6.Ex. 8.)
CMM, xvii, vol.3, p.39. (plus tenor part as re-constructed by the present author).

the first stanzas of the latter Mary is hailed as daughter (of the Father), mother (of the Son), spouse (of the Holy Spirit) and handmaid (of the Trinity): verse 1 reads 'Ave Dei Patris nobilissima, / Dei Filii mater dignissima, / Dei Spiritus sponsa venustissima, / Dei unius et trini ancilla subjectissima'. Each stanza except the fourth has a key word which appears in every line—'Dei' in verse 1 for example; and every line in stanzas 1–3 ends with a superlative. The basic pattern of 'Ave Dei Patris filia' is kept in verses 1–5 of the 'Lauda vivi' text; however the superlatives are maintained throughout, and are even more extravagant (for instance 'immaculatissima', 'praefulgidissima', 'mellifluissima', 'intemeratissima').

An interesting feature of Fayrfax's work is his linking of compositions belonging to different genres through shared material and common names. Thus we have a Mass, Magnificat and antiphon called *O bone Jesu*; a similar *Regali* set; and a Mass *Albanus* with a related antiphon.

The Mass *Regali* is called after its cantus firmus 'Regali ex progenie', third antiphon at Lauds on the feasts of the Conception and Nativity of the Virgin. In some manuscripts however, it is named *Regale*, as is the related Magnificat. The alternative spellings make it possible that both works were originally written for King's College, Cambridge or Eton, a play having been intended on the opening words of the antiphon and 'Collegium *Regale*', the Latin title of each foundation[7]— although so far no connection between Fayrfax and either College has been established. John Browne, almost certainly a scholar at Eton, also used the 'Regali ex progenie' plainsong in his four-part *Stabat virgo mater Christi*, conceivably with the same pun in mind. Fayrfax's *Regali* Mass and Magnificat had a third partner, an antiphon *Gaude flore virginali*, whose bass part alone, subtitled 'Regali', has survived. We cannot now tell the extent of the connection between the *Regali* Mass and *Gaude flore virginali*; but both works are in the same mode, and repeated *f*s come at the first entries of the bass in the Gloria and Credo of the Mass and in the antiphon. The 'Regali' plainsong can be made to fit what survives of *Gaude flore* between 'Gaude sponsa cara' and 'plenitudine' and again towards the end. The Mass and Magnificat *Regali* are musically linked, if only slightly: three full sections in the Mass ('Qui sedes', 'Et in unum Dominum', 'Et resurrexit') correspond very briefly with 'in De-(o salutari)' in the Magnificat; at 'Dominus Deus Sabaoth' there is a disguised reference to the same idea.

It is not clear which work from the *Regali* set was written first. But the supposed inclusion of a plainsong in the antiphon would perhaps imply that this work postdates the Mass, because Fayrfax like later composers does not normally base his antiphons on cantus firmi. Each Mass *does* incorporate a plainsong—except for *O bone Jesu*, which could be assumed to have been composed after rather than before the antiphon of the same name if it were not already clear that the Mass took its name from the antiphon anyway. The full extent of the links between the Mass and antiphon *O bone Jesu* cannot be shown, because only the mean part of the latter survives; but it is clear that the opening of the antiphon serves as Mass head-motif, and that a passage which recurs near the end of the Gloria, Credo and Agnus is also borrowed material. Several other correspondences may be found; for instance 'Crucifixus eti-(am)' in the Credo is derived from '(no)-men Jesu, nomen confor-(tans)'. The name *O bone Jesu* seems odd when applied to Magnificat, the Virgin's canticle, but its correctness is proved because the Magnificat shares material with the other *O bone Jesu* works. The music at 'in Deo (salutari)' is the same as that at 'O piissime' in the antiphon and as part of the Mass's head-motif; at '(mente cordis) sui' most of the Mass movements' common closing passage re-appears, although the upper voices are considerably re-modelled; and at 'Et di-(vites dimisit)' the beginning of the 'In nomine' section appears transposed up a fourth.

The Mass *Albanus* and the antiphon *O Maria Deo grata* (which is sub-titled *Albanus* in British Museum Additional MS. 34191) were obviously both written for Fayrfax's choir at St Alban's Abbey. The tenor

of the Mass is based on a nine-note plainsong theme (7(a).Ex. 8.) which had the name 'Albanus' as its original text, and which was extracted from 'Primus in Anglorum', an antiphon belonging to a rhymed Office of St Alban, 'Inclita martyrii recolentes'.[8] Fayrfax presents his theme backwards, in inversion, and in retrograde inversion as well as ordinarily, and makes it start at several different pitches. It appears forty times, in the full sections only. Much of the time statements are grouped in threes; for example the Sanctus has three 'ordinary' statements, three retrograde, and three in retrograde inversion. Each type of statement (ordinary, retrograde, etc.) has a basic rhythmic shape (7(b)-(e).Ex. 8.). Each shape is subject to diminution (for instance compare 7(b).Ex. 8. with 7(f).; and with a few exceptions statements become shorter as the work progresses, until in the 'Dona nobis pacem' the theme is given to each voice in turn in equal semibreves. The diminution recalls isorhythmic practice, but is less rigorously executed. The cantus firmus treatment of Albanus is without any exact precedent or parallel, although Continental composers did occasionally use such devices as retrograde movement (see for example Josquin's Mass Hercules Dux Ferrariae), and although both they and English composers after Fayrfax did sometimes adopt very brief 'ostinato-type' cantus firmi (for example Isaak in his Mass O praeclara and Alwood in his Praise Him Praiseworthy). Fayrfax was almost certainly acquainted with Dunstable's motet Albanus roseo rutilat / Quoque ferendus / Albanus, for the tenor of this begins with the 'Albanus' theme before quoting a little more of the 'Primus in Anglorum' antiphon. Although there appears to be no direct link between Dunstable's cantus firmus technique and Fayrfax's, it is probable that the younger composer knew the older man's piece and that his handling of diminution in some way shows a debt to Dunstable's genuinely isorhythmic practice.

O Maria Deo grata has statements of the 'Albanus' theme in the countertenor, mean and bass at bars 197, 200 and 205. Its tenor has not survived, but it clearly carried the same melody throughout the full sections. In view of what was said earlier about the order of composition of the Regali Mass and antiphon, the use of a cantus firmus in O Maria Deo grata suggests that this work was written after Albanus; its beginning not like the Mass with ordinary statements of the theme but with statements in retrograde inversion seems to confirm this secondary position.

NICHOLAS LUDFORD

Together Ludford and Fayrfax dominate the Lambeth and Caius choirbooks; but there are important differences between them musically and in personal circumstances. Ludford's music, while rarely very florid, is noticeably more so than Fayrfax's; his surviving output is

Table 7: Nicholas Ludford

Masses (Ordinary only)
à6: Benedicta, Videte miraculum
à5: Christi virgo, Inclina,* Lapidaverunt Stephanum, Regnum mundi†
à4: Leroy†

Lady Masses (Ordinary and Proper)
à3: seven settings: Dominica (Sunday), feria ii (Monday), feria iii (Tuesday), feria iv (Wednesday), feria v (Thursday), feria vi (Friday), sabbato (Saturday)

Votive Antiphons
à5: Ave cujus conceptio,* Ave Maria ancilla Trinitatis,* Domine Jesu Christe,* Salve regina,† Salve regina pudica mater†

Magnificat
à6: Benedicta

Lost
Masses: (?)Requiem aeternam, Sermone blando, Tecum principium.¶

Edition of Ludford: *CMM*, xxvii (vol. i, Seven Lady Masses, 1962).

*Imperfectly preserved.
†Fragmentary.
¶Hughes, 'An introduction to Fayrfax', p. 94.

more varied, for it contains some six-part writing and the set of three-part Lady Masses; and unlike Fayrfax (or indeed Taverner or any other major composer) he frequently sets the Mass Credo complete. While Fayrfax received every academic honour. Ludford had no degree; and while Fayrfax enjoyed very great royal recognition, Ludford was not even a Gentleman of the Chapel Royal, despite his being at St Stephen's, Westminster which adjoined the Royal Palace of Westminster.[9] His association with St Stephen's obviously began in the first quarter of the sixteenth century, for a Mass of St Stephen, *Lapidaverunt Stephanum*, is preserved in the Lambeth and Caius choirbooks. But it is only in 1547, in connection with the dissolution of the collegiate foundation, that we find a written record of Ludford's work at St Stephen's. He was then serving as verger, a post which apparently had special musical duties there. After the dissolution he received a pension until 1555–6, which is presumably the time of his death. The date of his birth is unknown, but *c.* 1480–5 is a reasonable conjecture: on the one hand he was probably older than Taverner (born in the 1490s) since much of his music is preserved in earlier sources, and on the other younger than Fayrfax because if born in or before the mid 1460s he would have been very old to be still in office in 1547.

Ludford's restricted circumstances resulted in his musical reputation being rather local and rather short-lived where Fayrfax's was wide and enduring. Most of his work is preserved in four Henrician sources, the Lambeth choirbook, which may have originated at St Stephen's; Caius, which is possibly related to this; British Museum Royal Appendix MSS. 45–48, which may conceivably be in Ludford's own hand (as explained below); and Peterhouse. There is no Ludford source later than Peterhouse. This neglect in the second half of the sixteenth century was unwarranted and unfortunate, because Ludford is a very accomplished composer. Much of the still very limited attention he has enjoyed in the twentieth century has been directed to the seven three-part Lady Masses, on account of the unique liturgical character and fascinating cantus firmus practice of these works.

The Lady Masses are the sole contents of Royal Appendix MSS. 45–48, four very neat and accurately copied partbooks which have the arms of Henry VIII and Catherine of Aragon stamped on their leather covers. Since a manuscript devoted to a single composer's works is exceptional, one wonders if Ludford himself produced them as a gift to the royal couple.[10] The presence of Catherine's arms as well as Henry's gives as the outside dates for the manuscript's production 1509, the year of the royal marriage, and 1533, the year of the divorce; but the latest probable date would be several years before 1533, because the two royal establishments were separate from 1531, and the divorce had been in Henry's mind since the late 1520s.

The Lady Masses constitute the only sizeable body of three-part church music surviving from sixteenth-century England. The scoring for treble, mean and countertenor, without use of the bass register, and the frequent presentation of cantus firmi in the lowest voice are traits as apparently old-fashioned as the choice of three parts itself; but the style and cadence practice of the Lady Masses are very much of the early sixteenth century; in particular imitation is often present, and there are occasional brief sequences. 8.Ex. 8. illustrates the grace and fluency of much of Ludford's writing in the Lady Masses, with that fondness for movement in parallel thirds which is slightly more pronounced in his work than in that of other composers.

Each Lady Mass is allocated to a different day of the week. It contains the Ordinary with Kyrie, plus an Alleluia and sequence. The chants for three Offertories (for Advent, Christmas to the Purification,

(8.Ex. 8.)   *CMM*, xxvii, 147.

Purification to Advent) and four Communions (the fourth being for use in Eastertide) are given in the soloist's book.

The Kyries, Alleluias and sequences were performed *alternatim*, as were the Glorias and Credos for all days except Wednesday and Friday. The polyphonic sections of the Alleluias and sequences incorporate or refer to their proper plainsongs. In sequences the three-part verses generally follow the plainsong throughout, very frequently beginning in equal notes (semibreves) and then becoming freer rhythmically and having touches of melodic decoration; the plainsong is usually but not always at the bottom. In two-part writing, which is adopted for the third verse of each sequence plus one or more later verses, the proper melodies are often abandoned after the first few bars. The Alleluias begin with their melodies in the lowest voice in semibreves, but thereafter the treatment is rather freer than in the three-part sections of sequences.

The movements of the Ordinary are built on squares. Each Kyrie has all three sections of its square in the soloist's book (with words 'Kyrie eleison', 'Christe eleison', 'Kyrie eleison') and also in the lowest voice of the polyphonic settings of these words which alternate with the solo passages. In the polyphony the square is usually decorated (*9.Ex. 8.*). Three squares (those of the Sunday, Monday and Thursday Masses) were specifically associated with the Kyrie text in British Museum Lansdowne MS. 462 (ff. 151v.–152); but Ludford re-uses them, as he does his other squares, in later movements, even though different squares belonging to these movements did exist. Ludford treats each square with considerable freedom, for it will sometimes return in a different rhythm

and metre from that in which it was presented in the Kyrie, and it may be much ornamented.

In the *alternatim* Glorias and Credos the usual method is for each of the soloist's passages to use one of the three sections of the square, and for each polyphonic passage to incorporate one as cantus firmus, generally in the lowest voice; most commonly a passage for the soloist and the following polyphony will share the same section of the square, and normally the three sections will appear in the same order in which they came in the Kyrie. But some of the two-part polyphony, used for one or more intermediate verses of each movement, is wholly or mostly free, and in the Sunday, Tuesday and Saturday Glorias some of the soloist's material appears to be unrelated to anything in the Kyrie, as for instance at 'Domine fili' in the Sunday Mass. The Gloria of the Saturday Mass does not refer to the Kyrie square either in its solo or polyphonic verses, and every verse has fresh material. Possibly Ludford is using some melody which belonged specifically to the Gloria, but it is not the same as either of the Gloria melodies in the Masses *Apon the square* by Mundy and Whytbrook.

Movements set in polyphony throughout generally use a square in their three-part sections, often presenting it very inexactly. In the Friday Mass, which has the Gloria and Credo in polyphony throughout as well as the Sanctus and Agnus, there seems to be scarcely any reference to the square. In each fully polyphonic movement the sequence of reduced and full textures follows the conventional pattern, and there is an intermediate triple-duple signature-change, but each *alternatim* Gloria and Credo has its own different scheme of between two and six changes involving C, Ø and ₵.

Ludford's other works include three for six-part choir, the Mass and Magnificat *Benedicta* (with two bass parts) and the Mass *Videte miraculum* (with two trebles). The full sections of the Magnificat are based neither on a faburden tenor nor on a psalm-tone, but on the same plainsong as the Mass, 'Benedicta et venerabilis', verse from the eighth respond at Matins of the Assumption, 'Beata es virgo Maria'; this exceptional rejection of normal Magnificat practice in favour of a Mass-style cantus firmus makes it almost certain that the Magnificat was written *after* the Mass. Another sign that the Magnificat came second is its beginning with reduced writing as a Mass commonly does instead of with the initial full texture conventional in a Magnificat. The first eight bars do indeed serve as the Mass's head-motif. Mass and Magnificat are further linked by the appearance of the first part of the 'Cum Sancto Spiritu' at 'et semini ejus (in saecula)'. The Mass was presumably first performed on the feast of the Assumption; the Magnificat could also have been sung on this feast at the first (and more important) Vespers: the canticle antiphon for this service, 'Ascendit Christus', is in the sixth mode, thus necessitating for the canticle itself tone 6, the very one which must be used for the odd-numbered verses of Ludford's setting if they are to agree in modality with the 'Benedicta' plainsong.

The style of the *Benedicta* Mass is broadly similar to that of Fayrfax's Masses, but there is a slightly greater feeling for florid detail and a tendency for more rapid declamation. There is a particularly delightful

(10.Ex. 8.)

passage at the end of the Credo (*10.Ex. 8.*) in which a little bell-like theme is worked in imitation, always off the beat in the bass parts.

The Mass *Videte miraculum*, based on the respond at first Vespers of the Purification, is in places far more florid than *Benedicta*, especially in solo passages involving the two trebles; here the rapidity of some

(11.Ex. 8.)

scalic writing almost recalls Davy's work, but the style is tighter, more imitative (11(a) and (b).Ex. 8.), and in 11(b). there is an equal-note cantus firmus. The presentation of a Mass cantus firmus in equal notes, which is an important feature of Taverner's *Gloria tibi Trinitas*, as in the famous 'In nomine' section, was something of a favourite with Ludford: possibly he pioneered it. In *Videte miraculum* he uses it at the first 'Qui tollis of the Gloria as well as at 'Benedictus qui venit'; and in *Lapidaverunt Stephanum*, a Mass based on the first antiphon at Lauds of St Stephen, at 'Benedictus'. In the 'Dona nobis pacem' of *Benedicta* the plainsong comes in dotted semibreves, under C signature against Ø in the other parts; there are several similar cases of cantus firmi in dotted semibreves elsewhere, notably in the ending of Taverner's *Ave Dei Patris filia* and the 'Cum Sancto Spiritu' of Avery Burton's Mass *Ut re mi fa sol la* (C against ₵) or at 'Dona nobis pacem' in Taverner's *Gloria tibi Trinitas* (C in all voices).

Ludford's *Christi virgo*, based on the ninth respond at Matins of the Annunciation, is a somewhat more compact setting than *Videte miraculum* or *Benedicta* which employs some interesting antiphonal

(12.Ex. 8.)

effects in the 'Et incarnatus' (*12.Ex. 8.*) and at 'Et in Spiritum Sanctum', the part of the Credo not normally set in large-scale English Masses. The antiphony does not involve any repetition as it does in Fayrfax's *Lauda vivi Alpha et O* or Taverner's *Mater Christi*.

The Mass entitled *Inclina* in Peterhouse has been widely referred to in error as *Inclina Domine*; but John Bergsagel has identified the missing tenor cantus firmus as 'Inclina cor meum Deus', an Epiphany respond.[11] *Inclina* is linked with the antiphon *Ave Maria ancilla Trinitatis* by a shared opening phrase. *Ave Maria* lacks its tenor part as *Inclina* does and as all Ludford's other antiphons do.

THE LAMBETH AND CAIUS CHOIRBOOKS: ANONYMOUS MUSIC AND LESSER COMPOSERS

Fayrfax and Ludford are the major contributors to the Lambeth choirbook, with at least ten of its nineteen pieces between them; in addition they composed eleven works out of fifteen in the Caius book. In Lambeth only three of the works by Fayrfax have his name attached, five other pieces being known as his, and two as Ludford's, from concordances in Caius and other manuscripts. It is possible that there are further works by Fayrfax and Ludford among the seven anonymous pieces for which no concordances have been traced: *Ave Dei Patris filia*, *Ave mundi spes Maria*, *Gaude flore virginali*, *Salve regina*, two Magnificats and *Vidi aquam egredientem de templo* (antiphon at the Aspersion before Mass during Eastertide).

Composers mentioned in Chapter 6 are still represented in both choirbooks: Sturton and Lambe in Lambeth (*Ave Maria ancilla Trinitatis* and *O Maria plena gratia* respectively, while Cornysh, Turges and their contemporary Henry Prentyce, who died in 1514, have Magnificats in Caius.

Caius also has a Mass by William Pasche, probably the man who was Fellow of New College, Oxford from 1494 to 1506.[12] This is based on 'Christus resurgens', a processional antiphon of Easter Day; one suspects that Pasche enjoyed the pun between his name and the Latin for Easter—'Paschae'!

9

John Taverner and Hugh Aston

JOHN TAVERNER

John Taverner is undoubtedly the greatest of England's early six-teenth-century composers by virtue of the uniquely compelling character of much of his work and the historical importance of a few pieces such as the *Meane Mass*. He stands very high indeed among English musicians of any age—although it would be idle to pretend that he rivals Dunstable or Byrd.

Life

Not a great deal is known of Taverner's life, but he is nevertheless the first English composer who begins to emerge as a real person rather than as just a name in a history book. Probably we even have some idea of what he looked like from the sketches (or caricatures) at the beginnings of all the parts of *Gloria tibi Trinitas* in the Forrest-Heyther part-books (Plate 5).

It is generally assumed that Taverner was born in the 1490s; he certainly had a brother William born between 1495 and 1505.[1] By 1525 Taverner was a clerk fellow at the Collegiate Church of Tatter-shall in Lincolnshire. In Autumn 1526, although apparently reluctant to relinquish this post and forgo the prospect of a 'good' marriage, he accepted Cardinal Wolsey's invitation to become the first master of the choristers at the newly-founded Cardinal College, Oxford (now Christ Church). While at the College he became involved in a small way with the Lutherans who were active there, and in 1528 had a lucky escape from punishment. John Foxe's comment that 'the Cardinal, for his music, excused him, saying that he was but a musician'[2] is well known; less well known, and even less complimentary, was Dean Higden's opinion that Taverner was 'unlearned and not to be regarded'.[3] Taverner's departure from the College in April 1530 may have been somehow connected with the disturbances of 1528. That the influence of Lutheranism was lasting is suggested by his working in the late 1530s as an agent of Thomas Cromwell, chiefly in dissolving monasteries. His efforts here have often led to his being labelled a fanatic and a cruel persecutor; in fact letters he wrote to Cromwell do not support this view, but show concern by him for the welfare of the dispossessed Boston friars. After his work for Cromwell was completed Taverner seems to have settled down to the life of a well-to-do citizen and small landowner in Boston. He served as an official in the influential Guild of Corpus Christi in the town, and became one of the twelve aldermen when Boston was made a borough in June 1545, four months before his death. He is buried with his wife Rose underneath the bell-tower of Boston Parish Church.

It has been widely assumed that Taverner completely abandoned musical composition as a result of his contacts with Lutheranism; this is largely on the strength of a marginal note in the 1583 edition of John Foxe's *Actes and Monuments* that he 'repented him very much that he had made songs to popish ditties in the time of his blindness'.[4] Some scholars however have considered that the term 'popish ditties', instead of extending to all types of church music for the Latin rite, would have applied mainly to such items as votive antiphons in honour of the Virgin or the Saints.[5] It is of course unclear exactly what Foxe himself understood by 'popish ditties'—and indeed whether the term was his or Taverner's own—but one imagines that at least in 1583 the texts of the *Mass* would have been considered 'popish'. The most important point perhaps is that Taverner did not, so far as we know, hold any musical post after 1530: so that (even if Foxe's marginal note were not just hearsay) Taverner's opportunities and motives for composing would have been limited, and it therefore remains likely that all or most of his church music *was* written before his leaving Oxford—when he was still only in his thirties. With Taverner then we apparently have the first known conflict between a musician's conscience and his work, and can see the first effects of the religious upheavals of the sixteenth century on music in England. Taverner's historical preeminence here is complemented by his being the first composer in whose work we can trace some of the important new stylistic trends of the sixteenth century.

Some Major Aspects of Taverner's Style

Most of Taverner's music, it is true, remains within the same tradition as Fayrfax's and Ludford's; but there is often greater textural unity because of an increased, sometimes a significantly increased, use of imitation, and these is some easing of rhythmic complexity resulting most obviously from a more cautious use than formerly of syncopated patterns involving dotted semibreves. Florid detail is more important to Taverner than to Fayrfax, but some passages, for example parts of *Ave Dei Patris filia*, are as restrained as anything by the older master. In a few of Taverner's smaller-scale works, including the *Meane Mass*, the stylistic advances are very marked; a quite new approach to imitation is the most momentous of these.

We turn first to the pieces of the former, large-scale group. These are at times more immediately forceful in their impact than the works of earlier men, partly because of their avoidance of the most difficult rhythms and their increased imitative and sequential activity. This strength and energy at its most impressive may be appreciated from *1.-4.Exx. 9.*, which are taken from *Gloria tibi Trinitas* and *Western Wynde*, two of Taverner's greatest works and indeed two of the

masterpieces of their age. *1.Ex. 9.*, from the Credo of *Gloria tibi Trinitas*, features triadic imitative points projected against a fairly slow-moving harmonic background, a kind of writing which Taverner used in several other places in this Mass, in *Western Wynde* and in *Corona spinea.* Triadic points themselves had been used before, but such intensive working of delightfully pithy figures like these was new. New also was the way Taverner concentrated much of his most striking motivic activity into full textures. Wide ranging scalic figures, again no novelty in themselves, are made the subject of imitation in several very impressive sections. At 'et ascendit' in *Gloria tibi Trinitas* for

(2.Ex. 9.)

example (*2.Ex. 9.*) the point, spanning a ninth, is appropriately a rising one, and moreover one which is heard first in the lowest voice before it climbs step by step to the top of the texture; the whole process climaxes in the very solid sound at 'in coelum' where the bass and tenor move in thirds.

Melodic sequence is sometimes remarkably persistent in Taverner, and powerful in shaping a passage of some length. An instance of the composer's enthusiasm for the device is given as *3.Ex. 9.*; there are several equally striking passages one could have chosen elsewhere in *Western Wynde*, or in *Gloria tibi Trinitas* or *Corona spinea.* Sometimes sequential repetition is made to underpin the texture by coming in the bass part. This happens for instance at '(Dominus Deus) Sabaoth' in the Sanctus of *Gloria tibi Trinitas* where there are four statements of a theme derived from the phrase currently in the cantus firmus part: these are accompanied by several entries of the same theme in imitation. The

(3.Ex. 9.)   *TCM*, i.18.

most outstanding instances of simultaneous imitative and sequential activity come in the Credo of *Gloria tibi Trinitas* at '(descendit de) coelis' (4.Ex. 9.) and the Agnus Dei at the first '(miserere) nobis'; in both cases there is much very energetic activity in the four lower parts, while the cantus firmus and the top part have slower, smoother lines to prevent 'over-heating'.

The most important of the smaller-scale and simpler works by Taverner are the antiphons *Mater Christi* and *Christe Jesu*, the Masses derived from them, the Mass *Playn Song*, and the *Meane Mass*. The last of these is the most obviously novel of Taverner's shorter pieces; it is natural to suppose that it is among the very last works Taverner wrote. The simpler works show limited similarities to some of the smaller-scale pieces mentioned in Chapter 7, notably to some antiphons from the final layer of the Ritson manuscript: they avoid the more complex rhythms (more carefully than Taverner's larger works do) and show only a limited interest in florid detail and other types of writing which involve very marked contrasts between long and short notes within short spaces. But Taverner's shorter works are also new and forward-looking because their composer places greater stress on imitation;

(4.Ex. 9.)

uses short and sharp antiphonal contrasts from time to time; pays closer attention to the words; and is at least occasionally influenced by Continental music. Additionally he uses five-part scoring for all shorter works except *Playn Song*, whereas this scoring was formerly restricted to works of 'festal' dimensions.

Imitation simplifies a texture by causing a reduction both in rhythmic and melodic diversity: where it is used the parts share rhythmic patterns and melodic shapes instead of all going their own ways. But in almost all music before Taverner, and in very much of Taverner's own, imitation is too infrequent or too limited in its power radically to shift the balance from a texture whose parts are essentially differentiated to a texture essentially unified. Entries are often very brief, as small points of detail at the head of a phrase or perhaps within its concluding melisma; or they are worked against a cantus firmus which ultimately controls the content of the texture; or they are projected against a static or slow-moving harmonic background. However, especially in the *Meane Mass*, sets of entries begin genuinely to shape entire phrases and short sections (*5.Ex. 9.*).

(*5.Ex. 9.*)

TCM, i.50.

One very important thing to notice about *5.Ex. 9.* is the 'pairing' of entries (something which happens where the relationship between entries 1 and 2 of an imitative passage is repeated between entries 3 and 4 but *not* between 2 and 3). In *5.Ex. 9.* the first and second entries are four beats apart, the latter beginning a fifth above the former; the same relationship exists between the third and fourth. Pairing of entries is the key feature of Josquin's imitation; and it is obvious that the imitation of the *Meane Mass* was derived from Continental practice. Indeed it is useful to compare *5.Ex. 9.* with a passage from Josquin such as the opening of his *Missa de Beata Virgine* (*6.Ex. 9.*). Although Taverner's Mass sets off with something of the same directness and purposefulness as Josquin's, it does not have the same economy of style and material, because the point is rather shorter and less sharply

(6.Ex. 9.)   *The Pelican History of Music*, ii.105.

defined, and because there is little overlapping of entries before the closer working towards the end which helps drive the music to its cadence. Taverner's choice of four-part scoring at 'Et in terra' and in a considerable number of other sections from the *Meane Mass*, unusual for a five-part work, is obviously very suitable for the working of paired imitation, and also recalls the Continental preference at the end of the fifteenth century and the beginning of the sixteenth for writing in this number of parts. Although Taverner retains the favourite English five-part texture for some sections, he dispenses with the charac-

(7.Ex. 9.)   *TCM*, i.62.

teristically English high treble line; the presence of a mean at the top accounts for the name of the Mass.

The passage shown in *7.Ex. 9.* is more obviously economical than that quoted in *5.Ex. 9.* There is also a new harmonic tension because of frequent suspensions highlighting the beginnings and ends of entries; this, which gives a forward thrust to the music in addition to that provided by the concluding stretto effect (and in place of the old Eton-style drive to the cadence in which all the parts simply move more quickly), has an obvious precedent in a section such as the 'Dona nobis pacem' from Josquin's Mass *Pange lingua*. Similar suspensions, used less persistently, are found elsewhere in the *Meane Mass*, and in the penultimate section of *O splendor gloriae* ('te prece precamur'), where the imitative writing is as economical as in *7.Ex. 9.*

Josquin's pairing of voices is often employed to give a kind of antiphonal effect: two parts will sing a short passage (not necessarily involving imitation) while the others rest, and then they themselves will rest as the second pair repeats the phrase (often at a higher or lower octave). Very commonly there is a slight dovetailing of the two phrases. Taverner tries this kind of antiphony once or twice in the

Meane Mass (8.Ex. 9.). In some other works, chiefly the short antiphons *Mater Christi* and *Christe Jesu* and the Masses derived from them, there is antiphonal writing which uses the type of scoring already seen in Fayrfax's *Lauda vivi Alpha et O (6.Ex. 8.* above), with the top two (boys') voices being answered by the lower three (for men). Short, pithy phrases which project the words with great clarity and give an unusually sharp contrast in vocal colouring are generally preferred (9.Ex. 9.) to the fairly long ones used in *Lauda vivi*.

(9.Ex. 9.)

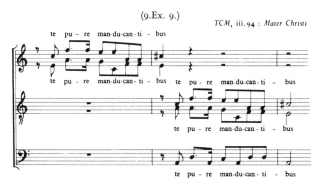

TCM, iii.94 : *Mater Christi*

The simpler rhythmic style of Taverner's shorter pieces leads occasionally to brief use of chordal writing, that simplest of all kinds of texture. Some antiphonal writing is chordal, as at the beginnings of several five-part sections in the antiphon *Mater Christi*. Homophony for the full choir is used at 'et homo factus est' in the Credo of *Small Devotion*; Continental Masses, for instance Josquin's *Pange lingua*, sometimes treated these words in the same way, but in earlier English Masses they had regularly been set contrapuntally for soloists. The Gloria and Credo of the *Meane Mass* have several short chordal (or mainly chordal) excursions into triple metre (⊙ or ₃⌀) within the basically duple metre; Continental music again provides obvious parallels. The

(10.Ex. 9.)

TCM, i.51.

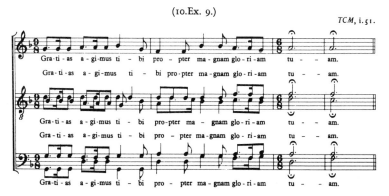

music of the 'Gratias' passages (*10.Ex. 9.*) is re-used in roughly the same position in the Credo at 'Et ex Patre natum' and again at 'Et exspecto', and in the third Agnus Dei; it thus strengthens the formal unity already given by the common openings and endings of the various movements.

In *Christe Jesu* and the Mass *Playn Song* simplicity of rhythmic structure is closely linked with the form of notation used. These two works employ what is essentially a white version of the black plainsong notation found in several works from the Ritson manuscript: the name of the Mass *Playn Song* clearly refers to this notation, for there is no chant present. Instead of Ritson's two symbols ▚ and ▚, Taverner uses mainly white breves and semibreves; but he does allow a few dotted breves (the Ritson scribe had to express the dotted breve as ▚▚), and we find the dotted semibreve followed by a single minim for a strong–weak pair of syllables. Towards the end of *Christe Jesu* (from the five-part entry at 'et ecclesiam piorum') there is less rhythmic severity, with groups of up to three minims and (as occasionally in *Playn Song*) one or two longs. While Taverner probably did have the Ritson works or others like them in mind when he wrote *Christe Jesu*

(II.Ex. 9.)

TCM, iii.73.

and *Playn Song*—there was even an example of white plainsong notation in Ritson—it is possible that he knew of Josquin's use of a form of white notation almost as simple in for example much of *O Domine Jesu Christe* and *Qui velatus facie fuisti*.

Christe Jesu is a small masterpiece, delightful in every detail and immediately attractive. It is made up mainly of very compact antiphonal and chordal passages (11.Ex. 9.), until the music briefly blossoms into imitative writing just before the end. The short antiphon *Mater Christi*, another of Taverner's very finest achievements, is again largely an essay in antiphony and homophony, but at about seventy bars it is twice as long as *Christe Jesu* and so the rhythmically freer imitative style is more widely used to give necessary variety. In the *Playn Song* Mass, naturally a much larger exercise in restricted values than *Christe Jesu*, Taverner again gives no impression of being uncomfortable or cramped; he even avoids some opportunities for contrast in weight and colour by employing reduced textures less than usual in the Gloria and Credo.

The notation of *Christe Jesu* and *Playn Song* is of course exceptionally narrow rhythmically. But in other shorter works Taverner is often more careful than in his larger ones to avoid very marked contrasts of pace and rhythm between parts; touches of floridity are more rigorously controlled, and movement within the single voice-part tends to be less diverse: everything is moving towards unity and away from differentiation.

Christe Jesu and *Playn Song* are notated predominantly in breves and semibreves, which gives them a very different appearance on paper from the other shorter works: in fact passages in *Small Devotion* which are derived from *Christe Jesu* have the original values halved. For in *Small Devotion* as in other works which begin with the signature ₵ (notably the *Mater Christi* pair, the *Meane Mass* and the Mass *Western Wynde*) Taverner takes the semibreve and minim as his leading values, using breves very much more sparingly than in the longer works, except where the sign of diminution $\frac{\emptyset}{3}$ rules). A similar emphasis on the semibreve and minim is found in some earlier pieces, especially short ones, and is pretty well universal in the mid sixteenth century.

It is obvious that, without any special effort on the composer's part, the words will come over much more clearly in Taverner's simpler works than in rhythmically complex writing. But there are signs that Taverner had *some* active concern with projecting his text clearly. There is more consistency in the matching of verbal and musical rhythms than in the work of earlier composers. (In fact there is some

Table 8: John Taverner

Masses

à6: Corona spinea, Gloria tibi Trinitas, O Michael
à5: Mater Christi,* Meane Mass *or* Sine nomine, Small Devotion*
à4: Playn Song, Western Wynde

Movements and Fragments of Masses

à4: Kyrie Leroy
à3: Agnus Dei, 3 settings of Christe eleison, Osanna in excelsis

Proper of the Mass

à4: Alleluia I, Alleluia II *Veni electa* (*Lady Mass*)
à3: Jesu spes poenitentibus (*v. 3 from Name of Jesus sequence 'Dulcis Jesu memoria'*), Tam peccatum (*v. 4 from Tract at Jesus Mass 'Dulce nomen'*), Traditur militibus (*v. 6 from sequence 'Coenam' from votive Mass of the Five Wounds*)
à2: Ecce mater (*verse of antiphon at Procession before Mass, Septuagesima, Sexagesima, Quinquagesima*)

Votive Antiphons

à5: Ave Dei Patris filia, Ave Maria,† Christe Jesu pastor bone,* Fac nobis secundum hoc nomen,† Gaude plurimum, Mater Christi, O splendor gloriae, Sancte Deus,† Sub tuum praesidium†

Fragments from Lost Antiphon(s)

à3: Prudens virgo, Virgo pura

Magnificats

à6: one setting* (version for men only à5 also exists)†
à5: one setting*
à4: one setting

Te Deum

à5: one setting*

Responds

à5: *Dum transisset* sabbatum I (version for men only à4 also exists) (*Easter*), *Dum transisset* sabbatum II, *Dum transisset* sabbatum III†
à4: Audivi *vocem* (*All Saints*), Hodie nobis coelorum *rex*/Gloria in excelsis (*Christmas*), In pace *in idipsum* (*Lent*)

Prose

à5: Sospitati dedit aegros (*St Nicholas*)

Lost

Mass 'for children'. Kyries and sequences.§††

Note

The Rex amabilis, Tu ad liberandum, Tu angelorum Domina and Esto nobis printed in Tudor Church Music, iii are by other composers‡‡; the (textless) Sanctus and Benedictus there are respectively a section from Gaude plurimum and Traditur militibus. The textless Quemadmodum, as suggested below, may well be an instrumental work. A fragmentary Ave regina coelorum à5 ascribed to Taverner in Tenbury MS. 1474 and printed in Tudor Church Music, Appendix is certainly not his.

Taverner's work is published in *TCM*, i and iii.

limited advance in this direction even in some of his longer works.) The dotted minim, crotchet pattern, very effective for clearly projecting a strong–weak pair of syllables, is more popular than before; it is of course especially successful when associated with chordal movement as in parts of *Mater Christi* and the *Meane Mass*.

An extremely important advance in text-treatment is the admission of verbal repetition, a device found already abroad in Josquin's work. It is in the Sanctus and Agnus of the *Meane Mass* that verbal repetition is employed most; but Taverner does use it a few times in the Gloria and Credo of *Small Devotion*, in *Christe Jesu*, in the final part of *O splendor gloriae*, in the *Dum transisset* settings and the *Te Deum*. Its adoption means that extended melisma is no longer inevitable in sections with few words, because each voice is no longer restricted to singing the text through once only; hitherto, for example, even in fairly short settings of the Mass, including Taverner's own *Mater Christi*, *Small Devotion* and *Playn Song*, the Sanctus and Agnus had consisted of one long melisma after another because of the extreme brevity of their texts. The removal of extended melisma in the *Meane Mass* furthers the other moves away from musical differentiation and complexity: instead of there being two separate approaches to the text there can now be one, the syllabic—the one which had always tended to bring with it the more concise and economical writing.

A Survey of Taverner's Work

Taverner's work is considerably more varied than that of any composer yet discussed, for we have not only eight Masses by him, but numerous votive antiphons in various degrees of completeness, and an important group of *alternatim* pieces among which Magnificats and responds are the most important items.

Masses

The Masses show the range of Taverner's achievement particularly well. The basic division is between the three six-part ones, large-scale

---

*Imperfectly preserved.
†Fragmentary.
§Harrison, *MMB*, pp. 432–3.
††Morley quotes from a Kyrie he ascribes to Taverner, but this work is probably spurious (*Thomas Morley, A Plain and Easy Introduction...*, p. 259).
‡‡Harrison, *MMB*, p. 334.

works based on plainsong cantus firmi, and shorter settings for four or five voices, in general less elaborate and never based in plainsong. But there is considerable variety within each group, particularly the latter, which consists of the *Meane Mass*, the two derived Masses *Mater Christi* and *Small Devotion*, *Playn Song*, and *Western Wynde*.

Gloria tibi Trinitas, the most widely known Mass of the former large-scale group, comes as the first item in the Forrest-Heyther part-books (which originated at Cardinal College during Taverner's stay), and it may have been written expressly for the collection. Its cantus firmus, as a Trinity Sunday antiphon, would be appropriate in this case, since the College was dedicated to the Trinity—although as a matter of fact Tattershall Collegiate Church had the same dedication. The 'Gloria tibi Trinitas' melody is the one which appears in many English instrumental works of the sixteenth and seventeenth centuries called *In nomine*; the name *In nomine* was given because it was the popularity of the 'In nomine Domini' section of Taverner's Mass (in various instrumental and vocal arrangements) which led composers to write pieces on the 'Gloria tibi Trinitas' plainsong.[6] Taverner puts the 'Gloria tibi Trinitas' melody in the mean, which is unusual. But he did not pioneer this placing: William Pasche gave the cantus firmus to the mean in his three works, including the Mass *Christus resurgens* from the Caius choirbook. Browne's *Stabat juxta Christi crucem*, for men only, had also had its cantus firmus in the second highest voice.

Several sections of *Gloria tibi Trinitas* end with impressive pedal-note *d*s in the cantus firmus part, most particularly at 'filius Patris' (Gloria) and 'descendit de coelis' (Credo) (*4.Ex. 9.* above). In the former case the progression begins and ends with D minor chord I; chord IV, sounded three times, has a 'Dorian' B natural instead of the 'Aeolian' B flat preferred almost everywhere else in the work; combined with the concluding tierce de Picardie this brightens the music most wonderfully. A similar use of the raised submediant is found in several later Aeolian works, notably in the final bars of Tallis's *Gaude gloriosa* and *Ave Dei Patris filia*; in both cases the tierce de Picardie is introduced before the final chord I is reached, to give additional brightness. At 'descendit de coelis' in *Gloria tibi Trinitas* the music ends on a chord of G, the subdominant, but the surprise effect is less pronounced than it is in *9.Ex. 5.* above from Browne's *O Maria salvatoris mater*, because the G chord is sounded more than the D chord in the course of the mean's pedal-note. B naturals are present in all G chords; some F sharps appear in the Forrest-Heyther books or in Forrest-Heyther and Christ Church, but others (printed small in our *4.Ex. 9.*) are editorial.

Corona spinea is on the same marvellous level as *Gloria tibi Trinitas*. It has some extremely effective writing for the trebles, notably in the gimel at 'In nomine Domini' and at 'Qui tollis' (second Agnus). The Credo ends with their soaring to top G; in fact the whole spacing of the final chord (G, B, g, d', g', g'') is very exciting, with the lightness and transparency of the octave gap between the top two voices counteracting the heavy effect of the first bass's B. The cantus firmus of *Corona spinea* has not been identified.[7]

O Michael is not at all in the same class as *Gloria tibi Trinitas* and *Corona spinea*. It must surely date from Taverner's 'apprentice' years, for there are some very untidy moments. One finds for example some rather rough dissonances and a large number of clumsy consecutive fifths and octaves. The Agnus has a couple of exceptionally rapid display passages with crotchets and quavers in all parts at once; these too are a little awkwardly handled and the contrast with the other solo sections rather violent—this kind of writing is used more successfully in the last verse of the six-part Magnificat. The retreat from rhythmic complexity in Taverner's large-scale works generally is not to be found in O Michael. Imitation and sequence are employed rather infrequently by the standards of *Gloria tibi Trinitas* and *Corona spinea*. The most striking example of sequence is at '(sepul)-tus' in the Credo: the second countertenor states an ascending four-note figure eight times, one step higher each time, in a very mechanical way which Taverner would normally have avoided, while the treble is singing two statements of a longer pattern. But in spite of its awkwardness O Michael is a promising work because it shows a composer willing to tackle all kinds of musical problems: at 'Dona nobis pacem' the basses divide to give the only example of seven-part writing by any of the composers mentioned in Chapters 8 and 9; strict canon, neglected by English composers after Nesbett and Horwood, is used throughout five long solo sections. The name O Michael is difficult to account for, because the cantus firmus is 'Archangeli Michaelis interventione'. 'Archangeli' is ninth respond at Matins of the important Sarum feast of St Michael in Monte Tumba (16 October), and was also sung at the Procession before High Mass when this feast fell on a Sunday.

Of the smaller-scale Masses the most widely known is *Western Wynde*; in fact if anyone knows or has heard of only one work by Taverner it is probably this. *Western Wynde* owes this favoured position to its unusual tunefulness and exceptionally clear formal construction, for it is basically a set of variations, a very attractive melody (quoted in full in the middle voice of *3.Ex. 9.*) being presented in thirty-six different settings, with no free sections at all. Its success in its own day is obvious, because Tye and Sheppard, younger composers, also wrote *Western Wynde* Masses.

No source for Taverner's theme has been traced; for although there is a tune with words beginning 'Westron wynd' in British Museum Royal Appendix MS. 58, f. 5, this bears few similarities to the melody in the Mass.[8] Taverner's choice of a *secular* tune for cantus firmus is a remarkable novelty for an English Mass. The inclusion of secular material in Continental Masses was common enough, but there is no particular case which seems a clear precedent for Taverner's handling of his melody. We cannot be certain in what circumstances a secular cantus firmus, so boldly presented, would have been accepted—or tolerated—by Taverner's superiors. Paul Doe has put forward some ingenious, but probably not very convincing, theories about this.[9] He considers that it would not have been possible 'in the repressive atmosphere of Wolsey's regime'; yet, so far as the arts are concerned, it is difficult to see that the atmosphere *was* repressive.[10] Doe is inclined to see Taverner, encouraged to return to musical composition at that time in the late 1530s when there seemed 'a real prospect that liturgical music might be steered in a Lutheran direction', putting into practice one of Luther's ideas by adapting a secular tune to sacred use, and turning to German music for inspiration regarding its treatment. He quotes the 'Domine Deus rex coelestis' of Taverner's Mass and Isaak's song *O weiblich Art* for comparison, pointing out that in each work the cantus firmus is presented in fairly short notes similar to those of the surrounding voices. However, the 'similarities of texture . . . with melodic lines that are independent and purposeful, but with very little formal imitation', seem insufficient to prove any connection between Taverner and Isaak. Doe remarks that Taverner's scoring for treble, mean, countertenor and bass was 'not common in England in the preceding decades'; admittedly: yet of the twenty-two four-part works listed in the Eton index seven, including the Passion, had twenty-one or twenty-two note compass, which implies the presence of both treble and bass voices. Doe goes on to say that Taverner's scoring 'accords well with the standard German four-part arrangement'; but Taverner keeps to the characteristically English high treble part, with plenty of f''s and a few g''s, while Isaak does not go above d''. In fact it is doubtful if there is anything in *Western Wynde* that Taverner could not have written at the time he composed *Gloria tibi Trinitas*, which at the latest was during his Oxford period; moreover we do not find those characteristics which, if not decisive, would be the most helpful in supporting a later date for *Western Wynde*: verbal repetition, or some other attempt to restrict melisma, and more imitation.

Western Wynde is a piece which it would be difficult to praise too highly. It shows astonishing resourcefulness of method and detail, each of the thirty-six variations sounding absolutely fresh and original. The principal means of obtaining variety are by sharing the melody between the treble (twenty-one statements, starting on *g′*), the counter-tenor (ten on *g*) and the bass (five on G); by using different vocal groupings; and by changing from the basic duple time to ₵ for the last sections of the Gloria, Credo, first Agnus and third Agnus. Each movement contains nine statements of the tune, one of which is always abbreviated by the omission of the third phrase. The Gloria and Credo both have four statements in each major section, one in the ₵₃ coda; the Sanctus has six in the first major section and three in the second, while this pattern is reversed in the Agnus. The melody thus appears seventeen times in the four first major sections, seventeen in the second sections, with the other two statements belonging to codas. The style of the work ranges from a fairly simple syllabic manner at the beginning to florid melisma in parts of the Sanctus and Agnus. In parts of the Agnus triplet movement, which Taverner used only rarely

(12.Ex. 9.)   *TCM*, i.25.

outside *Western Wynde*, is prominent; *12.Ex. 9.* shows one of the loveliest passages of the whole Mass.

The shorter Masses, unlike the six-part ones, appear to have no names which suggest connections with particular feasts; yet the curiously titled *Small Devotion* is almost certainly an exception. Its name has been explained as a corruption of 'S Will Devotio', which is itself an abbreviation of 'Sancti Willelmis Devotio'.[11] This is largely because of the Mass's derivation from the antiphon *Christe Jesu pastor bone* which is thought to have been originally in honour of St William of York. The statutes of Cardinal College ordained that an antiphon of St William, one of Wolsey's predecessors as Archbishop of York, should be sung every evening.[12] It is extremely probable that the words were those of an antiphon beginning 'O Willelme pastor bone',[13] and that the very similar text addressed to Christ now found in Taverner's piece was substituted for it when the College was re-founded by Henry VIII in 1532 after Wolsey's fall. *Christe Jesu* ends with a prayer for Henry, who is described as 'founder' ('Fundatorem specialem / Serva regem nunc Henricum'); in the first place the prayer probably referred to the College's original founder, and rhymed: 'Fundatorem specialem / Serva Thomam Cardinalem'.[14]

   Christe Jesu and *Small Devotion* can be dated 1526–30 on the grounds of the Cardinal College–St William connection. In fact the tercentenary of St William's canonisation, on 21 March, 1526–7, three or four months after Taverner's arrival at Oxford, is a possible occasion for the first performance of the Mass.

   The derived Mass *Mater Christi* is in many ways, including its almost identical length, the twin of *Small Devotion*. In particular the textural schemes of the Gloria and Credo of both Masses are very similar, notably in the placing of antiphonal passages.

Votive Antiphons

   Taverner's antiphons like his Masses may be divided into elaborate works of festal proportions and shorter simpler pieces. The former group comprises *Ave Dei Patris filia*, *Gaude plurimum* and *O splendor gloriae*.

   Ave Dei Patris filia is the most old-fashioned of these: it uses imitation least and, unusually for a sixteenth-century antiphon, incorporates a cantus firmus. The cantus firmus consists of verses 1, 2, 5, 14 and 29 of the Te Deum melody, plus the neuma of the fourth mode; the choice is appropriate because the first section of the Te Deum is a kind of hymn to the Trinity, while the antiphon text is Trinitarian in structure. *Gaude plurimum* was very popular throughout the sixteenth century, various parts of it turning up in a multitude of minor sources. Although it is more polished than *Ave Dei Patris filia*, one wonders why it was ever quite such a favourite.

   O splendor gloriae is a Jesus-antiphon[15] whose text is an account of our Lord's role in creation, his conception and birth, Passion, resurrection, ascension and his gift of the Holy Spirit. It is probably the finest of the long antiphons, and, judging from its style, one of Taverner's latest works. *O splendor gloriae* is much more compact than *Gaude plurimum*, extended melisma occurring only in the Amen; so that although the two works have texts of almost identical length, the former is the shorter by some sixty bars. Imitation is present most of the time, in full as well as solo sections, and tends to occupy a rather more powerful position in the texture than usually in Taverner—and a very much more powerful one in the penultimate section 'te prece precamur' which we mentioned earlier in this Chapter. John Baldwin, possibly because he was unable to believe that Taverner wrote a passage like 'te prece precamur', attributes *O splendor gloriae* to Taverner *and Tye* in his Christ Church partbooks. In British Museum, Royal Music Library MS. R.M. 24 d. 2, his musical commonplace book, he ascribed the opening trio to Taverner and the first part of the second major section to Tye. We know that the commonplace book has several mis-attributions, and in fact it is doubtful if Tye was involved in the composition of *O splendor gloriae*: the two other sources of the work mention only Taverner, and the piece does seem a genuine unity, even allowing for the exceptional character of the 'te prece' section.

Of the shorter antiphons only *Mater Christi* survives complete. *Christe Jesu* has lost its tenor, while four other works lack the treble as well.

Ave Maria and *Sancte Deus* were obviously written at Cardinal College, for settings of both were prescribed by Wolsey's statutes for use at an evening devotion. The former was to be sung kneeling after a polyphonic 'Salve regina' had been performed, the versicle 'Ave Maria' and a prayer said; it was to be interrupted twice by the ringing of a bell, for which Taverner provided suitable breaks in his setting. The music is short, fairly simple, and apparently without solo contrast. *Sancte Deus*, rather similar in style, is a Jesus-antiphon which was sung after *Ave Maria*, in front of the Crucifix in the nave.

The words of *Sub tuum praesidium* do not appear in the Sarum liturgy, but can be found in the modern *Liber Usualis*.[16] The melody given there can almost be made to fit between the two lowest surviving parts as a tenor cantus firmus, but it was clearly a slightly different version, the same as Obrecht used in his Mass *Sub tuum praesidium*, which Taverner employed, with the first part (to 'deprecationes') all in breves, the remainder in semibreves.[17] There appears to be no other link between Taverner's antiphon and Obrecht's Mass.

Alternatim Works

The *alternatim* works comprise Magnificats, responds, a prose and a Te Deum for the Office, and a few short pieces for the Lady Mass and for the Proper of other votive Masses. Important features of Taverner's contribution to music for the Office are the appearance of the first choral responds and the clearer statement of proper melodies than generally in the past.

In two of his Magnificats, those for four and six voices, Taverner abandoned the traditional elaborated faburden tenors. In the six-part setting the full-choir sections have the first tone, still with a little elaboration in places; in the four-part setting Taverner moves further away from traditional faburden practice by normally presenting tone 6 without decoration. The four-part Magnificat is the more modern in style, with imitation playing an important part; in full sections the two countertenors and the bass often enter in imitation ahead of the tenor, usually with different material from it, but at 'salutari meo' they do anticipate almost in chorale prelude fashion.

The five-part Magnificat survives minus its tenor, but was quite clearly faburden-based. The treble at 'et sanctum nomen' begins with part of the faburden of tone 2, first ending. A variant of this is used in imitation at 'ejus in saecula'. The entries, each three bars long, are placed end to end, and together with an earlier set of similar entries (possibly also derived from the faburden) condition an entire section of some thirty bars. Simultaneous use of briefer imitative and sequential patterning helps bring this somewhat ponderous passage to life.

Taverner's responds are the first to survive after those in the Pepys manuscript. Three, *Audivi vocem*, *Gloria in excelsis* and *In pace*, are solo responds, the others choral settings of *Dum transisset sabbatum*, the earliest of that type. All employ an equal-note cantus firmus. The solo ones have their cantus firmi in rather long notes—*Audivi vocem* in breves, *Gloria in excelsis* in dotted breves, *In pace* in longs—with often very florid lines against them, especially in the first and second (*13.Ex. 9.*), somewhat in the general manner of Norman's *Miserere* in Ritson (*3(c).Ex. 7.*). Taverner, following the rubrics closely, sets *Audivi vocem* and *Gloria in excelsis* for boys' voices only.

In the *Dum transisset* settings the cantus firmi move in the semibreves which became normal for choral responds. This encourages the 'compactness' of style with a fairly regular rate of harmonic change on the semibreve or minim which we also find in Taverner's shorter Masses and antiphons. It avoids excessive length, for the plainsong to

(13.Ex. 9.)   *TCM, iii.47 : Gloria in excelsis*

be set is longer than in the solo responds, and some polyphonic sections have to be repeated. Points of imitation appear quite frequently in the lovely first *Dum transisset*, but for Taverner, unlike Tallis and Sheppard, its working is not the primary concern. This is true of the second *Dum transisset* as well, but imitation is more important here, with several slightly more weighty points being used.

Dum transisset II does not have in either of its sources a break after 'aromata' to allow the repetition from 'ut venientes' to be made, for the mean has a phrase which bridges the two sections. Nor is there a really clear break at 'Jesum' before the Alleluia. The manuscripts must be corrupt, unless Taverner envisaged some abnormal mode of performance. The possibility that *Dum transisset* II originated as an instrumental piece cannot be ruled out: one of the sources, textless, is British Museum Additional MS. 31390, a book which contains much instrumental music; moreover Tye wrote four *Dum transisset* settings which appear to be instrumental, although these *do* have clear breaks after 'aromata' and 'Jesum'. Taverner's own *Quemadmodum* is more probably instrumental: it is completely textless in all three sources. It has been suggested that this work originally had words from Psalm 42 ('*Quemadmodum* desiderat cervus');[18] but it is unclear how these could be fitted in, and why they should have been omitted from all sources.

In *Sospitati dedit aegros*, a setting of the St Nicholas Prose which we encountered in Pepys, Taverner treats plainsong with unaccustomed freedom. Possibly this was because prose melodies did not have the same 'authority' as the main body of chant to which they were later additions. In verses 1, 2 and 3 some free material is included; verse 5 refers only briefly to the plainsong; while 7 and 8 disregard it altogether. In part of verse 2 and the whole of verse 4 the melody is treated canonically. *Sospitati dedit aegros* would have been inserted into the respond 'Ex ejus tumba'. It came part-way through the first repeat of the response after 'et debilis quisque' and was followed by the last words of the response 'sospes regreditur'. These two words, the only ones of the respond which Taverner set, have his normal equal-note cantus firmus, perhaps *because* they belong to the respond and not to the prose.

The Te Deum differs very greatly from Taverner's other pieces with equal-note cantus firmus[19] in its almost continuous use of imitation, and from the rest of his work in employing the new types of dissonance described in Chapter 10. On the other hand it is very similar in feeling to equal-note works of the Tallis-Sheppard generation, and one is tempted to wonder if it is in fact by either of these masters: as we saw earlier, Baldwin, the copyist of its single source, is known to have made several other misattributions.

HUGH ASTON

Hugh Aston, with seven large-scale works to his credit, is the most important of the less famous composers represented in the Forrest-Heyther and Peterhouse partbooks. He graduated Bachelor of Music at Oxford in 1510.[20] It was fitting therefore that the choirmaster's post at Cardinal College, Oxford which Taverner was persuaded to take was first offered to him. Aston was master of the choristers at St Mary Newarke College, Leicester in 1525, and remained there until the

Table 9: Hugh Aston

Masses

à6: Videte manus meas
à5: Te Deum

Votive Antiphons

à5: Ave Maria ancilla Trinitatis,† Ave Maria divae matris Annae,* Gaude virgo mater
     Christi* (survives also as Gaude mater matris Christi), O Baptista vates Christi,† Te
     matrem Dei laudamus† (survives also as Te Deum laudamus)

Aston's work is published in *TCM*, x.

*Imperfectly preserved.
†Fragmentary.

College was dissolved in 1548. In 1549 he was still receiving an annuity granted in 1544.[21]

Much of Aston's music is very vigorous and forceful, sometimes rather in the manner of Taverner, but with a fondness for tiny florid touches which sometimes produce rather rough unessential dissonances. Some of the imitative writing for full choir in the Mass *Videte manus meas* (cantus firmus an antiphon from Vespers of Easter Tuesday) is similar in its energetic quality to parts of Taverner's *Gloria tibi Trinitas*,

(14.Ex. 9.)

especially at 'rex coelestis' (*14.Ex. 9.*—compare *1.Ex. 9.*) or 'descendit de coelis'; but in general there is a far more mechanical handling of less interesting shapes.

The best of Aston is probably to be found in the antiphons *Gaude*

(15.Ex. 9.) TCM, x.86,88 : *Gaude virgo mater Christi.*

virgo mater Christi and *Ave Maria divae matris Annae*. The melodic style here occasionally points ahead quite strikingly to that of composers discussed in Chapter 11 in the new boldness of outline of some important melodic phrases; in particular one notes in several places a new kind of melodic expansion in which an important interval is enlarged when imitated to help create a sense of growth and climax. *15.Ex. 9.* shows two main instances, the prominent outline of the minor seventh at 'x' being not at all typical of the imitative ideas in earlier music. The Amens of both antiphons are based on ostinato figures in the bass which involve melodic expansion.[22] There is a limited use of verbal repetition in both works, notably several times in the concluding section of *Gaude virgo*, apparently to emphasise important words (notably 'O Maria virgo nobilissima' and 'O virgo sanctissima') rather than to curb extended melisma which elsewhere is very considerable.

Gaude virgo mater Christi follows the text set by Sturton, Horwood and Wylkynson, except that a concluding prayer is added; *Ave Maria ancilla Trinitatis*, which Sturton also set, is extended in a similar way. *Gaude virgo* survives in another version *Gaude mater matris Christi* addressed to St Anne, the Virgin's mother, in Bodleian Library MSS. Mus. Sch. e. 1–5, the latest of the four sources for the music. In both versions the prayer ends with a petition that the singers may be united in heaven 'in thy College', which suggests that the work was written for an earthly College dedicated to the Saint whose help was sought. The Marian version was probably used at St Mary Newarke, Leicester. The other may indicate that Aston was somehow connected with a College dedicated to St Anne—especially as another (Marian) antiphon mentions her in its opening line: 'Ave Maria divae matris Annae'. *O Baptista vates Christi* seems to be linked with some foundation dedicated to St John the Baptist: 'O Baptista . . . defende chorum istum / Cujus caput es post Christum / Et patronus optimus'.

The antiphon beginning *Te matrem Dei laudamus* in two manuscripts written during Aston's lifetime survives in the Bodleian MSS. Mus. Sch. e. 1–5 as *Te Deum laudamus*. The words of this latter are not those of the normal Te Deum from Matins of which *Te Matrem Dei laudamus* is a Marian adaptation, but were quite clearly derived (possibly for use as an antiphon of the Trinity at a time when Marian devotion was on the wane) from the 'Te matrem Dei' text: for example 'Te gloriosus apostolorum chorus omnipotentem Deum collaudat' is closely based on the Marian 'Te gloriosus apostolorum chorus creatoris matrem collaudat' not on the liturgical words 'Te gloriosus apostolorum chorus'.

The antiphon *Te matrem Dei laudamus* is linked with the Mass *Te*

Deum, for both use parts of the Te Deum plainsong as cantus firmus, and have a common opening phrase. Just possibly they were the Mass and antiphon which Aston was required to compose for his graduation ceremony at Oxford.[23] The Mass is built mainly on repetitions in long notes of the second verse of the Te Deum, which come in both full and solo sections. Although Aston varies his treatment of it, by letting voices other than the tenor occasionally have it, and by varying the note it starts on, his melody is unpromising material for such extended use. There is some dullness harmonically, especially where the melody appears in the bass, and some rather uninspired patterning and busy florid activity, notably in the Benedictus. In the antiphon the plain-song is largely restricted to the full textures, verse 2 again being favoured (in the first or second countertenor on g or c').

THE FORREST–HEYTHER PARTBOOKS: LESSER COMPOSERS

The first layer of the Forrest-Heyther partbooks (from the late 1520s) is probably the earliest source for Taverner and Aston. In addition to one Mass by each of these composers, it contains four Masses by Fayrfax and one each by Thomas Ashewell, John Marbeck, John Norman and William Rasor. The second (mid-sixteenth century) layer has a second Mass by Ashewell among further works by Taverner and Aston and music by younger composers, Sheppard, Tye (see Chapter 11) and Richard Alwood (see the final section of the present Chapter).

Thomas Ashewell was master of the choristers at Lincoln in 1508 and *cantor* at Durham in 1513.[24] His first Mass *Jesu Christe* is based on the short respond from Prime in Easter week. The second, again in six parts and a very impressive work, is *Ave Maria*, on an antiphon at Commemorations of the Virgin in Advent. The short plainsong appears in many solo sections as well as full ones, parts of it sometimes being used in imitation. It is worked in canon at 'Qui sedes', the bass moving a fifth below the tenor, first at three bars' distance, then closing the gap to two bars and finally to one and a half.

The Mass by Avery Burton (Gentleman of the Chapel Royal, 1494–1526)[25] is called *Ut re mi fa sol la* because its cantus firmus is simply a hexachord running from f to d' and down again. Burton presents the melody in equal notes, except where sections with many syllables require sub-division. In the first two movements the time-unit becomes progressively shorter in quasi-isorhythmic fashion. 'Abstract' cantus firmi such as Burton's hexachord theme were by no means rare in the early sixteenth century: they are found for instance in puzzle canons by Fayrfax and John Lloyd in British Museum Additional MS. 31922, and in Continental music including Josquin's Mass *La sol fa re mi*.

John Marbeck's Mass *Per arma justitiae* (on the antiphon at Terce in the first week of Lent) and his antiphons *Ave Dei Patris filia* and *Domine Jesu Christe* are competent and craftsmanlike, but of little positive interest. In the Preface to his Biblical Concordance, written in 1550 some years after his conversion to Calvinism, Marbeck clearly repudiated works such as these, saying that 'in the study of music and playing on organs ... I consumed vainly the greatest part of my life';[26] his *Book of Common Prayer Noted* of the same year, with its simple Communion setting which has made Marbeck's name so very widely known, was not so much composition as the arrangement of plainsong melodies to the words of the new English liturgy.

THE PETERHOUSE PARTBOOKS: LESSER COMPOSERS

Three lesser composers from Forrest-Heyther, Marbeck, John Norman and William Rasor, are represented by single works in Peterhouse. Each of the following also has a single work there: William Alen, Thomas Appleby, Richard Bramston, Catcott, Arthur Chamberlayne, John Dark, Edwards, Walter Erley, Robert Jones, Thomas Knyght, Edward Martyn, John Northbrooke, Hugh Sturmys and William Whytbrook. Richard Hunt, William Pasche and Richard Pygot have two works each, John Mason four.

There are also two Continental pieces which stand very much on their own in the collection—one wonders how the scribe came across them, and what he thought of them. One is a Mass modelled on an early sixteenth-century motet *Surrexit pastor bonus* by Andreas de Silva. It is ascribed to 'Lupus Italus', but it is not certain which of several composers this is. The motet *Aspice Domine*, although not so ascribed, is by Jaquet de Mantua.[27]

The works by Mason[28] include a setting of *O rex gloriose*, an antiphon with three verses used at Nunc dimittis in the last part of Lent and on the feast of the Holy Name of Jesus. Mason provides for a full liturgical performance, with repeats of various parts of the antiphon after each verse, and it is clear that he incorporated the proper plainsong as an equal-note cantus firmus, although the tenor is now lost; but it is possible that the work was sung in a votive context as well, because there are so many votive antiphons in Peterhouse but only one other ritual piece, an anonymous *Vidi aquam egredientem*; moreover *O rex gloriose* is included in the prayers and devotions in several early sixteenth-century Primers.[29]

William Pasche has an antiphon and a Magnificat to his name; both of them, like the Mass *Christus resurgens*, have the cantus firmus in the mean. The antiphon *Sancta Maria mater Dei ora pro nobis*, which begins as a kind of Marian litany, has its full sections based on repetitions of the phrase *f′ g′ a′ b′ flat a′*; all notes are breves, except where the presence of many syllables demands sub-division. The five-note motif may possibly have been attached in some prior context to the five-syllable phrase 'Sancta Maria' or to 'ora pro nobis'; but it is probably just an 'abstract' figure, because two other composers use it in works with quite different texts. In William Alen's *Gaude virgo mater Christi* for men's voices it comes a fourth lower again in the second highest part. Richard Alwood, who on stylistic grounds one assumes to be of the Tallis–Sheppard generation, bases his six-part Mass *Praise Him Praiseworthy* (Forrest-Heyther) on it. It is generally in the mean, but there is canonic treatment by the tenor and the mean at 'Et in unum Dominum' and 'pacem'. Unlike Pasche and Alen, Alwood varies the rhythm of the figure: it is given in a mixture of breves and semibreves at the ends of the first three movements; at 'Dona nobis pacem' each of the five notes is five minims long, or to be precise is a breve followed by a minim (*f′* breve, minim; *g′* breve, minim; etc.): the more complex form of notation involving coloration which enabled John Browne to write a note of five minims' length as a *single* symbol (see Chapter 4, section on Cantus firmus treatment) was avoided by the mid sixteenth-century scribe who copied Alwood's Mass into the second layer of Forrest-Heyther, or perhaps was not even known to him or understood by his singers.

Latin Church Music c. 1530–1575

The years 1530 to 1575 take us from Taverner's supposed abandonment of composition to the publication of the *Cantiones* which marks the end of Tallis's career and the beginning of Byrd's. They encompass all the principal religious events of mid sixteenth-century England.

LATIN CHURCH MUSIC AND THE REFORMATION

In the period under discussion we shall see a change from the dominance of Latin church music within a Latin liturgy to its occupying a very limited position under Edward VI and Elizabeth when the liturgy was English. In investigating its possible uses under Elizabeth we shall conclude that, since it was no longer closely tied to the liturgy, its perpetuation was due in some part to new aesthetic and antiquarian motives. Such motives have nothing to do with medieval thinking, but are certainly in accord with the spirit of Renaissance humanism.

The upheavals of the Reformation led, even before the Latin services were first discontinued in 1549, to changes in the kinds of church music produced, and to some changes in attitude towards it.

The decline of the votive antiphon would indeed have been hard to resist in the face of reforming legislation such as the Ten Articles of 1536, and the First and Second Royal Injunctions of 1536 and 1538.[1] None of these Acts prohibits votive antiphons—or even directly mentions them—but there is a new attitude to Saints and images (before which antiphons were often sung), an awareness of the dangers of 'superstition'.

The Festal Mass declined in importance after Taverner. The length and elaboration of such works as Taverner's *Gloria tibi Trinitas* or Fayrfax's *Tecum principium* would probably not have been encouraged in the new atmosphere of the 1530s.

Where then did composers divert the energies formerly channelled into the votive antiphon and festal Mass? Tallis and Sheppard in particular wrote many Office responds, mostly of the new choral type pioneered by Taverner, and *alternatim* hymns. Although we cannot date any one of these pieces precisely, many of them are probably pre-1549; there is a choral respond *Sint lumbi vestri praecincti* in Christ Church ascribed to John Redford, a composer chiefly famous for his organ music who died in 1547. Moreover since almost all hymns and responds clearly pre-date the final outlawing of the Sarum liturgy in 1559—certain exceptions and possible exceptions are detailed below—it would be very unwise to assign them all to the brief Marian Reaction of 1553–8. One or two non-liturgical, non-Scriptural motets are, or may well be, pre-1549: Tye's *Domine Deus coelestis* is mentioned a little later in this section, Wood's *Exsurge Domine* at the end of it. Settings of psalms, whose texts would naturally have been unexceptionable to Protestant opinion, and which like votive antiphons were obviously not intended for liturgical use because they are not *alternatim* and have no doxology, were probably first produced before 1549: there are several by Tye, most of whose Latin music is likely to have been written by that time. Psalms had been frequently set on the Continent since Josquin's time.

There are some interesting insights into attitudes towards church music in the book of *Ceremonies to be used in the church of England*. This unpublished work dates from the early 1540s, and was drawn up by a committee of bishops not as 'an attempt to formulate a system of ceremonies to suit the times, but as an explanation of those existing ceremonies which were to be observed "for a decent order" '.[2] The passage about church music comes in a section concerning the Office:

> The sober, discreet and devout singing, music and playing with organs used in the church, for the service of God are ordained to move and stir the people to the sweetness of God's word the which is there sung and not understanded, and by that sweet harmony both to excite them to prayers and devotion and also to put them in remembrance, of the heavenly triumphant church, where is everlasting joy with continual laud and praise to God.[3]

Much of this would have been familiar enough in the fifteenth century. But the phrase 'and not understood' shows an awareness of the objections since Erasmus's Cambridge days to the unintelligibility of Latin worship. The most fascinating point of all is that this phrase was deleted, probably very soon after it was written, as though the writer did not wish to become too deeply involved in a delicate question. The second word of the passage, 'sober', is also interesting, for it seems to have distinct reformatory undertones. At about the time the book of *Ceremonies* was produced Archbishop Cranmer, in a letter to Henry VIII, expressed a desire for musical 'sobriety': processional music should be 'not . . . full of notes, but, as near as may be, for every syllable a note'—although as le Huray points out, Cranmer was not actually referring to part-music.[4]

Edward VI's reign saw many Protestant hopes realised, including the introduction of an English liturgy in 1549. The English church music dating from this reign is marked by a deliberately austere style in which the words are normally quite clearly audible. Even before the Prayer Book was introduced, the Lincoln Cathedral Injunctions demanded the singing of anthems in English with 'a plain and distinct note, for every syllable one'.[5] For church music, to those Protestants who did not distrust it altogether, was a form of preaching and teaching instead of an expression of the glory of the church, a form of ceremonial, or a means of stirring people to an uncomprehending kind of devotion.

How far did these attitudes influence the composer of Latin church music? On the one hand any musician such as Tallis who composed for the English liturgy under Edward VI could hardly fail to be affected by the new disciplines imposed on him when he turned again to Latin composition. On the other we have already seen processes of musical simplification in Chapters 8 and 9 which were quite independent of reformatory influences.

In the first two years of Edward's reign, before the introduction of the Prayer Book, there would have been no legal impediment to the composition of Latin church music, but it can scarcely have been encouraged, while we know that experimental English forms of service had already been in use.[6] Nevertheless, it is almost certain that Tye's prayer for a king *Domine Deus coelestis* belongs to these years, and likely that his *Quaesumus omnipotens* does as well (see further Chapter 11). In a Scottish source, Thomas Wode's partbooks (1562–c. 1590) there is a setting of *Deus misereatur* (Psalm 67) by Robert Johnson, a priest who, the scribe tells us, fled to England 'long before Reformation . . . for accusation of heresy', which was 'set in England ten or twelve years before Reformation'.[7] 'Reformation' here presumably refers to the Scottish Reformation of 1560, not the English one to which no such precise date can be given. 'Ten or twelve years' before 1560, if interpreted strictly, gives a date within Edward's reign of 1548–50.

The 1549 Act of Uniformity made the Prayer Book the only authorised form of worship, but Mattins and Evensong could be said privately in Latin, or even Greek or Hebrew if one understood these languages. Latin, Greek or Hebrew could also be used publicly in College chapels at Oxford and Cambridge for Mattins, Evensong and all other services except the Communion 'for the further encouraging of learning in the[se] tongues'.[8] Thus even now the performance and composition of Latin music remained at least theoretically possible. The 1552 Act, which introduced a new, more Protestant Prayer Book, did not alter the position.

A few months after her accession in July 1553, Mary Tudor repealed both Edward's Acts of Uniformity and various other laws passed in his reign to restore liturgical usage to that of Henry VIII's last year. Latin church music could once again be widely used and composed; even a few votive antiphons date from this period. The Second Statute of Repeal (1554) abolished all post-1529 anti-papal legislation.

Just five years later the Elizabethan Settlement was passed: the papal supremacy was abandoned, the new Queen becoming 'Supreme Governor' of the Church of England, and the 1552 Prayer Book was restored with a few alterations to allow greater latitude in eucharistic belief.[9] Latin church music did continue to be written, although in a fairly small way. Points in its favour were the authorisation of a Latin Prayer Book, the unique position of the Chapel Royal, and probably its devotional value to Roman Catholics; but above all it was more rewarding from a purely musical angle than the rather limited kinds of composition generally written for the English service.

The Latin translation of the Prayer Book by Walter Haddon (*Liber precum publicarum*) appeared in 1560 with the Queen's permission for it to be used in the Oxford and Cambridge Colleges and at Winchester and Eton Colleges.[10] But while it probably saw little use in the Universities or schools—some Cambridge dons roundly condemned it as 'the Pope's dregs'[11]—it would undoubtedly have enjoyed considerable use in the Queen's own Chapel in view of her very conservative outlook.

The beginning and end of Morning and Evening Prayer provide the most obvious scope for Latin church music within the framework of Haddon's Prayer Book translation. A Royal Injunction of 1559 had established that 'for the comforting of such that delight in music . . . an Hymn, or suchlike song to the praise of Almighty God' might be sung at such times 'in the best sort of melody and music that may conveniently be devised, having respect that the sentence of the Hymn may be understood and perceived'.[12] It is impossible to say what kinds of Latin music might have been sung at Morning and Evening Prayer in the Chapel Royal, but one imagines that psalm-motets would have met with approval. Tallis's five-part Magnificat and Nunc dimittis may well have belonged to the Latin Evening Prayer: the much greater proximity in performance which they would have enjoyed there than in the Sarum order (for which in any case Nunc dimittis was not normally set) gives point to their sharing of material; for both works begin alike, and the music of 'salutari meo' (Magnificat) reappears, with its triumphant climax appropriately toned down, at 'salutare tuum' in the quieter first verse of the Nunc dimittis. Elizabeth, unlike Edward VI, permitted the Communion to be celebrated in Latin, and it is possible that Tallis's O sacrum convivium and O salutaris hostia were sung as motets at this service.[13]

The Chapel Royal undoubtedly had a most important place in the cultivation of church music, English and Latin, in Elizabeth's reign. All the leading church composers we shall discuss, except Whyte, belonged to it. There was a first-class choir, much better provided for than any other. And there was freedom from the harassments of those influential Puritans who tried hard during the 1562 session of Convocation to get rid of all organ-playing and non-congregational singing in church.[14]

Latin polyphony could in theory have been used at the Roman Catholic services which took place secretly after 1559; but such music normally requires a sizeable number of highly trained singers and its performance cannot often have been possible and can never have been easy. Catholics could more readily have sung Latin music outside a liturgical context as a form of private devotion or recreation.

But many singers, composers and manuscript copyists, non-Roman Catholics included, must surely have wanted for aesthetic reasons to avoid the death of the long and glorious tradition of Latin polyphony. The desire to preserve is clear from inclusion of pre-1559 music in Elizabethan manuscripts. The desire to compose new Latin music may have come at least in part from the restricted opportunities in English music. Again Latin church music was obviously more 'international'; under Elizabeth English composers were more responsive to external influences than at any time in our period, and we know that the printed Cantiones of 1575 were, according to the prefatory matter, intended partly to demonstrate English musical skill to the world.[15] Although it is not clear how far if at all the publication was a successful ambassador of English music abroad, it is clear that it was not a success commercially at home[16]—which indicates that, whatever its uses, Latin polyphony did not enjoy a very wide demand or a very assured position in 1575.

The Latin music which we suppose to date from after 1559 falls into two principal categories: psalm-motets, and settings of texts taken from liturgical sources. Choice of texts was therefore basically un-adventurous; composers seemed largely unaware of, or cautious in exploring, the new freedom now that they were working inde-pendently of the liturgical requirements which had earlier exercised most of their powers. Yet the considerable interest in rather doleful texts (Lamentations, texts about death and penitence) was one im-portant step, because these had a definite and sometimes quite strong emotional character—even though this was not often matched by a strongly expressive musical setting. Robert Parsons's three responds from the Office of the Dead (*Credo quod redemptor meus vivit, Peccantem me quotidie, Libera me Domine*) all employ the first person singular—the votive antiphon had hardly ever done this—but it is important to remember that Parsons's texts are liturgical in origin and do not contain a truly individual or personal note. Continental composers frequently had recourse to great tragic stories from the Bible such as those of Job or David lamenting for Jonathan or Absalom. The closest we come to this in England—and it is not very close at all—is in Parsons's *Magnus es Domine*, a setting of Tobit's prayer of thanksgiving from Chapter 13 of the Apocryphal Book of Tobit. Only the first section survives, but the work is clearly not influenced by any of the Continental Biblical settings, being a characteristically English work with reduced-full contrasts and an opening in triple time: we cannot even be sure that it does not predate Elizabeth's accession.

A psalm-motet normally has as text an entire short psalm or a section from Psalm 119. Composers of Tallis's generation and even of Whyte's appear to be unacquainted with the selective or critical approach used on the Continent and later in England especially by Byrd by which a text is assembled from verses belonging to several psalms or verses from a single psalm are chosen with some deliberate suggestive intent.[17] Wil-liam Mundy, it is true, extracts verses 1–9, 26–27 and 40–41 from the very long Psalm 37 ('Noli aemulari') and successfully captures its essence; but he is probably concerned chiefly with getting a text of manageable length. It is probably the desire for an easily manageable text that prompts him to base his *Adolescentulus sum ego* on only half a section from Psalm 119 and Parsons to set only the first four verses of Psalm 15 in his *Domine quis habitabit*. When Mundy omits verses 13 to 15 from Psalm 45 ('Eructavit cor meum') the only result is a loss of con-tinuity and grammatical sense.

Almost all psalm-motets follow the Vulgate wording used in the

Sarum services and in connection with the 1560 Latin Prayer Book. Mundy's *Miserere mei Deus* in places deviates from the Vulgate to follow a translation by the Hebrew scholar Vetablus (Vatable) of Paris; Stephanus (Estienne) printed this in 1556 alongside the Vulgate version, and Mundy may have been looking at a copy of this as he wrote his *Miserere*.[18] No motet uses Sebastian Münster's translation which was annexed to the Latin Prayer Books printed in 1571–2 by Wolf and 1574 by Vautrollier. This has been taken to imply that existing psalm-motets pre-date the early 1570s; this dating is strengthened by the fact that the lives and/or composing careers of Tallis, Tye, Whyte and Parsons all came to an end at about this time.

Despite the lack of imagination in the choice of psalm texts, it is perhaps not entirely fanciful to see one or two texts of liturgical origin as having been chosen with the intention of expressing some subversive 'hidden' meaning. Tallis's *In jejunio et fletu* may reflect the regrets and misgivings which Roman Catholics must have felt in Elizabeth's days: 'The priests prayed with fasting and tears, saying: Spare thy people, O Lord, and give not thine heritage to reproach . . .'. The texts of Tallis's Lamentations may possibly refer cryptically to the 'ruin' of the English church, the closing appeals to Jerusalem to turn to God stemming from a desire for the nation's return to papal allegiance.[19] But we cannot be sure—particularly since Whyte, who wrote two sets of Lamentations, is not known to have had any Roman Catholic associations or sympathies.

Works which use liturgical texts often differ in some important aspect of text-treatment or performance practice from those discussed in earlier Chapters: in fact these differences must be taken as the signs of non-liturgical performance and thus of an Elizabethan date. A few works have Roman not Sarum texts: Tallis's responds *Derelinquat impius* and *In jejunio* and Byrd's *Emendemus in melius* are of this type. A normal *alternatim* scheme may be changed, as in Parsons's *Peccantem me quotidie* and *Libera me Domine* where the soloist's beginning is set polyphonically as well as the main part of the response, or in Byrd's *Christe qui lux es* where the odd-numbered verses, except for the first, are set as well as the even. *Alternatim* practice may be discarded altogether along with the plainsong cantus firmus normal for liturgical responds and hymns and found in the three works just mentioned; this happens in some of Tallis's works and in Parsons's *Credo quod redemptor*. Tallis sets the responds *Derelinquat impius*, *In manus tuas*, *Spem in alium* and *In jejunio* complete, that is, including the verse and the opening words of the response; he does not allow for a re-statement of the closing words of the response, except in *In jejunio* where the re-statement of 'Parce populo tuo' is necessary to complete the sense of the verse, although even here the repeat is to a fresh setting contrary to the practice of the normal liturgical respond.

Occasionally in Elizabethan sources there are small 'irregularities' which may have originated simply as modernisations of earlier material instead of implying that the work *never* enjoyed liturgical performance. Thus in the *Cantiones* Tallis's respond *Honor virtus et potestas* has the repeat of the response printed in full and very slightly dovetailed into the first statement of the response, so that the verse cannot be interpolated; presumably Tallis was adapting an older work for a new, non-liturgical mode of singing—or was *Honor virtus* after all an Elizabethan work written in this way in the first place?

The Lamentations by Tallis and Osbert Parsley of Norwich (1511–85)[20] occasionally depart from the standard liturgical texts. In Parsley's case the Hebrew letters preceding the three verses are not those assigned to them in the Breviary (Aleph, Beth and Gimel), but those which fit their positions as thirteenth, fourteenth and fifteenth verses in the second Chapter of the Book of Lamentations, Mem, Nun and Samech. Yet despite this anti-liturgical feature Parsley incorporates the simple liturgical reading-tone of the Lamentations throughout in the highest voice; the prominence of the reciting-note *a'*, together with the almost total restriction of the top part to the interval of a fourth *f'* to *b' flat*, makes the setting rather monotonous and dull.

Works other than psalm-motets, hymn- and respond-motets and Lamentations include several settings of non-liturgical prayers, notably Tallis's *Absterge Domine* and *Suscipe quaeso*. Such texts were obviously first set before Elizabeth's reign: we have already noticed Tye's *Domine Deus coelestis* and *Quaesumus omnipotens*. In the Christ Church partbooks there is an *Exsurge Domine et dissipentur inimici* by John Wood, who was master of the children at Christ Church, Canterbury in about 1530.[21] It is a prayer for the concord of Christ's church (a pun intended?) based on Psalm 68 which is found in the 1546 Latin translation of Henry VIII's 1545 Primer and dates back to the *Precationes christianiae* of 1536.[22] Another piece which is indebted (very slightly) to Psalm 68 is a short three-part motet by Mundy in the Gyffard books, *Exsurge Christe defende nos*, in which the writer mentions the confounding of those who hate Christ, the ending of schism, and the revival of apostolic truth. These words might well have been written at a time when the church in England was 'schismatic' and yet there was prospect (officially expressible) of a return to full Roman allegiance—

possibly the very earliest days of Mary's reign before the Second Statute of Repeal. The text of Parsons's *Anima Christi*, which bears some resemblance to a modern Roman Catholic prayer, was described in Primers of 1494 and 1538 as a prayer at the Elevation of the Sacrament.[23]

MUSICAL STYLE

The movement away from rhythmic differentiation towards unity and directness of expression which we noted in Taverner's work is continued, intensified and widened in most of the Latin music written by his juniors.

This movement did not of course happen suddenly or uniformly. Some votive antiphons, Masses and psalm-motets, including works written under Mary and probably Elizabeth too in the case of some psalm-motets, still maintain in some degree the musical tradition established by the Eton composers. A few works, notably one or two by Tallis who must have been composing before Taverner stopped, contain little that is new. But in others, especially some psalm-motets by Whyte and Mundy, who were twenty to thirty years younger than

(1.Ex. 10.)

EECM, ii.120,138 : Mundy's *Eructavit cor meum*.

Tallis, there are times when the connection with the late fifteenth-century tradition does not extend very far beyond the continued alternation of full and reduced textures. Little of the old exuberance and expansiveness remains (*1.Ex. 10.*). Imitation is rarely absent, and its handling shows some similarities with the rather rigid, systematic working of the imitative motets discussed below. There are fewer and less abrupt differences of pace and character within the single voice, between voices or between sections—in particular the kind of quasi-cantus firmus foundation part which is still found in parts of Tallis's *Ave rosa sine spinis* and *Salve intemerata* is now abandoned, and the powerful drive to the cadence of much earlier music is absent or much reduced in force. There is more careful avoidance of 'difficult' rhythms; and extended melisma and floridity are much curtailed. These motets by Whyte and Mundy have lost much of the rhythmic appeal and dynamism of the old tradition without gaining all the cogency and directness of fully imitative pieces: one is very conscious of their transitional character. But on the credit side there tends to be, as in very much mid sixteenth-century music, some greater boldness in the most important melodic ideas—which now means chiefly imitative points—than generally found in earlier works. One finds a more frequent use of perfect fourths, fifths and larger intervals. The type of melodic expansion already noted in Aston (see *15.Ex. 9.* above) is not now uncommon.

One of the principal obstacles to the fullest textural unity is a cantus firmus. Several large-scale pieces, including Tallis's Mass *Puer natus est nobis*, still have a plainsong in mixed long notes. In many other works, chiefly *alternatim* ones by Tallis and Sheppard, the proper plainsong stands less obviously aloof because it is in equal notes of only moderate length. Imitation against the plainsong is important; it may even briefly dominate where there are entries in the free parts before the cantus firmus enters at the head of a piece, as in Tallis's *Honor virtus* or Sheppard's first *Non conturbetur cor vestrum*. Most works with equal-note plainsong were obviously written before 1559, but a few as we saw above must be Elizabethan; composition on a plainsong of course remained popular for instrumental music even into the 1600s.

It is in a fairly small group of psalm-motets and other non-liturgical motets chiefly from Elizabeth's reign that the concept of musical unity is furthest advanced. The reduced–full differentiation is abandoned for the unity of continuous full writing. There is no cantus firmus, and imitation normally dominates much or all of the time; where it does not, simple chordal textures are used. These are the works in which

English music approaches the mainstream of musical development abroad most nearly. The closest contacts of all are to be found in Byrd's 1575 *Cantiones* where the influence of Alfonso Ferrabosco the elder (in England between 1562 and 1578)[24] may be termed decisive. There are parallels between the music of the earlier generation of Gombert and Clemens and some of Tallis's motets in particular, not only in the adoption of continuously imitative full writing, but in some aspects of dissonance treatment and cadence practice. Despite the greater influence of Continental music, scarcely any examples of it survive in England between 1530 and 1575 apart from the two pieces in Peterhouse, two in Gyffard by Philip van Wilder, a Netherlander resident in England after 1525,[25] and a collection of songs by Lassus printed in London in 1570;[26] but so few manuscripts containing even English composers' works have reached us that this is not particularly significant. Large numbers of Continental works do appear in manuscripts from the latter part of Elizabeth's reign, including some of the Paston group.[27]

The novelty of so heavy a dependence on imitation in the motets of the early Elizabethan period is clear from Tallis's, and especially Whyte's, often very regular and rather mechanical working of entries: exact repetition of entire sets is important, and so is pairing of entries (which, fundamental to Josquin, was already largely discarded abroad by Gombert and Clemens). Byrd's imitation is much more flexible, even in his 1575 pieces, in response to more up-to-date Continental influences.

The continuously imitative works are the simplest, most restrained rhythmically, with as a rule only the tiniest florid touches. The brilliance of the treble voice, still found in many antiphons, psalms and responds, is usually absent, as in most English church music and in Continental works. The range of note-values is markedly narrower than in early sixteenth-century large-scale works. (Most mid sixteenth-century pieces which maintain something of the old tradition are less restricted, but they do show striking new signs of economy, especially in use of the longest notes.) The minim is the most widely used value; crotchets are common—single ones after dotted minims and pairs of crotchets often carry syllables, while little melismatic runs of between about three and six are common; quavers are rare; breves and longer notes are infrequently used except at ends of phrases. As in mid sixteenth-century music abroad, the metre is always ₵. Melismas other than the very shortest normally come in one or a few voices at a time against syllabic writing elsewhere, although something of the old long melismatic Amen occasionally survives (as in Whyte's *Domine quis habitabit* I and III) and in Lamentations the Hebrew letters at the heads of verses are given melismatic treatment.

Melodic lines almost always fit the words well enough, as they had done less regularly in the past, in that accented syllables attract metrically strong and/or long notes, unstressed ones weaker notes, and the highest pitches sometimes coincide with the strongest syllables. But many lines are a little pedestrian; Tallis in particular sometimes overdoes continuous minim movement (*2.Ex. 10.*); and one very rarely

(2.Ex. 10.)

TCM, vi.118 : *Lamentations II*

in - i - mi - ci il - li - us lo- cu - ple -ta - ti sunt, lo- cu- ple- ta - ti ⸺ sunt : ⸺

feels that text and melody enjoy the perfect spontaneous union that Byrd had in mind when he wrote in the Preface to the *Gradualia* of 1605: 'In sacred words . . . there is such a profound and hidden power that to one thinking upon things divine and diligently and earnestly pondering them, all the fittest numbers occur as if of themselves'.[28] Not surprisingly it is chiefly in parts of Byrd's 1575 pieces that we find a melodic line with genuinely expressive qualities. Joseph Kerman remarks on the 'monotone apostrophe and . . . guilt-ridden semitones'

(a)

(3.Ex. 10.)

TCM, ix.122 and vi.222.

Do - mi - ne,   se - cun- dum a - ctum me - - (um)

(b)

Su - sci- pe quae - so, Do - mi - ne, vo - cem con-fi - ten - - (tis)

of the opening subject (*3(a).Ex. 10.*) of *Domine secundum actum meum*, a penitential motet modelled on Ferrabosco's *Domine non secundum peccata mea*;[29] contrast the rather neutral melody of Tallis's penitential *Suscipe quaeso* (*3(b).Ex. 10.*).

Other important instances of a positive expressive response to a text come in Tallis's Lamentations and *In jejunio et fletu*, where repeated-note declamation and solemn chordal harmonies emphasise crucial words and phrases (further, see Chapter 11). Both works are in a minor 'key'; there are in fact no blatant contradictions between major/minor modality and cheerful/gloomy words in motets, as there sometimes were in votive antiphons. But even in motets we must not look for much vivid expressive writing: this is in any case not easy to achieve in continuous full-choir imitative writing where purely musical unity is paramount, and had to wait for the evolution of a more 'fragmented and dramatic style' in some of Byrd's music and especially in the work of his 'younger Anglo-Catholic contemporaries, Philips and Dering'.[30]

In much mid sixteenth-century music, as already in parts of Taverner's shorter works, the harmony tends to move more regularly and purposefully, in fact to be more tonal in feeling than in the past. The new harmonic sense is partly a by-product of the new textural unity. The bass line moves more regularly because extreme rhythmic contrasts within a part are far less common, and differs less in pace and character from the other voices because it is so frequently linked to them through imitation. In several places, especially in Tallis as detailed in Chapter 11, interest is polarised between the outer voices in a new way which, with hindsight, seems an interesting anticipation of seventeenth-century textural ideals. But the new harmonic sense is not merely the result of changed textural methods, a kind of accident. The insistence on sharpened leading-notes in the 1575 *Cantiones* is important, a clear contradiction of modal 'purity'. Byrd's limited use of other new accidentals is mentioned in Chapter 12. Pure Dorian modality is now rare, transposed Aeolian on D or G being preferred. Byrd uses untransposed Aeolian on A, not previously found in England, in *Da mihi auxilium* and *Domine secundum actum meum*. Where modality is genuinely chosen, and is not just dictated by the modality of a proper cantus firmus as in a respond or hymn, there is a quite strong preference for the minor; this is not simply connected with the feeling for gloomy texts in Elizabeth's reign—for example all Tallis's antiphons are minor, even though beginning with such words as *Gaude gloriosa* and *Ave dei Patris filia nobilissima*. Compare this preference for the minor with the love of major modes in Eton—and invent some suitable psychological explanation!

A new more positive attitude to dissonance, occasionally present in Taverner's *Meane Mass*, gives extra 'bite' to the harmony, particularly at cadences; it is felt chiefly in works with equal-note cantus firmus and in motets. Since the suspension is now valued more for its tension and pungency than as decoration, ornamental resolutions which minimise the effect of the dissonance proper are used much less, while configurations hitherto unknown or uncommon which compound and intensify it are quite widely employed. Most notably we find the sounding of the note of resolution against the suspension dissonance proper; the sounding of a fifth from the bass with the seventh of a 7–6 suspension, the progression in full being $\frac{7\text{–}6}{5\text{–}3}$; double suspensions, especially where 7–6 and 4–3 suspensions are combined. Leading-notes are now frequently doubled, and if those which rise are sharpened by *musica ficta*, semitonal clashes and false relations result. These are sometimes definitely required in Elizabethan sources, including the especially authoritative 1575 *Cantiones*. A 4–3 suspension, although always with decorative resolution, now sometimes disturbs the consonant purity of a work's final chord (in Tallis, Whyte and Byrd, although Sheppard and Tye avoid it). Tallis often tempers the sound with simultaneous 6–5 movement, which on its own had long been acceptable at a final chord; unlike Byrd he never resolves the 6–5 'suspension' ornamentally (to give $\frac{6\text{–}5\text{–}4\text{–}5}{4\text{–}3\text{–}2\text{–}3}$). Sometimes Tallis was prepared to tolerate 4–3–2–3 movement on its own. This concluding 4–3 suspension was used abroad occasionally by Gombert and frequently by Clemens, mainly without 6–5 movement; perhaps the idea of it came from them. In fact most of the other new dissonant situations are found abroad; even the semitonal clashes

(4.Ex. 10.)

TCM, vi. 218 : *Salvator mundi I* ; and vi.256 : *Domine quis habitabit.*

and false relations often thought of as typically English can be found there if rising leading-notes are sharpened.

An important aspect of mid sixteenth-century cadential practice is greater reliance on tonic pedals at important closes, particularly in cantus firmus pieces, where the final note of the plainsong is extended, and (most effectively of all) in some of Tallis's motets. Especially in these latter the handling is very similar to that of many cadences by Gombert and Clemens. The pedal may come at the top rather than in the tenor (*4(a).Ex. 10.*) or in two parts simultaneously (*4(b).Ex. 10.*). The pedal section may, as in *4(a).*, be a kind of little relaxatory coda, added on as it were to a perfect cadence with which the work *could* almost have ended; its effect is due in part to the lingering suspension on the final chord and the very prominent position of the sustained note at the top.

Thomas Tallis, John Sheppard and Christopher Tye

Tallis, Sheppard and Tye all started composing under Henry VIII, and all wrote English as well as Latin church music. But there are important differences between them in age, character, circumstances and nature of achievement. Tallis was active well into Elizabeth's reign, while Sheppard is last heard of in 1557, and Tye is unlikely to have composed much apart from English music after Henry VIII's death. Tallis is a far more significant figure historically and artistically than Sheppard. Sheppard in turn outweighs Tye—at least as far as Latin music is concerned—partly because so much of the latter's work survives only in fragmentary form.

THOMAS TALLIS

Tallis is generally agreed to have been born about 1505: he is described as 'very aged' in 1577, and he died in 1585.[1] He can have been only about ten years Taverner's junior, which means—and the style of a few works confirms this—that his career slightly overlapped Taverner's. The antiphon *Salve intemerata* appears in British Museum Harleian MS. 1709, a single partbook which 'seems to have been copied in the 1520s';[2] it is interesting to note that the work's text is found in a Book of Hours of 1527.[3] The first reference to Tallis comes in 1531, when he was organist of Dover Priory. All his early career seems to have been spent in the South-East. In 1536 he was at St Mary-at-Hill near Billingsgate. Afterwards he moved back to monastic employment at Waltham Abbey: we hear of his being pensioned off at the dissolution in 1540. The following year he was a singer at Canterbury Cathedral, and it was at about this time that he became a Gentleman of the Chapel Royal.[4] He held this rank under four monarchs until his death, serving some of the time as organist.

A tribute paid to Tallis at his death, as well as indicating the great

Table 10: Thomas Tallis

Masses

à7: Puer natus est nobis†
à5: Salve intemerata*
à4: unnamed setting

Proper of the Lady Mass

à4: Alleluia *Ora pro nobis*, Euge coeli porta (*v .2 from sequence 'Ave praeclara'*)

Votive Antiphons

à6: Gaude gloriosa
à5: Ave Dei Patris filia,† Ave rosa sine spinis,* Salve intemerata
à4: Sancte Deus

Canticles

à5: Magnificat *and* Nunc dimittis*
à4: Magnificat

Responds

à7: *Loquebantur* variis linguis (*Whitsun*)
à6: *Homo* quidam fecit coenam (*Corpus Christi*),* *Videte* miraculum (*Purification*)*
à5: *Candidi* facti sunt (*Apostles in Eastertide*), Dum transisset sabbatum (*Easter*), Honor virtus et potestas (*Trinity*)
à4: Audivi *vocem* (*All Saints*), Hodie *nobis coelorum rex* (*Christmas*), In pace *in idipsum* (*Lent*)

Hymns

à5: *Jam Christus astra*/Solemnis urgebat dies (*Whitsun*), *Jesu salvator saeculi Verbum*/Tu fabricator omnium (*Low Sunday to Ascension*), *Quod chorus vatum*/Haec Deum coeli (*Purification*), *Salvator mundi Domine*/Adesto nunc propitius (*Christmas Eve to Octave of Epiphany*), *Sermone blando*/Illae dum pergunt concitae (*Low Sunday to Ascension*), *Te lucis ante terminum*/Procul recedant I (*Compline*), *Te lucis*/Procul II

Psalm-Motets

à5: Domine quis habitabit (*Ps. 15*), Laudate Dominum (*Ps. 117*)

Motets

à40: Spem in alium
à7: Miserere nostri, Suscipe quaeso
à5: Absterge Domine, Derelinquat impius, In jejunio et fletu, In manus tuas Domine, Mihi autem nimis, O nata lux de lumine, O sacrum convivium, O salutaris hostia, Salvator mundi salva nos I, Salvator mundi II

Lamentations

à5: two sets

Fragment

à3: Rex sanctorum

Note

The Deus tuorum militum/Hic nempe mundi gaudia printed in Tudor Church Music, vi is almost certainly by Sheppard; Domine Deus is from Tye's Domine Deus coelestis

Tallis's work is published in *TCM*, vi.

*Imperfectly preserved.
†Fragmentary.

respect in which he was held, suggests that he was a modest, unassuming man: 'As he did live, so also did he die, / In mild and quiet sort . . .'.[5] This disposition certainly enabled him successfully to weather all the main religious storms of the century, for although he seems to have remained a Roman Catholic at heart to the end—his use of several Roman texts and his close friendship with Byrd in particular suggest this—he is not known to have been in any trouble on account of his beliefs, and clearly did not experience any crisis of conscience comparable to Taverner's.

Although Tallis is justly famous for his part in developing English church music, and is probably most widely known for this, it is above all for his Latin works that he deserves to hold one of the very highest places in the music of his country. In our period he stands alone in terms of the range and variety of his work: there are votive antiphons, including the brief *Sancte Deus* and the long and very rich *Gaude gloriosa*; Masses, with a simple four-part setting and the splendid seven-part *Puer natus est nobis* at opposite extremes; responds (solo and choral) and hymns; and motets, among them such masterpieces as the Lamentations and *In jejunio et fletu*. But the breadth of Tallis's achievement and the major stylistic changes which took place between the early antiphons and the late motets seem to mean that the essential Tallis is a little elusive. One remembers the tribute to his 'mild and quiet' life—and indeed one senses a less incisive personality than in the music of John Browne or Taverner. Tallis has above all a very fine feeling for the overall balance, shape and architecture of a piece: his tonal planning in *In jejunio* and the Lamentations is remarkable, as is his method of shaping whole sections of responds or verses of hymns by means of ostinato patterns; the use of repetition as a formal device is also very striking.

Any examination of Tallis's stylistic development is difficult because not a single work is precisely datable. But a rough chronological picture can be attempted. Some categories of works may be confidently labelled 'pre-1559': Masses, antiphons, works preserved in the Peterhouse and Gyffard partbooks. Most if not all hymns and responds designed for *alternatim* performance must also be from this period. Pieces with ritual texts which do not require *alternatim* performance, such as *In manus*, are presumably post-Sarum, as are works with Roman texts, such as *Derelinquat impius*. Other works, chiefly motets from the *Cantiones* and the Lamentations, are sufficiently similar to the two just mentioned to make a similar dating likely. The 1575 publication is almost certainly to some extent a retrospective collection so far as

Tallis is concerned—in particular note the presence of several *alternatim* hymns and responds. Whatever the date of the motets, even these are old-fashioned by Byrd's standards, for they do not show such 'modern' influences as the music of Ferrabosco.

Any attempt to say which Sarum pieces belong to Henry's reign and which to Mary's would be very hazardous. But since Mary's lasted for only five years, while Tallis was active for twenty years or more under Henry, the bulk of his Sarum pieces presumably dates from before 1547. The antiphon and Mass *Salve intemerata* and *Ave rosa sine spinis* are the only works for whose Henrician dating we have proof, because these alone are known from Henrician sources.

Sarum Works: Antiphons and Masses

Ave rosa, whose verse text is a troped form of the 'Ave Maria', is Tallis's most old-fashioned piece: imitation is less important than in the other antiphons, and extended melisma is cultivated rather more. It is much more successful than *Salve intemerata*, although the latter is much more widely preserved in sixteenth-century sources. Built on a long and somewhat rambling prose text, *Salve intemerata* runs to about 270 bars (one hundred more than *Ave rosa*), even with limited melisma: this is far too much for its content and interest, and one feels that Tallis is often ill at ease. He seems to find the hitherto little used Phrygian modality cramping, and too rarely manages to cadence away from E (note by contrast the adventurous 'tonal scheme' of the first set of Lamentations, as described below). There is also some stylistic indecision: the character of the imitation at 'misericors patrona' with its verbal repetition contrasts oddly with the much more old-fashioned material surrounding it. Disparities of material are greater in the parody Mass *Salve intemerata*, the newly composed sections being both better and more modern than the borrowed ones. And yet strangely the Mass is more successful than the antiphon. The change of scale is beneficial, for the fairly brief Mass movements (together only slightly longer than the parent work) show the borrowed material in a more favourable light than does the loose structure of the large-scale antiphon. Perhaps the most interesting of the new passages are the 'Crucifixus' and 'Benedictus': these resemble quite strikingly the corresponding sections of Taverner's *Meane Mass*. The Mass uses verbal repetition frequently, mostly in the Sanctus and Agnus, where the antiphon had virtually avoided it; from now on it becomes accepted practice.

Gaude gloriosa is in every respect a much finer, more mature work than *Ave rosa* or *Salve intemerata*—in fact it is probably the greatest of all sixteenth-century large-scale antiphons. It is almost certainly later than the two pieces it so greatly surpasses. Possibly it was even written in Mary's reign: it is after all generally similar to William Mundy's six-part antiphons which cannot be earlier than 1553. The main technical differences between *Gaude gloriosa* and the other antiphons are that imitative entries tend to be longer and a little more powerful in shaping the music, and that voices are more equally balanced, without the tenor tending to stand aloof as a cantus firmus-like part. Perhaps the most striking feature of all is the exciting treatment of rising inter-

(a)   (1.Ex. 11.)   *TCM*, vi.124,125.

(b)

vals, most especially in the passages quoted in *1.Ex. 11.*, where the text about Mary's Assumption and enthronement in heaven probably prompted them.

Although *Ave rosa* and the *Salve intemerata* pair are the only works we know to be Henrician, there seems no doubt that *Sancte Deus* and the fragmentary *Ave Dei Patris filia* are also from this period.

The unnamed Mass for four voices is in a very severe style broadly similar to that of some English music which Tallis wrote in Edward VI's reign, such as the four-part Benedictus. It is likely therefore that it is not far removed in date from such pieces. Clear text projection as in the English pieces is ensured by letting chordal and other straight-forward full-choir textures predominate (*2.Ex. 11.*); the imitation

(2.Ex. 11.)

TCM, vi.31.

which provides a contrast is only very simple. In the last two movements verbal repetition is used copiously to keep melisma to a near-minimum, and the words 'Sanctus, Sanctus, Sanctus' are set to three tiny chordal phrases, each ending with a pause mark. Although Tallis's Mass, like some Edwardine English music, is of only limited appeal and interest, Harrison's description of it as 'rather uncomfortable'[6] is unduly harsh; and perhaps even Doe's doubts about its style's standing up to 'such extended use'[7]—to which the scale of the internal repetitions seems to lend weight—can be answered by the fact that the four movements were not to be sung in immediate succession. Five quite long sections from the Gloria, which together make up almost all that movement, recur in later movements, so that the Gloria stands in much the same 'parental' relationship to the rest of the Mass as the antiphon *Salve intemerata* does to the entire Mass of that name.

Tallis's Mass *Puer natus est nobis* for two means, two countertenors, tenor and two basses, was clearly one of his greatest achievements, but unfortunately parts of the Credo are lost, and some editorial reconstruction has been needed in the Sanctus and Agnus.[8] The tenor is the Introit from the third Mass of Christmas[9]—the only case discovered so far where a cantus firmus comes from the Mass Proper instead of from the Office. It has been suggested that *Puer natus* was performed at Christmas in 1554 while Philip II of Spain, to whom Mary had been married five months earlier, was still in England. We know that Philip's chapel had joined with Mary's and with the choir of St Paul's on the first Sunday in Advent; another such collaboration might account for the unusual splendour of the seven-part Mass. Paul Doe thinks it possible even that 'the choice of Introit, 'Puer natus est nobis et filius datus est nobis cuius imperium super humerum eius . . .', may not have been wholly unconnected with the then highly topical news that Mary was expecting an heir'.

Musical considerations certainly suggest that the Mass is as late as Mary's reign. Philip's singers would have taken to it easily enough: Doe has suggested the influence of Gombert, who almost certainly spent some time in Madrid—and indeed the similarities he sees between *Puer natus* and the seven-part Agnus of Gombert's *Quam pulchra es* are quite marked. *Puer natus* is the only English festal Mass which dispenses with reduced–full contrasts; the three movements we have all begin in duple time; text repetition is fundamental in all sections, with extended melisma eliminated. The main technique is imitation against the cantus firmus, which is present almost all the time. The cantus firmus is very slow-moving; there are not many notes longer than the breve, but it is common for a note to be extended over two or three bars by repetition. This slowness sometimes makes the music rather limited harmonically, but it does give a very solid, almost monumental quality to some sections, just as the occasional introduction of homophony and antiphony does. Towards the end of the first Agnus the tenor, which has reached a point in the plainsong where there are nine consecutive *f*s, begins an *f* which it maintains, apart from four quite short rests, for fifteen bars; even during the silences there are few moves away from F major, B flat and D minor chords (3.Ex. 11.). The cantus firmus treatment is unusual in other ways than its very slow pace. As Doe has pointed out, we find some retrograde movement in the Sanctus and the repetition of various neumes. Both the Gloria and the Sanctus use only part of the 'Puer natus' melody, as far as 'humerum ejus'. The Agnus, which came to light after Doe examined the Gloria and Sanctus, uses the remainder of the melody from 'et vocabitur', and has some repetition of neumes, chiefly near the end.

(3.Ex. 11.)

Presumably the Credo also used the second half of the chant, so that the whole Mass had two complete statements of 'Puer natus' (compare John Lloyd's plan in the early sixteenth-century Mass *O quam suavis*).

Puer natus is a most remarkable piece, quite unlike any other English festal Mass. Most interesting of all is the contrast between its modern style and the basically old-fashioned manner of other music supposed to date from Mary's reign, notably the Mundy antiphons and (perhaps) Tallis's *Gaude gloriosa*.

Sarum Works: Responds and Hymns

Three responds are of the old solo type. *Hodie*, which is independent of the proper plainsong, is short and fairly restrained, with brief imitative points worked unobtrusively into rather solid four-part writing. *Audivi vocem* and *In pace* both use imitative points which paraphrase the proper chant, a technique probably derived from Continental practice, although it is impossible to be precise about the nature or timing of this influence. In *Audivi* imitative paraphrase is not used in a thoroughgoing way, and at 'clamor factus est' Tallis even reverts to cantus firmus style. But with *In pace* every phrase of the chant is paraphrased, and imitation dominates the piece to an extent that it has not in any work so far discussed. The whole shape and content of the individual phrase is governed by the working of the imitative point,

(4.Ex. 11.)

TCM, vi.260.

and formally the piece becomes simply a succession of short imitative sections, each more or less dovetailed into the next. All this Tallis manages quite without rigidity or awkwardness; strangely there is not the pairing of entries or the repetitive techniques on which he relied in the motets.

The six choral responds follow Taverner's *Dum transisset* settings in adopting a cantus firmus in semibreves, but they show a much greater emphasis on imitation. There is some fondness, more noticeable still in a few verses from the hymns, for ostinato-like procedures, particularly in closing sections. For example at 'et perenni' in *Honor virtus* the top part has five statements of a quite long phrase derived from the plainsong, all beginning on c'' and working within the fourth c'' to f''; and there are repeated entries on B flat in the outer parts at 'quia parata' in *Homo quidam*. The Alleluia of *Dum transisset* (4.Ex. 11.) is very neatly managed, especially near the end where the entries are made to come lower and lower as the music subsides to the final cadence. Interest is polarised between the outer voices, cantus firmus at the top instead of in the tenor as with the other responds, imitative entries continuously in whichever is the lowest voice singing. The nature of the imitative point makes for a simple harmonic structure, and for a clear, clipped word-setting instead of the melisma traditionally associated with the word 'Alleluia'.

Tallis's hymns do not have such regular cantus firmi as the choral responds: they begin in ₵ with the plainsong, occasionally slightly decorated, in mixed note-values, only changing later to ₵ with equal semibreves for the cantus firmus if more than one verse is set. The cantus firmus is always at the top. If three verses have to be sung in polyphony, the first and second are musically the same (except in *Salvator mundi Domine*). *Sermone blando*, with four polyphonic verses, has the same setting for the second pair of verses as well as for the first, except that for each repeat the two countertenors exchange parts.

Hymn melodies are mainly syllabic and have a regular phrase structure; accordingly polyphonic settings of them tend to be simpler and more compact than those of the irregular and melismatic responds. The simplest hymn of all is the second *Te lucis ante terminum*. Its single polyphonic verse has the simpler (ferial) tune for the hymn in slightly decorated homophony. Each line occupies two bars and is separated from the next by a rest in all parts. Appropriately the setting of the festal tune (*Te lucis* I) is less severely functional. The lines are still punctuated by rests, but each begins with the mean anticipating the first three notes of the melody.

(5.Ex. 11.) *TCM*, vi.193.

In verse 2 of *Sermone blando* the anticipations are developed into brief imitations, and the breaks between lines are never total (5.Ex. 11.). In verse 6 the texture is continuous, with imitation against an equal-note cantus firmus. All the themes could be seen as derivatives of the one used at the beginning; such prolonged treatment of a single idea is important also in the equal-note verses of *Jesu salvator saeculi* and *Quod chorus vatum*.

Jam Christus astra ascenderat begins with a canon between the treble and countertenor. Each line of the tune is followed by a short rest, but the canonic working and the skilful imitation of the tune in other parts keep up a continuous flow, and the texture is more complex than anywhere else in the hymns.

Motets and Lamentations

Tallis's remaining Latin works, which come principally from the 1575 *Cantiones*, contain much of his greatest music. They form a very varied group, including works with continuously imitative writing such as the lovely *O sacrum convivium* and the psalms *Domine quis habitabit* and *Laudate Dominum*; pieces with some contrasting chordal textures, notably *In jejunio* and the Lamentations; and such deliberate demonstrations of technical skill as the canonic *Miserere nostri* and the forty-part *Spem in alium*.

Tallis tends to work on a more modest scale than his English (or foreign) contemporaries. This might be thought to indicate loss of energy and 'staying power' in an ageing composer; but the excellence of the music argues strongly against any deterioration. Neither does Tallis's considerable reliance on fairly rigid imitative and repetitive schemes signify failing powers: other composers write similarly.

The basis of two works is canon, the strictest of all contrapuntal devices. The second setting of *Salvator mundi salva nos* (antiphon from the feast of the Exaltation of the Holy Cross) has a canon at the octave between the top part and the tenor, worked so neatly and naturally that the piece is one of Tallis's most fresh and attractive. By contrast the seven-part *Miserere nostri* (whose text comes from verse 27 of the Te

(6.Ex. 11.)   *TCM*, vi.216.

Deum) is chiefly a *tour de force*. The top two voices, in canon at the unison, provide the only clearly audible sign of the work's learned character; four others, which all begin at the same time, are more subtly related by augmentation (rather in the manner of Ockeghem's *Missa Prolationum*)[10] and by inversion. The seventh part is free.

The first *Salvator mundi* shows the extent to which Tallis was sometimes prepared to rely on regularity and repetition. It also shows that their use can be interesting and varied. The opening quite weighty set of entries is repeated virtually unchanged, except that Tallis devises additional material to support the re-statement of the first new entries so that the texture does not become too sparse when the repetition begins (6.Ex. 11.). There follows a single, more compact set of entries at 'qui per crucem'; but the point here is immediately re-adopted for 'redemisti nos', and this latter passage is then repeated: both at 'qui per crucem' and 'redemisti nos' the imitation is so managed that continuous five-part texture is maintained. At 'auxiliare nobis' we find the polarisation of interest between the outer parts noted elsewhere in Tallis, with the outer voices alone having melodically exact entries; these entries and some of the inner material are sung twice, the second time a fourth higher than at first. The last section of *Salvator mundi* ('te deprecamur') has two very similar statements of an important new set of entries which together occupy roughly a third of the entire piece.

Such repetition of a particularly substantial passage at the end of a motet is a feature also of *O sacrum* and *In manus*, for in both of these statement and repetition take up about half the piece. Such an arrangement may be compared (and is perhaps connected) with the 'A B B' scheme of some English anthems, among them Edwardine pieces like Tallis's own *If ye love me*. Possibly there is also some connection between such anthem- and motet-structures and the form a choral respond takes if its verse is omitted and the repeat of the response leads straight on from its first statement, as happens in *Honor virtus*. Incidentally although repetition was an essential feature of some Continental secular music, the 'A B B' pattern is rare.[11] Whole sets of entries are occasionally repeated in Continental church music, but this seems to be chiefly at ends of sections (for example at 'Dona nobis pacem' in Josquin's *Pange lingua*) rather than at the beginning of a piece in the manner of Tallis's *Salvator mundi*.

The skilful joinery of *Salvator mundi* may best be appreciated by contrast with *O salutaris hostia*. The latter has all its sets of entries of much the same character and weight; almost all are repeated, and the texture is allowed to thin out each time as the re-statement begins (7.Ex. 11.). Even the order of the entries re-inforces the work's pre-

(7.Ex. 11.)

TCM, vi.279.

dictability with its strong preference for entries in descending order from treble to bass. The first four voices to enter frequently form two sets of paired entries.

Repetition may be considerably freer than in the works so far mentioned, as in *Absterge Domine* and *Mihi autem nimis*. The latter, whose texts was originally the Introit for the Common of one Apostle, has for example a very much modified repeat of the opening entries which moves considerably more smartly and pointedly: the first note of each entry is abbreviated, and at 'honorati' a striking octave leap not present before is introduced (8.Ex. 11.).

Although we have assigned Tallis's motets to Elizabeth's reign, in accordance with the general view, it is worth pointing out that the techniques they employ apparently originated before that time. The concluding repetition of a long section, as already mentioned, is found as early as Edward's reign. Repetition of opening paired entries without

(8.Ex. 11.)   *TCM*, vi.204.

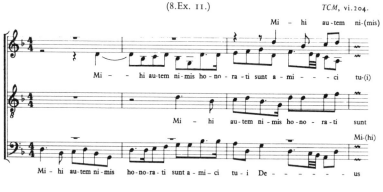

much overlap between first statement and repetition is found in Tye's
O God be merciful unto us, which is preserved in British Museum Royal
Appendix MSS. 74–76 of *c.* 1550 (*9.Ex. 11.*); the similarity with *O*

(9.Ex. 11.)

salutaris hostia is obvious; one would compare also the beginning of
Robert Johnson's *Deus misereatur* of *c.* 1548–50 (*10.Ex. 11.*). Tye's
Praise ye the Lord ye children employs re-statement with overlap as in
Tallis's *Salvator mundi*; this work cannot be dated as confidently as *O
God be merciful*, but most of Tye's English music is likely to date from

(10.Ex. 11.)

MB, xv.106.

Edward's reign. Sheppard's psalm-motets, which are probably pre-1559 since no reference to their composer after 1557 has been traced, again show similarities with Tallis's practice (see *18.Ex. 11.* below). Again it is interesting to compare the imitation in *6. and 7.Exx. 11.*

(11.Ex. 11.)

TCM, vi.257.

above with that of *11.Ex. 11.* from Tallis's own *Dum transisset,* a Sarum work and therefore presumably pre-1559.

In some pieces, notably *In jejunio*, the Lamentations, *Suscipe quaeso* and *Derelinquat impius*, there is much greater flexibility because repetition is either absent or less important, and greater textural variety is obtained through some use of chordal or antiphonal writing.

In jejunio, whose words form the seventh respond at (Roman) Matins of the first Sunday in Lent, is possibly Tallis's finest work. The solemnity of the text is reflected in the insistent repeated-note declamation at the beginning and at 'inter vestibulum', and in the rich chordal textures here and elsewhere. The work is basically in the Aeolian mode on G, but repeated A flat chords appear near the beginning and at

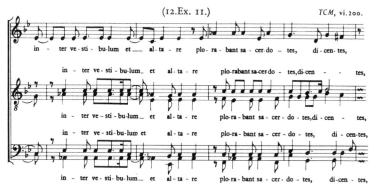

(12.Ex. 11.)   *TCM*, vi.200.

'inter vestibulum' (*12.Ex. 11.*) where they are almost certainly intended to point up these crucial words. In each case the remoteness of the A flat chords from the main 'key' centre is emphasised by their proximity to cadences on G, C or D. It is possible also that cadences well on the sharp side of G minor (on A and E) are meant to balance these moves to A flat: such a feeling for overall tonal structure is evident in the first set of Lamentations.

At 'inter vestibulum' a single part is set off against chordal movement in the other four, a device which Tallis uses in several other places in *In jejunio* and the Lamentations. The single part, which always enters first, is usually imitated by one of the others. Often, as at 'inter vestibulum', the treble is the leading part, and the bass imitates it, so that interest is again polarised between the outer parts.

The very moving first set of Lamentations has in common with *In jejunio* not only the 'one against four' antiphonal method, but an adventurous tonal scheme and some telling use of repeated notes; above all the handling of its pivotal section 'Plorans ploravit' is remarkably close to that of 'inter vestibulum'. In the Lamentations Tallis moves from an initial Phrygian modality on E through A and D cadences to a

B flat cadence at 'Beth'. The following words 'Plorans ploravit', in B flat (*13.Ex. 11.*), form the tonal climax, for after them the earlier

(13.Ex. 11.)

TCM, vi. 106.

movement away from E is reversed. The tonal climax is made to co-incide with the most highly-charged words in the piece, just as in *In jejunio* other words about weeping are harmonically underscored. The centrality of 'Plorans ploravit' is stressed also by the unusually deliber-ate pace of the music; the *b'* flats in the top part are also remarkable because *a'* is normally the summit and because *f'* had been the highest note for some long time before. Tallis uses repeated-note declamation and 'one against four' antiphony at the end, in the solemn appeal to Jerusalem to turn to God. The first part of the section is repeated a fourth lower to make the ending particularly sombre. This is Tallis's love of repetition transmuted into something quite new, rich and expressive.

The first set of Lamentations uses the two verses 'Aleph' and 'Beth' which formed the first lesson of Maundy Thursday Matins. The second set, on the verses 'Gimel', 'Daleth' and 'Heth', is in a different key and was clearly conceived separately from the first; it is similar in general style to this, but is tonally conventional, and does not attain the same heights of inspiration.

The seven-part *Suscipe quaeso* is the longest of Tallis's *Cantiones*. Its text, partly an adaptation of verse 3 from the penitential Psalm 130, is a personal plea for forgiveness; it is not 'in the form of a collect' (a formalised liturgical prayer) as Doe claims, and it is doubtful if it 'would have served admirably' for Cardinal Pole's absolution of England in 1554.[12] A date in Mary's reign might however be supported by the similarity of scoring between *Suscipe quaeso* and *Puer natus* and the associated deduction that both works could have been linked in performance. The style certainly shows considerable similarities to that of *Puer natus*, but this cannot be regarded as conclusive evidence. *Suscipe quaeso* has spacious imitation at the beginning and at the head of the second major section (or 'pars' to use the Continental term, as the *Cantiones* does); dramatic homophony at 'peccavi, peccavi'; and bold antiphonal contrasts at 'qui se dicere'.

Spem in alium, Tallis's legendary forty-part motet, uses the words of the fourth respond at Matins of Hystoria Judith.[13] Various attempts have been made to explain the significance of the forty parts; but there is no clear evidence to show in what conditions this enormous work was performed. The work is scored for eight five-part choirs, which from time to time are all in use at once. Elsewhere Tallis exploits various antiphonal effects, and employs an interesting range of 'reduced' imitative textures.

JOHN SHEPPARD

John Sheppard was a much more prolific composer than Tallis, but his achievement is comparatively limited. His Latin music consists predominantly of *alternatim* works with equal-note cantus firmus, especially responds and hymns; and there is, perhaps inevitably, a certain sameness about much that he wrote. Nevertheless there can be no doubt that Sheppard deserves far greater notice than he has so far enjoyed; his style is forthright and vigorous, the full-blooded sound of six-part writing with trebles being a favourite.

Sheppard was almost certainly considerably younger than Tallis or Tye, because unlike them he was not yet represented in the Peterhouse partbooks of *c.* 1540–7. He was probably born in about 1520: reference is made to his twenty years' study of music in his supplication for the Oxford Music Doctorate in 1554.[14] He was master of the choristers at

Table 11: John Sheppard

Masses

à6: Cantate
à4: Be not afraide, French Mass, Playnsong Masse for a Mene, Western Wynde

Fragments of Masses

à5: Kyrie
à3: Agnus

Proper of the Mass

à6: Haec dies (*Easter Gradual*)
à4: Alleluia Confitemini Domino (*Easter Eve, Whitsunday Eve*), Alleluias *Per te Dei, Posuisti Domine, Veni electa, Virtutes coeli* (*Lady Mass*)
à2: Laudes Deo (*troped lesson for Midnight Mass*)

Votive Antiphons

à6: Gaude virgo christipera*
à4: Gaudete coelicolae omnes

Fragments of Antiphons

à3: Igitur O Jesu, Illustrissima omnium, Singularis privilegii

Magnificats

à6: one setting†
à4: one setting

Fragment of Magnificat (not from either setting above)

à5: Esurientes

Te Deum

à6: one setting*

Responds

à6:   *Christi virgo* dilectissima (*Annunciation*),* *Dum transisset* sabbatum I (*Easter*),* *Dum transisset* sabbatum II, *Filiae* Jerusalem venite (*One Martyr or Confessor from Low Sunday to Whitsun*), *Gaude gaude gaude Maria* virgo cunctas haereses, with prose Inviolata (*Purification*),* *Non conturbetur* cor vestrum I (*Eve of the Ascension*),* *Non conturbetur* cor vestrum II,* *Reges Tharsis* et insulae (*Epiphany*),* *Spiritus Sanctus* procedens a throno (*Whitsun*),* *Verbum* caro factum est (*Christmas*)*
à5:   *Impetum* fecerunt unanimes (*St Stephen*),* *Justi* in perpetuum (*All Saints*),* *Laudem dicite* Deo nostro (*All Saints*), *Spiritus Sanctus* procedens a throno (*Whitsun*)*
à4:   Audivi *vocem* (*All Saints*), *Hodie* nobis coelorum rex/Gloria in excelsis (*Christmas*), In manus tuas *Domine* I (*Lent*), *In manus tuas* Domine II, In pace *in idipsum* (*Lent*)
à3:   *In manus tuas* Domine III

Hymns

à8:   *Sacris solemniis*/Noctis recolitur (*Corpus Christi*)*
à7/à8: *A solis ortus cardine*/Beatus auctor saeculi (*Christmas*)*
à7:   *Beata nobis gaudia*/Ignis vibrante (*Whitsun*)*
à6:   *Adesto sancta Trinitas*/Te coelorum militia I (*Trinity*),* *Adesto*/Te coelorum II,* *Ave maris stella*/Sumens illud Ave (*Annunciation*),* *Hostis Herodes impie*/Ibant magi (*Epiphany*),* *Jam Christus astra*/Solemnis urgebat dies (*Whitsun*),* *Jesu salvator saeculi Verbum*/Tu fabricator omnium (*Low Sunday to Ascension*),* *Martyr Dei qui*

unicum/Tui precatus munere (*One Martyr*),* *Salvator mundi Domine*/Adesto nunc propitius (*Christmas Eve to Octave of Epiphany*)*

à5:   *Aeterne rex altissime*/Scandens tribunal (*Ascension*),* *Christe redemptor omnium Conserva*/Beata quoque agmina (*All Saints*),* *Deus tuorum militum*/Hic nempe mundi gaudia I (*One Martyr*),* *Deus tuorum*/Hic nempe II—ascribed in one source to Tallis, *Jesu salvator saeculi Redemptis*/Coetus omnes angelici (*All Saints*), *Sancte Dei pretiose*/Funde preces pro devoto (*St Stephen*)*

Ritual Antiphons

à7:   *Libera nos salva nos* I (*Trinity*),* *Libera nos salva nos* II*
à6:   Media vita in morte sumus (*Lent*)*

Processional Psalms with Antiphons

à4:   In exitu Israel (*Pss. 114 and 115, Easter*)—composed jointly with William Mundy and Thomas(?) Byrd, Laudate pueri (*Ps. 113, Easter*)

Processional Hymn

à4:   Salve festa dies . . . *qua Deus infernum vicit* (*Easter*)

Psalm-Motets

à5:   Beati omnes qui timent (*Ps. 128*),* Confitebor tibi Domine quoniam iratus es mihi (*Canticle of Isaiah, Isa. 12*),* Deus misereatur (*Ps. 67*),* Inclina Domine I (*Ps. 86: 1–6*), Inclina Domine II,† Judica me Deus (*Ps. 43*)*

Fragments

à4:   Domine labia (no other text)
à?:   Pater noster

Note

An Esto pater à3 in British Museum, Royal Music Library MS. R.M. 24 d. 2, ascribed to Sheppard, is from John Wood's Exsurge Domine.

*Imperfectly preserved.
†Fragmentary.

Magdalen at various times between 1542 and 1556;[15] the interruptions to his service were probably connected with disciplinary infringements, for the College registers record several charges against him. Although granted his degree, he may not actually have received it, for he is never referred to as 'Doctor', even in the College records of 1555 and 1556. Sheppard became a Gentleman of the Chapel Royal in about 1552. The Check Book does not list him, and so he had presumably left, or died, before 1561 when its record of appointments and resignations begins.[16] The last reference to him is in 1557 when he made a gift of music to the Queen.

The responds form Sheppard's largest group of works and contain some of his most impressive writing. Sixteen are choral responds, twelve with texts not previously set. The basic technique of working imitation against a plainsong in semibreves resembles that of Tallis's responds; but Sheppard's textures tend to be more consistently dense, and to be a little more florid.

Gaude gaude gaude Maria is the crowning work among Sheppard's responds. Most of it is exciting, densely-textured six-part writing, with the tune in the tenor, but verses 3–8 of 'Inviolata integra', the prose incorporated into it, are by contrast for divided trebles, divided means and a supporting lower part, with the melody alternately in the

(14.Ex. 11.)

first and second mean. The ending of the response (*14.Ex. 11.*) is particularly memorable for a telling touch of harmonic colour and the exceptionally wide spacing at the climactic moment when the treble sings *g″* and the bass *E flat*.

Where Sheppard makes two settings of a respond (or hymn) he uses a different scoring for each, or gives the cantus firmus to a different voice. One *Dum transisset* for example has the melody in the tenor (the favourite place for it in the responds), while the other has it in the mean (very unusually). Both are fine works, but the Alleluia of the former is

(15.Ex. 11.)

especially good, with its pealing imitations (15.Ex. 11.) which, like a
number of other passages by Sheppard, exploit the top of the treble
register fairly ruthlessly. The ostinato character of the treble recalls
some passages in Tallis's responds, but it is less common in Sheppard
than in Tallis.

The first *Non conturbetur cor vestrum* has the melody in the treble (the second most common place for it in responds). The closing Alleluia eschews the rhythmic variety and melisma of *15.Ex. 11.* for movement predominantly in minims: it recalls the Alleluia of Tallis's *Dum transisset* (*4.Ex. 11.* above), but it lacks the same sense of overall planning, direction and shape, while the point itself has much less character, and is weakened by being treated very inexactly.

The four solo responds are most delightful small-scale pieces without equal-note cantus firmus. *In pace* and *In manus*, which form a pair liturgically because they are both for Compline in Lent, are linked musically as well by common scoring, similarity of general method and the sharing of an important musical phrase. Each is basically imitative, with paired entries predominating; a few points paraphrase the plainsong. Chordal phrases come at the most important sectional endings: they follow rests, and repeat the preceding words as a kind of

(16.Ex. 11.)

summing-up. *16.Ex. 11.* demonstrates this, and also shows at 'x' the lovely phrase with parallel thirds which appears four times in each piece.

In their hymns Tallis and Sheppard differ sometimes quite markedly. While Tallis always has the cantus firmus at the top, Sheppard sometimes has it in the tenor, the mean or even the bass. Sheppard almost always presents the proper plainsongs in equal notes throughout; most commonly the signature is ¢ in all verses, but ¢ appears in the final verses of *Aeterne rex altissime* and several other hymns (see Chapter 3, section on Tempo). The major prolation signature ℂ is used in the *last* verses of *Beata nobis gaudia* and *Jesu salvator saeculi Verbum*, while with Tallis it always comes at the beginning. Decoration of the plainsong under ℂ is generally more limited than in Tallis; phrase structure is less simple and clear-cut. Sheppard's scoring is the more adventurous.

In *Sacris solemniis* for example trebles and means divide from time to time to make eight-part writing possible, although because of rests more than six real parts are rarely sounding. In *A solis ortus cardine* the outer verses are for seven parts; the inner two have divided trebles and therefore an eighth line. Each pair of verses is musically the same, apart from the usual but not invariable practice of having the two counter-tenors exchange parts for the repeat. Incidentally identical *outer* verses, which are also found in *Sacris solemniis*, are never a feature of Tallis's hymns; and even in Sheppard's three other settings with repeated verses it is neighbouring verses which are the same.

The hymn *Jesu salvator saeculi Redemptis* and the respond *Laudem dicite* form a kind of pair, because both works belong to first Vespers of All Saints, and both employ the same vocal forces. Other hymns and responds linked in this way by common scoring and common liturgical placing are *Ave maris stella* and *Christi virgo dilectissima*, *Hostis Herodes impie* and *Reges Tharsis*. One wonders if these pairs are isolated survivors from some yearly cycle of hymn-respond pairs for Vespers at Magdalen College or the Chapel Royal.

Sheppard's other works with equal-note cantus firmus include several ritual antiphons. *Libera nos salva nos* for Trinity Sunday exists in two settings: the first has the plainsong in breves in the bass, the second, a mere eleven bars long, has a faburden bass in semibreves. *Media vita in morte sumus* is a most masterly six-part setting of the long antiphon used at Nunc dimittis in the third and fourth weeks of Lent, and its three verses. Sheppard's setting the text complete—without leaving the beginning or the verses in plainchant—does not mean that performance was extra-liturgical and composition therefore post-1559 as might be imagined from various comments in Chapter 10. John Mason's setting in Peterhouse of *O rex gloriose*, the other antiphon with three verses which was sung at Nunc dimittis in the last part of Lent, is similar to Sheppard's *Media vita* in form. In other ritual antiphons without verses such as the *Miserere* settings in Ritson—but not Sheppard's own (*Libera nos*) *salva nos*—the beginning is set. Sheppard's use in *Media vita* of a cantus firmus in breves instead of semibreves not only contributes to the work's exceptional length, but also encourages a more spacious harmonic rhythm than normal—most notably in the fittingly broad and solemn treatment of the opening words. The 'Sancte Deus' section hints at the subsequent variety of linear activity with its initial measured style and its later more animated writing. 'Sancte fortis' is remarkable for its appropriately lively motifs with dotted rhythms (*17.Ex. 11.*). The verses 'Ne projicias' and 'Noli

(17.Ex. 11.)

claudere' are for the lower voices only, and virtually ignore the plainsong, while 'Qui cognoscis' is for divided trebles and divided means,
with the bass paraphrasing the chant.

The remaining *alternatim* works also ignore the plainsong, or state it
less directly than those with equal-note cantus firmus. The processional
psalms at second Vespers of Easter Day, *Laudate pueri* and *In exitu
Israel*, have the faburdens of the psalm tones in the bass; each even-
numbered verse is set, with a single Alleluia appended, in simple
functional style. The four-part Magnificat has the first half of tone 1
in the bass at 'Sicut erat', but although the plainsong may occasionally
be traced in decorated form, as at 'Fecit potentiam', normally neither
it nor the faburden appears to be present.

Psalm-motets, votive antiphons and Masses make up the comparatively small group of works whose texts Sheppard sets complete. The
psalms employ full texture continuously, with rather stiff imitation
basically similar to that of Tallis's motets. *Beati omnes* and *Judica me*

(18.Ex. 11.)

Deus (*18.Ex. 11.*) have some repetition, usually of very brief passages,
although in the former a repeat of the whole of verse 1 (words and
music) follows on without a break after the last verse (compare Robert

Johnson's *Domine in virtute tua*). Harrison points for comparison to the arrangement in 'an antiphon with psalm *Ipsum*',[17] where the antiphon, heard in full at the end, has the same words as the opening of the psalm. But liturgical performance is *not* implied, because the Gloria Patri, which must follow a psalm and precede its antiphon, has been omitted and cannot be inserted.

Confitebor tibi is something of a mystery. Its text is the Canticle of Isaiah (Isaiah 12), but it deviates considerably from the Vulgate version used as one of the psalms at Lauds on Mondays. *Confitebor tibi* includes Sheppard's only experiments with 'two plus three' antiphonal writing in the manner of Taverner.

Since Sheppard was probably not active before about 1540, it is not surprising that there are, apart from fragments, only two votive antiphons by him. *Gaude virgo christipera*, which unusually for so late a piece has a rhyming text, appears to be broadly similar to Tallis's *Gaude gloriosa*, except that there is more melisma; unfortunately the treble part has been lost. *Gaudete coelicolae omnes*, a smaller-scale piece, is an antiphon of All Saints.

The Masses range from the alternatim *Playnsong Masse for a Mene*, a setting in black plainsong notation plus a few single (white) minims with a mean as the highest of four voices, to the exciting six-part *Cantate*. The latter is in the festal tradition because it is more richly scored and longer than the other settings, but like Tallis's *Puer natus* it is on a much smaller scale than Taverner's longer Masses or Fayrfax's (some 400 bars instead of 600 or 700).

The name *Cantate* ('Sing!') is possibly connected with the melodic material on which the work is based. The three themes quoted in

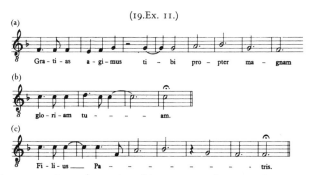

(19.Ex. 11.)

(a) Gra - ti - as   a - gi - mus   ti – bi   pro – pter   ma – gnam

(b) glo - ri - am   tu - - - - am.

(c) Fi - li - us ___ Pa - - - - - - - tris.

19.Ex. 11. constitute the main subject-matter. In some six-part writing these themes function as a long-note tenor; in other full passages and in some reduced ones they are the subjects of imitation. The magnificent

(20.Ex. 11.)

ending of the Gloria (*20.Ex. 11.*) shows the former approach at 'x' and the latter at 'y'.

Western Wynde is the only other Mass to use pre-existing material. It is the least interesting of the three *Western Wynde* settings, and probably the least accomplished of Sheppard's major works. Apart from obvious inferiority in style and finish, important differences from Taverner's *Western Wynde* are more frequent imitation, including anticipatory imitations worked during brief rests in the melody part, and less use of reduced textures. Sheppard's setting is little more than half as long as Taverner's, having only twenty-four statements of the tune, fourteen of them without the final phrase. There is a much reduced use of sequence and triplet passages, an unfortunate unwillingness to let the tune move away from the treble, and a simpler style than Taverner's in the $\frac{\emptyset}{3}$ sections.

The two remaining Masses are stylistically much more advanced than *Western Wynde* and presumably later in date. Reduced scoring is now virtually eliminated, verbal repetition is adopted (as indeed it is in *Cantate* and the *Playnsong Masse*), and imitation is much more important. The very title of one of them signals deliberate experiment, and acknowledges the source of inspiration: the *French Mass*, in its polished imitative writing, recalls the shorter Masses of such Frenchmen as Gombert.[18] As in Taverner's *Meane Mass*, the imitation is effectively set off by occasional chordal passages, although Sheppard employs the signature C for them instead of Taverner's $\odot$ and $\frac{\emptyset}{3}$. The strangely titled *Be not afraide* is a less interesting work, lacking the chordal passages and having a somewhat limited melodic vocabulary.

CHRISTOPHER TYE

After Tallis Christopher Tye is the most widely known composer from the mid sixteenth-century period, largely because of his important contribution to the earliest music of the Reformed church. His Latin work has suffered a number of bad losses, but what remains complete shows a very considerable technical command.

Tye was born about 1500, if he was the choirboy of that name who sang at King's, Cambridge from 1508 to 1513.[19] He was certainly a lay-clerk there in the late 1520s and the 1530s, and received the Cambridge degrees of Bachelor and Doctor of Music in 1536 and 1545. From 1541 to 1561 he was master of the choristers at nearby Ely Cathedral. Tye was a member of Edward VI's Chapel, and dedicated his *Acts of the Apostles* to the young king. He may even have been Edward's music teacher. Tye's fragmentary *Domine Deus coelestis*, a prayer for a king, must have been written with Edward in mind because it seems to have been written at or near the beginning of a reign and for a young king, as the following passage indicates, in which the

Table 12: Christopher Tye

Masses

à6: Euge bone
à5: unnamed setting*
à4: Western Wynde

Proper of the Lady Mass

à4: Alleluia *Per te Dei*, Kyrie *Orbis factor*, Tellus flumina *and* Unde nostris (*vv. 4a nd 8 from sequence 'Post partum'*)

Votive Antiphons

à7: Peccavimus cum patribus
à6: Ave caput Christi,† Te Deum laudamus†
à4: Sub tuam protectionem

Magnificats

à6: two settings†

Respond

à4: In pace *in idipsum* (*Lent*)

Processional Antiphons

à6: Christus resurgens (*Easter*)
à5: *Salve regina* . . . Ad te clamamus

Processional Hymn

à4: Gloria laus et honor (*Palm Sunday*)

Psalm-Motets

à6: Cantate Domino canticum novum laus ejus (*Ps. 149*),* In quo corriget (*Ps. 119: 9–16*)†
à5: Miserere mei Deus miserere (*Ps. 57*), Omnes gentes plaudite (*Ps. 47*)

Motets

à6: Domine Deus coelestis†
à5: Quaesumus omnipotens*

Christopher Tye, The Latin Church Music, 2 vols., has complete pieces, plus complete sections from a few fragmentary ones including *Domine Deus coelestis* and *In quo corriget*.

*Imperfectly preserved.
†Fragmentary.

writer asks that the king may be 'sharpsighted in executing the affairs of the realm, circumspect and scrupulous in giving justice': 'Da ut . . . perspicax in obeundis regni negotiis, consideratus et diligens in judicia afferenda, constans et sedulus in tua, Domine, Catholica fide et religione restauranda et tuenda vehemens et invictus'.[20] (It is probably no accident that the opening of *Domine Deus coelestis* briefly corresponds with the opening of the psalm-motet *In quo corriget* ('Wherewithal shall *a young man* cleanse his way?')). Use of the word 'Catholica' in our quotation does not contradict an Edwardine dating; it appears in the English Prayer Book Creeds, and the Anglican Church considers itself both Catholic and Reformed. The 'restoring of the Catholic faith' mentioned in Tye's piece was not a plea for the return to papal allegiance, but for that restoring of the church to its primitive state, free of medieval abuses, which was the aim of the Reformers. *Domine Deus coelestis* must be the only Latin composition definitely assignable to Edward's reign, but *Quaesumus omnipotens*, whose text is discussed later, may be contemporary with it.

In 1560 Tye was ordained, and the following year became Rector of Doddington in Cambridgeshire, He died in 1572 or 1573. One imagines that Tye's work as a composer was more or less finished by the time he resigned his Ely post and moved to the country. His regular membership of the Chapel Royal had apparently ceased before 1561 as he is never mentioned in the Check-Book. However Anthony à Wood's well-known anecdote, despite its author's reputation for unreliability, suggests that the break with London was not total: 'Dr Tye was a peevish and humoursome man, especially in his latter days. And sometimes playing on the organ in the chapel of Queen Elizabeth, which contained much music, but little delight to the ear, she would send the verger to tell him he played out of tune: whereupon he sent word that her ears were out of tune'.[21]

Tye is unlikely to have written much Latin church music after the death of Henry VIII. He did remain at Ely during Mary's reign, but his personal position may well have been strongly Protestant: this is suggested by his close connections with Edward VI and his acquaintance with the Protestant firebrand Richard Cox, who was first Archdeacon of Ely and later Bishop.

Probably Tye's most important Latin work is the six-part Mass *Euge bone*, which has been supposed widely, but without any definite evidence, to have been his Doctoral exercise of 1545. The title is a mystery. There was no ritual item 'Euge bone'; but the Common of one Confessor or Bishop had a respond and antiphon 'Euge *serve* bone'.[22] The melody of neither is used in the Mass however, and there appears to be no other borrowed material in it. The six-part scoring implies use on an important occasion, but the Mass is a fairly compact one. The desire for compression led most obviously to the employment of just six chords for 'Sanctus, Sanctus, Sanctus' (compare the treatment of the same words in Tallis's four-part Mass, and of 'Holy, Holy, Holy' in the English arrangements of Taverner's *Small Devotion* and *Meane Mass* (Bodleian Library MSS. Mus. Sch. e. 420–2) made about three years after Tye is supposed to have composed *Euge bone*). There is some limited repetition of sets of imitative entries; but this technique is unusual in Tye's Latin music, other examples being confined to the textless, probably instrumental, *Amavit* and *Rubum quem*. Antiphony in which the lower three voices answer the upper three, is found in a few places, but the second statement is less of an exact repetition than it is in antiphonal writing by Taverner.

In his two other Masses however, Tye does seem to be in Taverner's debt. One is a setting of *Western Wynde* which stylistic considerations indicate is later than Taverner's work. In fact it seems designed to complement or 'answer' Taverner's similarly-scored piece, because all twenty-nine statements of the tune come in the mean, the one voice from which Taverner excluded it. Another link between the two Masses is the treatment of the opening of the Sanctus, where Tye has six statements of a descending figure (from *b flat* to G) in the bass, Taverner five ascending ones of the same compass in the same voice. Tye's is an accomplished piece, but less varied than Taverner's: one notes in particular its very limited use of sequence and the lack of triplets. Some rhythmic contrast is however again provided by occasional changes from ₵ to ₃°. The statements with ₵ signature all have their rhythmic regularity disturbed by the extra semibreve's rest which is always inserted between the second and third phrases.[23] Tye differs from Taverner (and Sheppard) here, as he does in usually making the third phrase rhythmically similar to the second by re-using the dotted minim, crotchet, minim, minim figure and an intermediate minim rest. He is also much more inclined to ornament the melody, particularly at the end to make a suspension possible.

The Mass in the Peterhouse partbooks is scored for the same voices as Taverner's *Meane Mass*, which it resembles in many other ways. One has the impression that Tye's work is deliberately based on Taverner's; but the novel technical features are handled much less convincingly. The 'Et in terra' (*21.Ex. 11.*)—compare *5.Ex. 9.*—is a similar kind of fugal opening to Taverner's, but becomes rather bogged down on a G minor chord in the middle and ends in free melisma instead of maintaining the imitation. Tye like Taverner uses the signature ☉ for short chordal five-part sections; occasionally introduces passages in ₃°; likes four-part textures, so far as one can judge with the tenor lost; and has a common ending to the movements as well as a head-motif. He does not however link any of the ☉ or ₃° passages by repetition as Taverner does.

The text of the short antiphon *Sub tuam protectionem* begins by

(21.Ex. 11.)

following that of a Marian antiphon from the feasts of the Virgin's Conception and Nativity, and the opening of the proper plainsong is even referred to; but the work continues as an independent Jesus-antiphon. *Ave caput Christi*, now fragmentary, was a much longer piece with a text of four-line stanzas each hailing some aspect of Christ's Passion. Although the opening words of *Peccavimus cum patribus* come from a psalm, the work seems to be another Jesus-antiphon, its second section ending with the words 'ad te supplices confugimus, benignissime Jesu'. *Te Deum laudamus*, of which only a single voice survives, has the text of that great hymn complete, not in *alternatim* fashion, and must have been an antiphon of the Trinity or a motet (compare Aston's *Te Deum* mentioned in Chapter 9). The *Salve regina* is likely to have been sung as a processional antiphon, the original use of its words before their adoption in votive antiphons: *alternatim* performance is indicated by the setting only of the section 'Ad te clamamus . . . lachrymarum valle'; but the proper plainsong is not incorporated or even paraphrased.

Tye's psalm-motets, like some by Whyte and Mundy and unlike Tallis's or Sheppard's, still somewhat resemble the votive antiphon, with the traditional contrast between solo and full sections being main-tained except in the imperfectly preserved *Cantate Domino*. The brief *Omnes gentes plaudite* is perhaps the best of them, the jubilant words inspiring very attractive vigorous music, most especially in the final section which culminates in triumphant homophony (*22.Ex. 11.*). The limited use of homophony, the size of the work and the voices

(22.Ex. 11.)

needed to sing it recall Taverner's *Mater Christi* and *Christe Jesu*, but the imitation is more highly developed, and verbal repetition is prominent at times. And although the four solo sections all involve first the top two voices and then the lower three, lack of shared material, or limited use of it, makes the effect rather different from that of Taverner's similarly scored antiphonal writing.

Tye wrote two other extra-liturgical motets whose texts are prayers. One is *Domine Deus coelestis* which, although now fragmentary, clearly resembled the larger antiphon in scale and manner. The second section 'Da illi Domine pectus' is a canon for mean and countertenor with a supporting bass; there are very similar canonic passages in Mundy's *Maria virgo sanctissima* (at 'te Pater in filiam'), *Vox Patris coelestis* ('ex corde purissimo') and *Eructavit cor meum* ('Audi filia'), and we have already noticed canonic writing in Tallis. *Quaesumus omnipotens* is similar in style to *Domine Deus coelestis*, but rather shorter. It begins and ends like a prayer for Henry VII found in one copy of the Sarum Missal (1508)[24] which was an expanded and individualised version of the Collect at the Mass *pro Rege*. No king is mentioned, and the prayer is now offered for 'thy servants' instead of only for a king; but such adaptation of a royal collect might well require royal acquiescence: *Quaesumus omnipotens* might therefore have been performed in the Chapel Royal, perhaps even under Edward VI.

SOME LESSER COMPOSERS AND ANONYMOUS MUSIC

The Gyffard and Christ Church partbooks contain a number of works by lesser composers who, like Tallis, Sheppard and Tye, are known or assumed to have been active before the death of Henry VIII.

Gyffard has works by four men known also from Peterhouse: Knyght (with three works, including a stylish Alleluia *Obtine sacris*), Appleby (whose *Mass for a Mene* is a rather pedestrian effort in something of the same style as Taverner's similarly titled piece), Bramston, and Whytbrook (composer of a Mass *Apon the square* briefly noticed in Chapter 12, section on William Mundy). Other composers, most of them represented by single works, include Philip Alcoke, Robert Barber, (?Thomas) Byrd (joint composer with Sheppard and Mundy of *In exitu Israel*), Robert Cooper (probably the oldest composer in Gyffard, having graduated Doctor of Music at Cambridge in 1502;[25] his work is a rather old-fashioned *Gloria in excelsis* for boys' voices), John Ensdale, John Hake, Christopher Hoskins, Hyett, Robert Okeland, Stenings, and Thomas Wryght. Finally there are three composers known also from the Christ Church partbooks and mentioned in Chapter 10 or earlier in this Chapter: Robert Johnson, John Redford and Philip van Wilder. Gyffard has unusually many anonymous pieces for a mid or late sixteenth-century source, eighteen out of ninety-four. There is a St Matthew Passion and four settings of the Asperges (these seem to be among the oldest works in the manuscript),[26] a *Vidi aquam*, a setting of the Jesus Mass Proper, a Kyrie, a Te Deum on the faburden, several responds and short antiphons.

Christ Church contains Wood's *Exsurge Domine* (see Chapter 10) and a *Dum transisset* by John Strabridge. There are a few Continental pieces including *In convertendo* and *Ubi est Abel*, ascribed to (Robert) Douglas, a Scot, but by Lassus.

Robert Whyte, William Mundy, Robert Parsons, William Byrd's 1575 pieces

Whyte, Mundy and Parsons were too young to have written much if anything in Henry VIII's reign; Byrd was only four when the king died. So some of the music discussed below was written during Mary's reign, some of it after the Elizabethan Settlement. This music is on the whole less interesting and less varied than that surveyed above. Whyte, Mundy and Parsons are all proficient composers, justly quite widely known in the sixteenth century and worthy of more than an occasional hearing today, but none can inspire great enthusiasm. And Byrd's 1575 pieces, although containing much of interest, are less rewarding than the later music of his maturity which has gained him such enduring love and esteem.

ROBERT WHYTE

When Robert Whyte applied for the Cambridge Bachelor's degree in 1560, he had studied music for ten years; so he may well have been born between about 1530 and 1535, by which time Tallis and Tye were in their twenties or thirties. In 1561 Whyte became master of the choristers at Ely in succession to his father-in-law, Tye; and before his death in 1574 he had occupied similar posts at Chester and Westminster.[1]

Whyte's works fall into two main groups: those which could have been used in Sarum services and devotions under Mary, and those (psalm-motets and Lamentations) which one would imagine were written in Elizabeth's reign.

The Sarum works comprise antiphons, hymns and a respond, all on equal-note cantus firmi, and a large-scale six-part Magnificat which, like two of Taverner's settings, has a psalm tone as the tenor of the full-choir sections. The Magnificat bears the date 1570 in the fragmentary source Bodleian Library MS. Mus. Sch. e. 423, but the style makes it

Table 13: Robert Whyte

Votive Antiphons
à6: Tota pulchra es*
à5: Regina coeli*

Magnificat
à6: one setting*

Respond
à4: *Libera me* Domine (*Office of the Dead*)

Hymn
à5: four settings of *Christe qui lux es*/Precamur sancte Domine (*Compline*)

Psalm-Motets
à6: Ad te levavi oculos (*Ps. 123*),* Deus misereatur (*Ps. 67*), Domine non est exaltatum (*Ps. 131*), three settings of Domine quis habitabit (*Ps. 15*)*
à5: Appropinquet deprecatio mea (*Ps. 119: 169–76*), Exaudiat te Dominus (*Ps. 20*), Justus es Domine (*Ps. 119: 137–44*), Manus tuae fecerunt me (*Ps. 119: 73–80*), Miserere mei Deus (*Ps. 51*), Portio mea Domine (*Ps. 119: 57–64*)

Lamentations
à6: one set*
à5: one set

Whyte's work is published in *TCM*, v.

*Imperfectly preserved.

very much easier to take this as the year of copying than as the year of composition. For example at 'Sicut locutus', a four-part section with the plainsong in the mean, mostly in longs and breves, the accompanying parts have numerous crotchet runs which, although considerably more numerous and more hectic, give something of the same effect as the similarly scored 'Et incarnatus' of Taverner's *Gloria tibi Trinitas*. But there are also traces of the repetitive techniques so characteristic of Whyte in his full-choir motets. The key point here is the exchanging of material between pairs of voices of equal range throughout a four-part or six-part texture (as shown in *1.Ex. 12*. below); Tallis and Sheppard of course had reversed a *single* pair of (countertenor) parts when the music for one verse of a hymn was re-used, or very occasionally when a set of entries was re-stated.

The words of *Tam pulchra es* were used as the first antiphon at first Vespers of the Assumption; but Whyte's piece was probably for votive use, like his *Regina coeli*, whose text is not in the Sarum liturgy. The *Tam pulchra* text came originally (as basically did the words of Mundy's *Vox Patris coelestis*) from the Song of Solomon, that rich source of Marian imagery so oddly neglected by other English composers since Dunstable. Whyte's setting has well-worked six-part writing with the plainsong in the tenor, and ends with an impressive tonic pedal. *Regina coeli* is also very stylish, with lively runs for some of the Alleluias. Votive antiphons with equal-note cantus firmus are rare; apart from Whyte's and those by Mower in Ritson there are three in Gyffard: Wryght's *Nesciens mater*, Hoskins's *Speciosa facta es*, and Knyght's *Sancta Maria virgo*.

Whyte deserves to be remembered most of all for his large and important contribution to the psalm-motet. His motets fall into a group of seven with solo–full textural contrasts and five with continuous full textures and very strictly worked imitation.

The former group may in turn be sub-divided. The three longest works, *Domine non est exaltatum*, *Domine quis habitabit* II and *Exaudiat te*, all have an intermediate change of signature from triple to duple. *Domine non est exaltatum* is the longest of all, with about 110 bars for five verses; its size results partly from Whyte's frequent use of more than one set of entries for each imitative point (often with the expansion of a crucial melodic interval the second time). There are tiny traces of the repetitive technique of exchange between equal voices, as also in *Domine quis habitabit* II. *Exaudiat te* employs this method a little in some of the four-part writing; it also hints at it in the closing passage, which by retaining the divided countertenors and tenors of the preceding gimel, is in seven parts instead of the five used in other full sections.

The four rather shorter reduced–full motets are settings of sections from Psalm 119. All have between seventy and ninety bars for eight verses, and all begin in duple time. One naturally wonders if these, together with settings of other sections from Psalm 119 by Mundy (three), Parsons (one) and Tye (one), all formed part of some joint effort at treating the longest Psalm complete. Points, all of them dubious admittedly, which suggest that this may *not* be so are the survival of comparatively few sections (nine out of a required twenty-two); the fact that all survivors do not have the same scoring, even among Whyte's group; that those by Parsons and Tye have triple–duple structure while the others do not; that we should not expect Tye to be collaborating with men so much younger than himself.

Four of Whyte's full-choir motets (*Ad te levavi oculos*, *Deus misereatur*, the first and third settings of *Domine quis habitabit*) are continuously imitative. All are in six parts, which allows Whyte to use more pairing of entries than Tallis could within the five-part grouping he preferred.

Repetition is used more widely than by Tallis, sometimes a little in-
sensitively and often rather differently: while the interchanging of
equal voices is important in *Deus misereatur* and *Domine quis habitabit*
III, the re-statement of long sections to produce 'A B B' structure for
example is avoided. *Ad te levavi* begins with three pairs of entries (on an
appropriately rising point of very strong character); these are all
repeated after the music has come to a virtual stop, and the passage is
saved from being completely square and predictable only because
paired entries are a semibreve apart, while the pairs themselves are
five semibreves distant. (This odd five-semibreve interval was used by
Whyte for several similar fugal openings, for instance in the *Miserere*.)
Deus misereatur has all six initial entries evenly spaced, and repeats all
of them, but 'exposition' and 'counter-exposition' are more neatly
dovetailed than in *Ad te levavi*. In *Deus misereatur* the voices are sometimes split into two groups of three (first mean, second countertenor,
second bass; second mean, first countertenor, first bass). Since each
group has one of each type of voice, we have here a kind of double-choir
effect, possibly suggested by the *decani-cantoris* arrangement of English
church music. But the two 'choirs' never actually alternate as in say
Tallis's Dorian service, for six-part writing is maintained throughout;
instead there is frequent repetition with exchange, because each group
often has the same entries, the supporting parts also tending to recur
(*1.Ex. 12.*).

(1.Ex. 12.)   *TCM*, v.66.

Domine quis habitabit III uses the same double-choir technique most of
the time. The first eight imitations (up to 'corde meo') all have the
second mean, countertenor and bass answering the first mean, countertenor and bass. At 'in lingua sua' the order is reversed. After this, until
near the end, membership of each 'choir' is varied. In turn every singer

finds himself grouped with hitherto opposing forces; thus if the choir *were* split into *decani* and *cantoris* sides, the shifting spatial contrasts would be most fascinating. In this way, and by his varied and interesting themes, Whyte transcends the apparently cramping imitative method: *Domine quis* III comes to life as an exciting and originally conceived work.

The remaining psalm-motet, *Miserere mei Deus*, is less uniform texturally than the others. The influence of Tallis is strongly suggested: we find the 'one against four' technique noted in *In jejunio* and the Lamen-

(2.Ex. 12.)   *TCM*, v.149.

tations, *2.Ex. 12.* even showing Tallis's love of repeated notes for solemn declamation. But Whyte uses the techniques he borrows rather indiscriminately, instead of reserving their very special but essentially limited effect for a few key words or phrases. The work seems too long by the time all twenty verses are set.

Both sets of Lamentations treat the six verses 'Heth' to 'Mem'. The first is for five-part full choir throughout, mainly with imitation, but with a little use of 'one against four'. It is about as long as both Tallis's sets of Lamentations together, and like the *Miserere seems* rather long, but its sheer insistency can be quite moving when it is sensitively sung. The second set has some sections for reduced groupings and an initial triple signature; in general manner it is closest to the three psalms which share these characteristics.

WILLIAM MUNDY

William Mundy was head chorister at Westminster Abbey in 1543, and so was born probably *c.* 1528–30. In 1548 he became parish clerk at St Mary-at-Hill, where his father Thomas Mundy had already been sexton and musician for twenty years and where Tallis was in 1536. He moved to St Paul's in about 1560, and was a Gentleman of the Chapel Royal from 1563 to 1591, probably the year of his death. His son John continued the family's musical tradition: he held appointments at Eton and Windsor, and graduated Doctor of Music at Oxford.[2]

Table 14: William Mundy

Masses
à4: Apon the square I, Apon the square II

Proper of the Mass
à4: Alleluias *Per te Dei* and *Post partum* (*Lady Mass*), Kyrie (*Easter*)

Votive Antiphons
à6: Maria virgo sanctissima,* Vox Patris coelestis
à5: Gaude virgo mater Christi†

Magnificats
à5: two settings†
à4: one setting

Respond
à5: *Videte* miraculum (*Purification*)*

Hymn
à5: *A solis ortus cardine*/Beatus auctor saeculi (*Christmas*)*
Processional Psalm with Antiphon
à4: In exitu Israel (*Pss. 114 and 115, Easter*)—composed jointly with John Sheppard and Thomas(?) Byrd

Psalm-Motets
à6: Adolescentulus sum ego (*Ps. 119: 141-4*), Domine non est exaltatum (*Ps. 131*), Domine quis habitabit (*Ps. 15*),* Eructavit cor meum (*Ps. 45: 1-12, 16-18*),* Miserere mei Deus (*Ps. 51*)†
à5: Adhaesit pavimento (*Ps. 119: 25-32*),* /((*25-32*),* Beati) Beati immaculati(*Ps. 119: 1-8*),* Memor esto verbi tui (*Ps. 119: 49-56*),* Noli aemulari (*Ps. 37: 1-9, 26-27, 40-41*)*

Motets
à5: Beatus et sanctus (*Rev. 20: 6*),* Sive vigilem sive dormiam*
à3: Exsurge Christe defende nos

The psalm-motets (except *Miserere*) and the antiphons *Maria virgo* and *Vox Patris* are published in *Early English Church Music*, ii.

*Imperfectly preserved.
†Fragmentary.

William Mundy wrote some pieces for the old services, psalm-motets, and a considerable body of English church music (some of this in Edward VI's reign).[3] His Latin work is all very accomplished technically, and avoids some of Whyte's rigidity, having fewer paired entries and very little exchanging of material between voices of equal range. Although it commands considerable respect, it is likely to inspire little positive enthusiasm. In the 1580s however, Robert Dow, compiler of Christ Church MSS. 984–8, thought Mundy second to Byrd, and punned on 'Mundy' and 'Monday' as follows: 'Dies lunae / Ut lucem solis sequitur lux proxima lunae / Sic tu post Birdum Munde secunde venis'.

The most important Sarum works are the long six-part antiphons. They invite comparison with Tallis's *Gaude gloriosa*, but melisma is limited a little more strictly through greater use of verbal repetition, except in the Amens. Mundy's antiphons are probably the only surviving ones in the 'old style' by so young a composer: Whyte, as we have seen, built his on equal-note cantus firmi. The text of Mundy's *Vox Patris coelestis* is a troping of the Assumption antiphon 'Tam pulchra es' which originally came from the Song of Solomon. *Maria virgo sanctissima* is so extravagantly worded even for a votive antiphon that the writer is forced to remind us that Mary is not actually a goddess, although anything good which the world has it has through her because she is the mother of the Saviour.

The basis of Mundy's Masses is indicated in the title of each: *Apon the square*. Contrary to Ludford's practice, the Kyrie squares are not re-used in later movements; instead each movement has a different melody. (The Sanctus melodies are among those squares preserved in the fifteenth-century British Museum Lansdowne MS. 462 (f. iv.).) Mundy employs the squares more or less continuously, most frequently in the lowest voice. Four-part textures are little used, three-part writing being the favourite. The Mass *Apon the square* by Whytbrook, grouped with Mundy's Masses in Gyffard, is similar in construction; it employs the same squares as Mundy's second Mass, except in its Kyrie.[4]

Mundy's psalm-motets, like Whyte's, may be divided between a group with reduced–full textural contrasts and another without. But the differences tend to be less marked; for instance *Beati immaculati* has some reduced writing in the second major section, but its first section is full throughout. Technically there is sometimes less difference. The extreme rigidity of the imitation in Whyte's full-choir pieces is avoided by Mundy in his full motets, while his reduced–full works have even less of the old exuberance than Whyte's. In fact the closest approach to the 'double choir' method of Whyte's full motets comes in the six-part triple gimel section 'Tota die miseretur' of a reduced–full work, *Noli aemulari*. But on the other hand two full works, *Adolescentulus sum ego* and *Domine quis habitabit* begin with 'double subject' imitation, a technique described in connection with Byrd's work, and presumably learned either from him or from Ferrabosco.

ROBERT PARSONS

Parsons became a Gentleman of the Chapel Royal in 1563,[5] the same year as Mundy, and so was probably about the same age. It is in any case clear that he was still a fairly young man at the time of his death in 1570 from the little eulogy at the end of his *Retribue servo tuo*

Table 15: Robert Parsons

Votive Antiphons
à5: Ave Maria, O bone Jesu illumina

Magnificat
à6: one setting†

Hymn
à6: *Jam Christus astra*/Solemnis urgebat dies (*Whitsun*)*

Psalm-Motets
à6: Domine quis habitabit (*Ps. 15: 1–4*)*
à5: Retribue servo tuo (*Ps. 119: 17–24*)

Motets
à6: Anima Christi,† Credo quod redemptor meus vivit,*
à5: Libera me Domine, Peccantem me quotidie*
à? Magnus es Domine in aeternum†

*Imperfectly preserved.
†Fragmentary.

in one of Robert Dow's partbooks: 'Qui tantus primo, Parsone, in flore fuisti / Quantus in autumno ni morerere fores'. Today most of Parsons's Latin pieces are incomplete or fragmentary, but such works as *Credo quod redemptor* and *Domine quis habitabit*, as well as the English First Service with its eight-part Nunc dimittis and seven-part Gloria in excelsis, help us to understand something of Dow's enthusiasm.

We know that Parsons was active before 1552—his first English service follows the 1549 text[6]—and so some of his Latin music, including the antiphons, Magnificat and *Jam Christus astra*, presumably dates from Mary's reign. The three responds from the Office of the Dead were clearly set after the Sarum rite was abandoned (see Chapter

10). We can probably give a post-1562 dating to *Credo quod redemptor*, a full-choir motet without plainsong cantus firmus, because it shows a debt to Ferrabosco's setting of these words, which Parsons is most likely to have encountered after the Italian had come to England. Parsons models his opening theme very closely on Ferrabosco's[7] (*3.Ex.*

(3.Ex. 12.)

Parsons

Cre - do quod re-demptor me - us vi-(vit)

Ferrabosco

Cre - do quod re-dem - - - ptor

12.), but it is interesting to note that he maintains the characteristically English 'A B B' form. *Ave Maria*, unlike any other antiphon, is basically in this form as well; the 'B' section begins at 'Et benedictum fructum ventris tui', the Amen standing as an additional short coda section. The fact that Parsons has left three works with texts from the Office of the Dead, but only two psalm-motets (the full-choir *Domine quis habitabit* and the reduced–full *Retribue servo tuo*) may suggest some Roman Catholic sympathies on his part.

WILLIAM BYRD: A NOTE ON THE 1575 CANTIONES

The career of William Byrd (1543–1623), who is unquestionably the greatest composer of the Elizabethan–Jacobean Golden Age and arguably the greatest of all English composers, just overlaps that of Tallis. We shall look briefly at the most important point of overlap only, the 1575 pieces. These works are unimportant compared with those published in 1589, 1591, 1605 and 1607, but already show an impressive and adventurous technique and incorporate several novel features.

Little is known of Byrd before 1575 except that he was organist of Lincoln Cathedral from 1563 until 1572 when he moved to London, having become a Gentleman of the Chapel Royal in 1570.[8] Like many of his contemporaries, he was both a Roman Catholic and a loyal and trusted subject of the Queen.

It is possible that Byrd was Tallis's pupil,[9] but there are not many signs of the older man's influence in his music. Regularity of imitation and repetition have largely been discarded. Only in *Laudate pueri*, an adaptation of an instrumental fantasia,[10] are they central; and even here there is perhaps a closer resemblance to Whyte than to Tallis. But it was probably in emulation of Tallis's canonic works that Byrd wrote *Diliges Dominum* and *Miserere mihi Domine*. The eight-part *Diliges Dominum*, frankly a very dull piece, is a crab canon; that is to say the music of the first section is repeated backwards for the second, each of the pairs of equal voices exchanging lines. Towards the end *Miserere mihi* has canonic treatment of the proper plainsong in the top two voices over two free parts and another independent two-part canon. Earlier the plainsong had been presented in equal notes, first in the highest, then in the lowest part.

Joseph Kerman has suggested[11] that Byrd was indebted to Robert Parsons, for he seems to have modelled his *Libera me Domine* on the older composer's setting, incorporating the beginning of the plainsong into the polyphony and devising a similar imitative opening. We know that Byrd made a keyboard arrangement of Parsons's most famous *In nomine*; we have thought it possible that Parsons's sympathies were Roman Catholic as Byrd's certainly were; and we have noted Parsons's contact with Alfonso Ferrabosco, the most powerful influence on Byrd's early development.

Alfonso Ferrabosco, Byrd's exact contemporary, who was in the Queen's service between 1562 and 1578, was by no means an outstanding composer, but his style, incorporating some of the most up-to-date Continental ideas, would have seemed very novel and challenging to young Englishmen in the 1560s and 70s; later his madrigals had some limited influence on the development of the English madrigal. By 1575 Byrd had learned about 'double subject' imitation; *nota nere* notation; a new form of accidentalism; and the progression $\frac{7\text{-}6\text{-}5}{3\text{-}4\text{---}}{}_{-3}$ over a dominant pedal, with its very strong dominant seventh at the beginning.

In 'double subject' imitation, as the name implies, two distinct points are used simultaneously. These may be announced together, or as usual in Byrd, the second may initially follow the first and subsequently be used to some extent independently of it: the opening of *Domine secundum actum meum*, which is closely modelled on the beginning of Ferrabosco's *Domine non secundum peccata mea*,[12] is one example, the 'et rursum' section of *Libera me Domine et pone me* another (4.*Ex.* 12.). Byrd's handling of double subject imitation in the 1575 motets is less confident and less polished than it later became, but its introduction is a most important step which gives enormous new scope for contrapuntal development, because a substantial passage can now be built on

(4.Ex. 12.)   *TCM*, ix.70.

a small unit of text without recourse either to extended melisma or straight repetition.

The *nota nere* or 'black note' manner originated in the 1540s in the Italian madrigal: it involved a marked shift to shorter values than formerly, with the black notes, crotchets and quavers, assuming much greater weight and importance. Ferrabosco used this kind of notation in his hymn *Ecce jam noctis*,[13] of which Byrd's *Siderum rector* (5.Ex. 12.) is in many ways the twin. *O lux beata Trinitas* also employs the new form of notation, and the influence of it is briefly felt elsewhere.

The new boldness in the use of accidentals shows itself most clearly at the beginning of *Aspice Domine*, especially where two parts have the notes A A F sharp G sharp A; the F sharps in the first two bars of 4.Ex. 12. and the c'–c' *sharp* movement are again not typical of earlier English music. But none of these accidentals would have surprised Ferrabosco in the least: in fact the latter's *Benedic anima mea* has one section which even uses D, A and E sharps to take it into F sharp major![14]

Si-de rum re-ctor,De - us al-me no - stris   Par-ce jam cul-pis, vi - ti - a re - mit-tens:

Continuous imitation within a full-choir texture is Byrd's basic technique in the 1575 motets. But some use is made of homophony, antiphonal contrasts and other short passages of reduced scoring. *Emendemus in melius*, the setting of a Lenten respond complete with verse which is Byrd's first item in the *Cantiones*, is basically homophonic throughout. It is punctuated by short rests in all parts. Here one is reminded of Tallis's hymns; but the general effect is very different: there is no single dominant rhythm, Byrd being much more obviously responsive to the changing demands of the words, for example introducing a brisker rhythm than anywhere else at the word 'subito', 'suddenly'.

Notes

The following abbreviations are used in notes:

CMM: Corpus Mensurabilis Musicae;
Harrison, *MMB*: F. Ll. Harrison, *Music in Medieval Britain*;
JAMS: Journal of the American Musicological Society;
MB: Musica Britannica;
MD: Musica Disciplina;
MGG: Die Musik in Geschichte und Gegenwart;
ML: Music and Letters;
NOHM: The New Oxford History of Music;
PRMA: Proceedings of the Royal Musical Association;
TCM: Tudor Church Music.
Full details of publications mentioned in notes may be found in the Bibliography.

Chapter 1 (pp. 1-7)

1. J. A. Froude, *Life and Letters of Erasmus*, p. 116.
2. John Major, *Historia Majoris Britanniae tam Angliae quam Scotiae*, Paris, 1521. A fuller quotation may be found in *The Treasury of English Church Music*, i. p. xiii.
3. Over twenty manuscripts are described in inventories from King's College, Cambridge (1529) and Magdalen College, Oxford (1522-4)—see Harrison, *MMB*, pp. 431-3—yet not one survives today.
4. See for example Harrison, *MMB*, pp, 177-8, 429.
5. Harrison, *MMB*, pp. xiv-xv.
6. Harrison, *MMB*, p. 2 and Chapter 4.
7. Translation from O. Strunk, *Source Readings in Music History*, p. 195.
8. *MB*, x. pp. xv-xvi.
9. Froude, p. 116.
10. Harrison, *MMB*, p. 219.
11. J. Stevens, *Music and Poetry in the Early Tudor Court*, p. 64.
12. A. Seay, *Music in the Medieval World*, p. 21.
13. There is a good discussion of the problem in W. Apel, *The Harvard Dictionary of Music*, p. 635.
14. J. Lees-Milne, *Tudor Renaissance*, p. 42.
15. A. R. Myers, *England in the Late Middle Ages*, pp. 243-9, gives a brief account of the progress of the New Learning in the early Tudor period.
16. O. Chadwick, *The Reformation*, p. 38. This book has a most useful summary of the Reformation in England to 1559 (pp. 95-136).
17. A. G. Dickens, *The English Reformation*, p. 100.
18. P. le Huray, *Music and the Reformation in England 1549-1660*, pp. 13-17.
19. A. G. Dickens and D. Carr, *The Reformation in England*, p. 132.

Chapter 2 (pp. 8–20)

1. Harrison, *MMB*, p. 1.
2. *The First and Second Prayer Books of Edward VI*, p. 4.
3. Harrison, *MMB*, p. 77.
4. Published as *Graduale Sarisburiense*, ed. W. H. Frere. The books mentioned in notes 4–5, 16, 18–19 below are the sources for most of the liturgical references in this book (descriptions of liturgical forms, identification of cantus firmi, etc.). All are so well indexed that no further references are normally given.
5. *Missale ad Usum . . . Sarum*, ed. F. H. Dickinson.
6. M. and I. Bent, 'Dufay, Dunstable, Plummer—A New Source', *JAMS*, xxii, 1969, pp. 406–7.
7. A most valuable article is H. Baillie, 'Squares', *Acta Musicologica*, xxxii, 1960, p. 178.
8. Harrison, *MMB*, p. 201.
9. Harrison, *MMB*, pp. 432–3.
10. For example, see Harrison, *MMB*, pp. 176–8, 210, 215.
11. See D. Stevens, 'A Unique Tudor Organ Mass', *MD*, vi, 1952, p. 167.
12. The subject has been treated, perhaps somewhat over-imaginatively, in R. Hannas, 'Concerning Deletions in the Polyphonic Mass Credo', *JAMS*, v, 1952, p. 155.
13. Bent, p. 413; *MB*, viii. 21.
14. See Chapter 8, section on Ludford, including note 11.
15. F. Ll. Harrison, 'Music for the Sarum Rite: MS. 1236 in the Pepys Library, Magdalene College, Cambridge', *Annales Musicologiques*, vi, 1958, p. 109.
16. Published as *Antiphonale Sarisburiense*, ed. W. H. Frere.
17. Not available in modern edition. The melodies of some Sarum hymns do, however, appear in *Hymns Ancient and Modern* and the *English Hymnal*.
18. *Use of Sarum*, ed. W. H. Frere, ii (Appendix).
19. *Breviarium ad Usum . . . Sarum*, ed. F. Procter and C. Wordsworth.
20. The words of the hymns and the Psalter are, however, included in *Breviarium ad Usum . . . Sarum*.
21. Harrison, *MMB*, pp. 65, 216–7.
22. 'The term 'response' has no liturgical authority but is used here to distinguish the choral part from the 'respond' or 'responsory', meaning the complete form' (P. Doe, *Tallis*, p. 29).
23. Harrison, *MMB*, pp. 81–88.
24. Harrison, *MMB*, p. 168. The original Latin may be found in *Statutes of the Colleges of Oxford*, ii, section on 'Cardinal and King Henry VIIIth's Colleges', p. 57.
25. E. Hoskins, *Horae Beatae Mariae Virginis or Sarum and York Primers*, p. 128. Other Primer texts (traced in Hoskins) which were used as votive antiphons include the following: *Gaude flore virginali* (set by numerous composers), *Gaude virgo mater Christi* (Horwood, Wylkynson, Sturton, Aston), *Salve regina* (numerous composers), *Stella coeli* (Lambe, Hawte)—all from a Primer of 1494; *Ave cujus conceptio* (Fayrfax, Ludford)—1497; *Stabat mater* (Browne, Davy, Cornysh, Fayrfax)—1501; *Ave caput Christi* (Tye)—1503; *Ave rosa sine spinis* (Tallis), *Ave Maria ancilla Trinitatis* (Sturton, Ludford, Aston)—1510; *O Willelme pastor bone* (Taverner: further see Chapter 9)—1511 and 1528; *Salve intemerata* (Tallis)—1527. The date of a text's appearance in a Primer does not necessarily give us any help in dating a votive antiphon based on it; but see a remark on the Tallis *Salve intemerata* in Chapter 11.
26. *MB*, xii. 172.

Chapter 3 (pp. 21–37)

1. *The Pelican History of Music*, ii, ed. A. Robertson and D. Stevens, p. 61.

2. The following discussion is much indebted to Harrison's description of the manuscript in *MB*, x, p. xvi.
3. Harrison, *MMB*, p. 162.
4. G. Chew, 'The Provenance and Date of the Caius and Lambeth Choirbooks', *ML*, li, 1970, pp. 109–10.
5. Chew, pp. 112–3.
6. See the inventory of 1522-4 (Harrison, *MMB*, p. 431).
7. 1529 inventory (Harrison, *MMB*, pp. 432–3).
8. Fully described and discussed in J. D. Bergsagel, 'The Date and Provenance of the Forrest-Heyther Collection of Tudor Masses', *ML*, xliv, 1963, p. 240.
9. R. Bray, 'British Museum Add. MSS. 17802-5 (The Gyffard Part-Books): An Index and Commentary', *RMA Research Chronicle*, vii, 1969, p. 50.
10. Bray, 'British Museum Add. MSS. 17802-5. . .', pp. 49–50.
11. Dom A. Hughes, *Catalogue of the Musical Manuscripts at Peterhouse, Cambridge*, pp. 2–3.
12. P. Doe, 'Latin Polyphony under Henry VIII', *PRMA*, xcv, 1968–9, p. 83.
13. R. Bray, 'The Part-Books Oxford, Christ Church, MSS. 979–83: An Index and Commentary', *MD*, xxv, 1971, pp. 194–7.
14. A copy is bound in with the Christ Church partbooks.
15. See list in le Huray, p. 403.
16. *The Pelican History of Music*, ii. 67.
17. The articles 'Mensural Notation' and 'Notation' in Apel, pp. 439, 493 are useful readable accounts; they include references to more detailed studies.
18. Harrison, *MMB*, p. 215.
19. M. Bukofzer, *Studies in Medieval and Renaissance Music*, p. 178.
20. *MB*, x, p. xvi.
21. Harrison, *MMB*, p. 27.
22. Harrison, *MMB*, pp. 36–37.
23. See le Huray, pp. 112–3. 'Double C fa ut' is modern C not C_1, as le Huray says.
24. J. Caldwell, 'The Pitch of Early Tudor Organ Music', *ML*, li, 1970, p. 157.
25. Harrison, *MMB*, p. 173.
26. le Huray, pp. 121–2.
27. Notably by the Clerkes of Oxenford.
28. Caldwell, p. 163.
29. D. Wulstan, 'The Problem of Pitch in Sixteenth-Century English Vocal Music', *PRMA*, xciii, 1966–7, pp. 101–9.
30. *Thomas Morley, A Plain and Easy Introduction to Practical Music*, ed. R. Harman, p. 243.
31. le Huray, pp. 103–6.
32. R. Bray, 'The Interpretation of Musica Ficta in English Music c. 1490–c. 1580', *PRMA*, xcvii, 1970–1, p. 30.
33. Apel, pp. 465–6.
34. G. Reese, *Music in the Middle Ages*, pp. 381–2.
35. P. Doe, 'Another View of Musica Ficta in Tudor Music', *PRMA*, xcviii, 1971–2, p. 118.
36. See Doe, 'Another View . . .', pp. 116, 119–21 (especially Examples 3–6 and note 14).

Chatper 4 (pp. 38–57)

1. T. Messenger, 'Texture and Form in the Masses of Fayrfax', *JAMS*, xxiv, 1971, p. 282.
2. Seay, p. 21.
3. In making the count fermata-marked chords followed by a double-bar have been disregarded as probably being 'extra tempus' (compare Harrison, *MMB*, p. 314.

Where the signature is Ø a 'bar' consists of three semibreves; where it is ₵ of four. ø/3 has two dotted breves to a bar.

4. H. Benham, 'The Formal Design and Construction of Taverner's Works', *MD*, xxvi, 1972, p. 198.
5. E. H. Sparks's masterly study *Cantus Firmus in Mass and Motet 1420–1520* deals with this Continental practice, and with English practice before our period.
6. See F. Ll. Harrison, 'An English "Caput" ', *ML*, xxxiii, 1952, p. 203.
7. J. D. Bergsagel, 'On the Performance of Ludford's *Alternatim* Masses', *MD*, xvi, 1962, p. 37. The present paragraph and the next are much indebted to Bergsagel's article.
8. References are to the Forrest-Heyther partbooks. The Christ Church books show the same kinds of textual peculiarities, but the precise arrangement is often different (see H. Benham, *The Music of John Taverner, A Study and Assessment* (unpublished thesis), p. 222).
9. Concerning the composer's identity see Harrison, *MMB*, p. 267.
10. *Missa O Quam Suavis*, ed. H. B. Collins, pp. xxiv–xxv.
11. *NOHM*, iii. 131.
12. All parodies listed in Benham, 'The Formal Design . . .', pp. 206–7.
13. Harrison, *MMB*, pp. 287–8.

Chapter 5 (pp. 58–73)

1. See list in *NOHM*, iii. 309.
2. Bent, p. 394.
3. Dom A. Hughes, *Medieval Polyphony in the Bodleian Library*, p. 43.
4. See partial transcription in Harrison, *MMB*, p. 260.
5. Hughes, *Medieval Polyphony . . .*, pp. 31–32.
6. M. Bukofzer, 'Caput Redivivum: A New Source for Dufay's Missa Caput', *JAMS*, iv, 1951, p. 97.
7. Seay, p. 38.
8. J. Stevens, p. 102.
9. *CMM*, xix, p. i.
10. Harrison, *MMB*, p. 325.
11. G. Reese, *Music in the Renaissance*, pp. 185–6.
12. Harrison, *MMB*, p. 323.
13. Reese, *Music in the Renaissance*, p. 13.
14. Strunk, p. 195.
15. See Bukofzer, *Studies . . .*, pp. 285–6.

Chapter 6 (pp. 74–97)

1. Harrison, *MMB*, pp. 179–80.
2. H. Baillie, 'A London Gild of Musicians, 1460–1530', *PRMA*, lxxxiii, 1956–7, p. 20.
3. *MB*, x, p. xviii.
4. H. Baillie and P. Oboussier, 'The York Masses', *ML*, xxxv, 1954, p. 24.
5. S. R. Charles, 'The Provenance and Date of the Pepys MS. 1236', *MD*, xvi, 1962, pp. 63–64.
6. W. H. G. Flood, *Early Tudor Composers*, p. 15.
7. Harrison, *MMB*, p. 309.
8. Charles, pp. 63–64.
9. Harrison, 'An English "Caput" ', pp. 210–4.
10. *MB*, x, p. xvii; Harrison, *MMB*, p. 459.

11. *MB*, x, pp. xvi–xvii.
12. Harrison, *MMB*, p. 419.
13. Harrison, *MMB*, p. 455; *MB*, xi, p. xiii.
14. The author is grateful to Dom Anselm Hughes for confirming this.
15. *Missale ad Usum . . . Eboracensis*, ii. 209.
16. Reese, *Music in the Middle Ages*, p. 389.
17. *MB*, xii. 174.
18. *MB*, x. 146.
19. *MB*, xi, p. xiii.
20. Harrison, *MMB*, p. 329.
21. *MB*, xii. 164, 170–1.
22. *The British Museum Manuscript Egerton 3307*, ed. G. S. McPeek, pp. 48, 54. The manuscript's date is discussed on pp. 14–16.
23. *MB*, xi. 181.
24. *MB*, x, pp. xvii–xviii.
25. Harrison, *MMB*, p. 328.
26. *MB*, x, pp. xvi–xvii.
27. *MB*, x. 147.
28. F. Ll. Harrison, 'Faburden in Practice', *MD*, xvi, 1962, p. 22.
29. *MB*, x, p. xviii.
30. *MB*, x, p. xix.
31. *MB*, xi, p. xiii.

Chapter 7 (pp. 98–113)

1. Harrison, 'Music for the Sarum Rite . . .', p. 100.
2. Charles, p. 58. The first two paragraphs of the present section are considerably indebted to Charles.
3. Bukofzer, *Studies* . . ., pp. 128–9.
4. Discussed in detail in Harrison, *MMB*, pp. 149–53 and *NOHM*, iii. 95–99.
5. British Museum Lansdowne MS. 763, ff. 116–116v. See pp. 46–48 of B. Trowell's Faburden and Fauxbourdon', *MD*, xiii, 1959, to which the remainder of this paragraph is indebted.
6. Harrison, 'Faburden in Practice', pp. 20–22.
7. Harrison, 'Faburden in Practice', p. 17.
8. Contents transcribed in C. K. Miller, *A Fifteenth-Century Record of English Choir Repertory* (unpublished thesis).
9. Miller, i. 2.
10. Harrison, *MMB*, p. 421.
11. Harrison, *MMB*, p. 421.
12. Harrison, *MMB*, p. 278.
13. i.e. the setting in *MB*, viii. 152.
14. Harrison, *MMB*, p. 461.
15. Baillie and Oboussier, p. 19. The first two paragraphs of the present section are much indebted to Baillie and Oboussier.
16. Harrison, *MMB*, p. 261.

Chapter 8 (pp. 114–133)

1. Harrison, *MMB*, p. 340; Reese, *Music in the Renaissance*, pp. 278, 280–1, 301.
2. *NOHM*, iii. 347.
3. *NOHM*, iii. 304.

4. Harrison, *MMB*, pp. 338–40.

5. Biographical information from E. B. Warren, 'Life and Works of Robert Fayrfax', *MD*, xi, 1957, p. 134.

6. The fragmentary Mass *Sponsus amat sponsam* may possibly have been written for the marriage of Catherine of Aragon to Prince Arthur in 1501 or to Henry VIII in 1509, since the title means 'the Bridegroom loves the Bride' and the cantus firmus comes from the Office of St Catherine. But for any major royal wedding it is more likely that a sumptuous Mass for at least five voices would have been provided, instead of one which, from what survives, does not look particularly impressive.

7. Dom Anselm Hughes suggested a link between *Regali* and King's ('An Introduction to Fayrfax', *MD*, vi, 1952, p. 101).

8. *MB*, viii. 189.

9. For this and the few other facts about Ludford's life, see J. D. Bergsagel, 'An Introduction to Ludford', *MD*, xiv. 1960, p. 105.

10. Bergsagel, 'An Introduction . . .', p. 115.

11. In a letter to the author.

12. Harrison, *MMB*, p. 461.

Chapter 9 (pp. 134–161)

1. Benham, *The Music of John Taverner. . .*, p. 5. Accounts of Taverner's life are published in *TCM*, i, p. xlviii and *MGG*, xiii, col. 152.

2. John Foxe, *Actes and Monuments*, 1563 edition, p. 497b.

3. Letter to Wolsey (Public Record Office, SP/1/47, f. 111).

4. Foxe, 1583 edition, ii. 1032.

5. For example see Doe, 'Latin Polyphony. . .', p. 87.

6. R. Donington and T. Dart, 'The Origin of the In Nomine', *ML*, xxx, 1949, p. 101.

7. It may possibly be a square. It is unlikely to be a sequence melody as suggested in H. Benham, 'The Music of Taverner: A Liturgical Study', *The Music Review*, xxxiii, 1972, p. 256.

8. Benham, 'The Formal Design. . .', p. 192.

9. Doe, 'Latin Polyphony . . .', pp. 88–90.

10. See for example Lees-Milne, pp. 40–45.

11. See F. Ll. Harrison's letter in *ML*, xlvi, 1965, p. 382.

12. See Chapter 2, note 24.

13. Originally of York Use (see Harrison, *MMB*, p. 341), but found in several Sarum Primers, including those of 1511 and 1528 (see Hoskins, pp. 125, 147).

14. D. Stevens, *Tudor Church Music*, p. 16.

15. Not an antiphon of the Trinity as Harrison says (*MMB*, p. 332).

16. *Liber Usualis*, p. 1861.

17. Taverner's tenor is reconstructed and compared with Obrecht's melody in Benham, 'The Music of Taverner: A Liturgical Study', p. 263.

18. H. B. Collins, 'John Taverner (Part II)', *ML*, vi, 1925, p. 316.

19. The tenor has been reconstructed (*TCM*, iii. 26), but with unnecessarily frequent departures from equal-note presentation.

20. Harrison, *MMB*, p. 335.

21. Harrison, *MMB*, pp. 29–30.

22. Harrison, *MMB*, p. 334, Examples 116–7.

23. Harrison, *MMB*, p. 335.

24. Harrison, *MMB*, pp. 41, 454.

25. *NOHM*, iii. 332.

26. H. Byard, 'Farewell to Merbecke?', *Musical Times*, cxiii, 1972, p. 301.

27. L. Lockwood, 'A Continental Mass and Motet in a Tudor Manuscript', *ML*, xlii, 1961, p. 336.

28. Concerning the identity of this composer see B. Rose, 'John Mason: A Clarification', *Musical Times*, cxiii, 1972, p. 1231.
29. Hoskins, pp. 112, 167, 218, 247.

Chapter 10 (pp. 162–176)

1. Dickens and Carr, pp. 74–85.
2. *The Rationale of Ceremonial*, ed. C. Cobb, p. lxiv.
3. *The Rationale . . .*, p. 14.
4. le Huray, pp. 5–7.
5. le Huray, p. 9. See also H. Benham, 'Latin Church Music under Edward VI', *Musical Times*, cxvi, 1975, p. 477.
6. le Huray, pp. 9–10.
7. *MB*, xv. 205.
8. Dickens and Carr, p. 135.
9. le Huray, pp. 31–32.
10. The *Liber* is printed in *Liturgical Services of the Reign of Queen Elizabeth*, ed. W. K. Clay, pp. 299–431.
11. *Liturgical Services . . .*, p. xxxi.
12. H. Gee and W. J. Hardy, *Documents Illustrative of English Church History*, p. 435.
13. Doe, *Tallis*, p. 38.
14. le Huray, pp. 35–36.
15. The prefatory matter is briefly summarised in *NOHM*, iv. 480–1. Facsimiles of the original Latin are in *The Collected Works of William Byrd*, ed. E. H. Fellowes, i, between pp. 118 and 119.
16. See the Petition which Tallis and Byrd addressed to the Queen in 1577: referring to the printing licence, the composers said that 'the same hath fallen out to our great loss and hindrance to the value of two hundred marks at the least' (*TCM*, vi, p. xiv).
17. A subject discussed in J. Kerman, 'The Elizabethan Motet: A Study of Texts for Music', *Studies in the Renaissance*, ix, 1962, p. 273.
18. *Early English Church Music*, ii, p. ix.
19. H. B. Collins, 'Thomas Tallis', *ML*, x, 1929, p. 163.
20. *TCM*, x. 231–2.
21. Harrison, *MMB*, p. 43.
22. Hoskins, pp. 242, 254.
23. Hoskins, pp. 107, 174.
24. *NOHM*, iv. 489.
25. Harrison, *MMB*, p. 341.
26. J. Kerman, 'An Elizabethan Edition of Lassus', *Acta Musicologica*, xxvii, 1955, p. 71.
27. P. Brett, 'Edward Paston (1550–1630): A Norfolk Gentleman and his Musical Collection', *Transactions of the Cambridge Bibliographical Society*, iv, 1964, pp. 61, 68–69.
28. Strunk, p. 328.
29. J. Kerman, 'Byrd, Tallis, and the Art of Imitation', *Aspects of Medieval and Renaissance Music . . .*, p. 533.
30. le Huray, p. 146.

Chapter 11 (pp. 177–211)

1. *TCM*, vi, pp. xi, xiii–xiv.
2. Doe, 'Latin Polyphony . . .', p. 83.
3. Hoskins, p. 134.
4. *Early English Church Music*, xii, Introduction.

5. Full text in *TCM*, vi, p. xv.
6. Harrison, *MMB*, p. 288.
7. Doe, *Tallis*, p. 20.
8. Parts of the Gloria, Credo and Sanctus are in *TCM*, vi. 49-61, minus the tenor and second bass parts. I am grateful to Mr David Wulstan for lending me a copy of his edition of the entire Gloria, Sanctus and Agnus.
9. Our comments on *Puer natus* are much indebted to Doe, *Tallis*, pp. 20-25.
10. Described in Reese, *Music in the Renaissance*, pp. 133-5.
11. le Huray, p. 181.
12. Doe, *Tallis*, p. 40.
13. The most thorough investigation of this work is in P. Doe, 'Tallis's "Spem in alium" and the Elizabethan Respond-Motet', *ML*, li, 1970, p. 1.
14. *MGG*, xii. col. 637 gives a useful outline of Sheppard's life.
15. Harrison, *MMB*, p. 36.
16. le Huray, p. 205.
17. Harrison, *MMB*, p. 345.
18. Harrison, *MMB*, pp. 289-90.
19. A good account of Tye's life appears in *MGG*, xiii. col. 1006.
20. There is some confusion of gender in the text in both (Elizabethan) sources of the work, as though there was some half-hearted attempt at making the work applicable to a queen (e.g. 'exaudi preces nostras pro famul*a* tu*a*, Domine rex noster'—not 'regina nostra' which has two extra syllables; or 'constans et sedul*a*, constans et sedul*us*'). See Benham, 'Latin Church Music under Edward VI', p. 477.
21. *MGG*, xiii. col. 1007.
22. *Mass to Six Voices 'Euge bone'*, ed. G. E. P. Arkwright, p. 3.
23. Preface to *The Western Wind Mass . . . by Christopher Tye*, ed. N. Davison.
24. *Missale ad Usum . . . Sarum*, coll. 561-2. See also Preface, p. lxi. The prayer is altered in favour of Henry VIII in Missals of 1516, 1527, 1529 and 1533 (p. liv).
25. Bray, 'British Museum Add. MSS. 17802-5 . . .', p. 43.
26. Bray, 'British Museum Add. MSS. 17802-5 . . .', pp. 47-48.

Chapter 12 (pp. 212-223)

1. *TCM*, v, pp. xi-xiii.
2. *Early English Church Music*, ii, p. viii.
3. le Huray, p. 212.
4. Baillie, 'Squares', p. 182.
5. le Huray, p. 191.
6. le Huray, p. 191.
7. Kerman, 'The Elizabethan Motet . . .', p. 285.
8. le Huray, p. 228.
9. le Huray, pp. 227-8.
10. Kerman, 'Byrd, Tallis, and the Art of Imitation', p. 525.
11. Kerman, 'The Elizabethan Motet . . .', pp. 283-4.
12. Kerman, 'Byrd, Tallis, and the Art of Imitation', pp. 529-32.
13. The beginning is quoted in *NOHM*, iv. 493-5.
14. Quoted in *NOHM*, iv. 491-2.

Bibliography

Antiphonale Sarisburiense, ed. W. H. Frere, London, Plainsong and Medieval Music Society, 1901–24 (re-published, 6 vols., Farnborough (Hants), Gregg, 1966).
APEL, W. *The Harvard Dictionary of Music*, London, Heinemann, 1944.

BAILLIE, H. 'A London Gild of Musicians, 1460–1530', *Proceedings of the Royal Musical Association*, lxxxiii, 1956–7, p. 15.
— 'Squares', *Acta Musicologica*, xxxii, 1960, p. 178.
BAILLIE, H. and OBOUSSIER, P. 'The York Masses', *Music and Letters*, xxxv, 1954, p. 19.
BENHAM, H. 'The Formal Design and Construction of Taverner's Works', *Musica Disciplina*, xxvi, 1972, p. 189.
— 'Latin Church Music under Edward VI', *Musical Times*, cxvi, 1975, p. 477.
— *The Music of John Taverner, A Study and Assessment*, unpublished Ph.D. thesis, University of Southampton, 1970.
— 'The Music of Taverner: A Liturgical Study', *The Music Review*, xxxiii, 1972, p. 251.
BENT, M. and I. 'Dufay, Dunstable, Plummer—A New Source', *Journal of the American Musicological Society*, xxii, 1969, p. 394.
BERGSAGEL, J. D., 'The Date and Provenance of the Forrest-Heyther Collection of Tudor Masses', *Music and Letters*, xliv, 1963, p. 240.
— 'An Introduction to Ludford', *Musica Disciplina*, xiv, 1960, p. 105.
— 'On the Performance of Ludford's Alternatim Masses', *Musica Disciplina*, xvi, 1962, p. 36.
BRAY, R. 'The Interpretation of Musica Ficta in English Music c. 1490–c. 1580', *Proceedings of the Royal Musical Association*, xcvii, 1970–1, p. 29.
— 'British Museum Add. MSS. 17802–5 (The Gyffard Part-Books): An Index and Commentary', *RMA Research Chronicle*, vii, 1969, p. 31.
— 'The Part-Books Oxford, Christ Church, MSS. 979–83: An Index and Commentary', *Musica Disciplina*, xxv, 1971, p. 179.
BRETT, P. 'Edward Paston (1550–1630): A Norfolk Gentleman and his Musical Collection', *Transactions of the Cambridge Bibliographical Society*, iv, 1964, p. 51.
Breviarium ad Usum Insignis Ecclesiae Sarum, ed. F. Procter and C. Wordsworth, 3 vols., Cambridge, C.U.P., 1879–86.
The British Museum Manuscript Egerton 3307, ed. G. S. McPeek, London, O.U.P., 1963.
BUKOFZER, M. 'Caput Redivivum: A New Source for Dufay's Missa Caput', *Journal of the American Musicological Society*, iv, 1951, p. 97.

— *Studies in Medieval and Renaissance Music*, New York, Norton, 1950.
BYARD, H. 'Farewell to Merbecke?', *Musical Times*, cxiii, 1972, p. 300.

CALDWELL, J. 'The Pitch of Early Tudor Organ Music', *Music and Letters*, li, 1970, p. 156.
CHADWICK, O. *The Reformation*, The Pelican History of the Church, iii, Harmondsworth (Middlesex), Penguin, 1964.
CHARLES, S. R. 'The Provenance and Date of the Pepys MS. 1236', *Musica Disciplina*, xvi, 1962, p. 57.
CHEW, G. 'The Provenance and Date of the Caius and Lambeth Choirbooks', *Music and Letters*, li, 1970, p. 107.
COLLINS, H. B. 'Thomas Tallis', *Music and Letters*, x, 1929, p. 152.
— 'John Taverner's Masses', *Music and Letters*, v, 1924, p. 322.
— 'John Taverner (Part II)', *Music and Letters*, vi, 1925, p. 314.
Corpus Mensurabilis Musicae [*CMM*], i: 'Guillaume Dufay, Opera Omnia', 6 vols., ed. G. de Van and H. Besseler; iv: 'Jacobus Clemens non Papa, Opera Omnia', 21 vols., ed. K. Ph. Bernet Kempers; vi: 'Nicolas Gombert, Opera Omnia', ed. J. Schmidt-Grörg; xvii: 'Robert Fayrfax, Collected Works', 3 vols., ed. E. B. Warren; xix: 'Walter Frye, Collected Works', ed. S. Kenney; xxvii: 'Nicholas Ludford, Collected Works', ed. J. D. Bergsagel; xl: 'The Pepys MS. 1236', ed. S. R. Charles'; xlvi: 'The Old Hall MS.', 3 vols., ed. A. Hughes and M. Bent; l: 'Lionel Power, Complete Works', 2 vols, ed. C. Hamm. Series published by American Institute of Musicology, 1947–

DICKENS, A. G. *The English Reformation*, London, Batsford, 1964.
DICKENS, A. G. and CARR, D. *The Reformation in England to the Accession of Elizabeth I*, London, Arnold, 1967.
DOE, P. 'Another View of Musica Ficta in Tudor Music', *Proceedings of the Royal Musical Association*, xcviii, 1971–2, p. 113.
— 'Latin Polyphony under Henry VIII', *Proceedings of the Royal Musical Association*, xcv, 1968–9, p. 81.
— *Tallis*, London, O.U.P., 1968.
— 'Tallis's 'Spem in alium' and the Elizabethan Respond-Motet', *Music and Letters*, li, 1970, p. 1.
DONINGTON, R. and DART, T. 'The Origin of the In Nomine', *Music and Letters*, xxx, 1949, p. 101.

Early English Church Music, i: 'Early Tudor Masses (Part I)' [Ashewell, Alwood], ed. J. D. Bergsagel; ii: 'William Mundy (Latin Antiphons and Psalms)', ed. F. Ll. Harrison; iv: 'Early Tudor Magnificats (Part I)' [Lambeth Anonymous, Fayrfax O bone Jesu, Cornysh, Turges, Prentyce, Ludford], ed. P. Doe; xii–xiii: Thomas Tallis, English Sacred Music, ed. L. Ellinwood. Series published London, Stainer & Bell, 1962–

The First and Second Prayer Books of King Edward VI, London, Dent, 1910.
FLOOD, W. H. G. *Early Tudor Composers*, London, O.U.P., 1925.
FOXE, John. *Actes and Monuments*, 1563 and 1583 (modern edition *The Acts and Monuments of John Foxe*, ed. S. R. Cattley, 8 vols., London, Seeley & Burnside, 1837–41).

FROUDE, J. A. *Life and Letters of Erasmus*, London, Longmans Green & Co., 1894.

GEE, H. and HARDY, W. J. *Documents Illustrative of English Church History*, London, Macmillan, 1914.
Graduale Sarisburiense, ed. W. H. Frere, London, Quaritch, 1894 (re-published Farnborough (Hants), Gregg, 1966).

HANNAS, R. 'Concerning Deletions in the Polyphonic Mass Credo', *Journal of the American Musicological Society*, v, 1952, p. 155.
HARRISON, F. Ll. 'An English "Caput" ', *Music and Letters*, xxxiii, 1952, p. 203.
— 'Faburden in Practice', *Musica Disciplina*, xvi, 1962, p. 11.
— 'Music for the Sarum Rite: MS. 1236 in the Pepys Library, Magdalene College, Cambridge', *Annales Musicologiques*, vi, 1958, p. 99.
— *Music in Medieval Britain* [*MMB*], London, Routledge, 1958.
HOSKINS, E. *Horae Beatae Mariae Virginis or Sarum and York Primers*, London, Longmans Green & Co., 1901.
HUGHES, Dom A. *Catalogue of the Musical Manuscripts at Peterhouse, Cambridge*, Cambridge, C.U.P., 1953.
— 'An Introduction to Fayrfax', *Musica Disciplina*, vi, 1952, p. 83.
— *Medieval Polyphony in the Bodleian Library*, Oxford, Bodleian Library, 1951.
HUGHES-HUGHES, A. *Catalogue of Manuscript Music in the British Museum*, 3 vols., London, published by order of the Trustees of the B.M., 1906-9.

Josquin des Prés, Werken, ed. A. Smijers, 44 fascicles, Amsterdam, Vereeniging voor Nederlandsche Muziekgeschiedenis, 1921-56.

KERMAN, J. 'Byrd, Tallis, and the Art of Imitation', *Aspects of Medieval and Renaissance Music: A Birthday Offering to Gustave Reese*, London, Dent, 1967, p. 519.
— 'An Elizabethan Edition of Lassus', *Acta Musicologica*, xxvii, 1955, p. 71.
— 'The Elizabethan Motet: A Study of Texts for Music', *Studies in the Renaissance*, ix, 1962, p. 273.

LEES-MILNE, J. *Tudor Renaissance*, London, Batsford, 1951.
LE HURAY, P. *Music and the Reformation in England 1549-1660*, London, Jenkins, 1967.
Liber Usualis, ed. Benedictines of Solesmes, Tournai, Desclee, 1961.
Liturgical Services of the Reign of Queen Elizabeth, ed. W. K. Clay, Parker Society, Cambridge, C.U.P., 1847.
LOCKWOOD, L. 'A Continental Mass and Motet in a Tudor Manuscript', *Music and Letters*, xlii, 1961, p. 336.
LYON, M. E., *Early Tudor Church Music, the Lambeth and Caius Manuscripts*, 2 vols., unpublished Ph.D. thesis, University of California, 1957.

Mass to Six Voices 'Euge Bone', ed. G. E. P. Arkwright, London, Joseph Williams, 1893.
MESSENGER, T. 'Texture and Form in the Masses of Fayrfax', *Journal of the American Musicological Society*, xxiv, 1971, p. 282.

MILLER, C. K. *A Fifteenth-Century Record of English Choir Repertory: B.M. Add. MS. 5665; a Transcription and Commentary*, 2 vols., unpublished Ph.D. thesis, Yale University, 1948.

Missale ad Usum Ecclesiae Eboracensis, ed. W. G. Henderson, 2 vols., Surtees Society, Durham, 1874.

Missale ad Usum Insignis et Praeclarae Ecclesiae Sarum, ed. F. H. Dickinson, Burntisland, Pitsligo Press, 1861–83.

Missa O Quam Suavis, ed. H. B. Collins, London, Plainsong and Medieval Music Society, 1927.

MORLEY, Thomas. *A Plaine and Easie Introduction to Practicall Musicke*, 1597 (modern edition *Thomas Morley, A Plain and Easy Introduction to Practical Music*, ed. R. A. Harman, London, Dent, 1952).

Musica Britannica [MB], viii: 'John Dunstable, Complete Works', ed. M. Bukofzer; x–xii: 'The Eton Choirbook', ed. F. Ll. Harrison; xv: 'Music of Scotland, 1500–1700', ed. K. Elliott; xviii: 'Music at the Court of Henry VIII', ed. J. Stevens. Series published London, Stainer & Bell, 1951– .

Die Musik in Geschichte und Gegenwart [MGG], Kassel, Bärenreiter, 1949–68.

MYERS, A. R. *England in the Late Middle Ages*, The Pelican History of England, iv, Harmondsworth (Middlesex), Penguin, 1952.

The New Oxford History of Music [NOHM], iii: 'Ars Nova and the Renaissance 1300–1540', ed. Dom A. Hughes and G. Abraham; iv: 'The Age of Humanism 1540–1630', ed. G. Abraham. London, O.U.P., 1960, 1968.

Johannes Ockeghem, Complete Works, ed. D. Plamenac, 3 vols., New York, American Musicological Society, 1947– .

Jakob Obrecht, Werken, ed. J. Wolf, 30 vols., Amsterdam and Leipzig, 1912–21.

The Pelican History of Music, ii: 'Renaissance and Baroque', ed. A. Robertson and D. Stevens, Harmondsworth (Middlesex), Penguin, 1963.

The Rationale of Ceremonial, ed. C. Cobb, Alcuin Club Collections, xviii, London, Longmans Green & Co., 1910.

REESE, G. *Music in the Middle Ages*, London, Dent, 1941.

— *Music in the Renaissance*, London, Dent, 1954.

ROSE, B. 'John Mason: A Clarification', *Musical Times*, cxiii, 1972, p. 1231.

ROUTH, F. *Early English Organ Music from the Middle Ages to 1837*, London, Barrie & Jenkins, 1973.

SEAY, A. *Music in the Medieval World*, Englewood Cliffs (N.J.), Prentice-Hall, 1965.

SPARKS, E. H., *Cantus Firmus in Mass and Motet 1420–1520*, London, C.U.P., 1963.

Statutes of the Colleges of Oxford, printed by desire of H.M. Commissioners for inquiring into the State of the University of Oxford, 3 vols., London, 1853.

STEVENS, D. *Tudor Church Music*, London, Faber, 1961.

— 'A Unique Tudor Organ Mass', *Musica Disciplina*, vi, 1952, p. 167.

STEVENS, J. *Music and Poetry in the Early Tudor Court*, London, Methuen, 1961.

STRUNK, O., *Source Readings in Music History*, London, Faber, 1950.

236   LATIN CHURCH MUSIC IN ENGLAND

The Treasury of English Church Music, i: '1100–1545', ed. D. Stevens; ii: '1540–1650', ed. P. le Huray. London, Blandford, 1965.

TROWELL, B. 'Faburden and Fauxbourdon', *Musica Disciplina*, xiii, 1959, p. 43.

Tudor Church Music [*TCM*], ed. P. Buck, E. H. Fellowes, A. Ramsbotham, R. R. Terry, S. Townsend Warner, i: 'John Taverner (Part I)'; iii: 'John Taverner (Part II)'; v: 'Robert White'; vi: 'Thomas Tallis'; ix: 'William Byrd (Masses, *Cantiones Sacrae*, Motets)'; x: 'Hugh Aston, John Marbeck and Osbert Parsley'. Series published London, O.U.P., 1923–9.

Christopher Tye, The Latin Church Music, ed. J. Satterfield, 2 vols., Recent Researches in the Music of the Renaissance, xiii, Madison (Wisconsin), A-R editions Inc., 1972.

Use of Sarum, ed. W. H. Frere, 2 vols., Cambridge, C.U.P., 1898–1901.

WARREN, E. B. 'Life and Works of Robert Fayrfax', *Musica Disciplina*, xi, 1957, p. 134.

The Western Wind Mass for Four Voices by Christopher Tye, ed. N. Davison, London, Chester, 1969.

WULSTAN, D. 'The Problem of Pitch in Sixteenth-Century English Vocal Music', *Proceedings of the Royal Musical Association*, xciii, 1966–7, p. 97.

Index of Works

General Index